W9-BVP-921

A12901 608370

9/04

Withdrawn

# FINAL ACCOUNTING

AMBITION,
GREED,
AND
THE FALL
OF ARTHUR
ANDERSEN

# FINAL

# ACCOUNTING

BARBARA LEY TOFFLER

WITH JENNIFER REINGOLD

WITHDRAWN

I.C.C. LIBRARY

BROADWAY BOOKS
*New York*

HF
5616
.U7
A288
2003

FINAL ACCOUNTING. Copyright © 2003 by Barbara Ley Toffler. All rights reserved. No part of this book may be reproduced or transmitted in any form or by any means, electronic or mechanical, including photocopying, recording, or by any information storage and retrieval system, without written permission from the publisher. For information, address Broadway Books, a division of Random House, Inc.

PRINTED IN THE UNITED STATES OF AMERICA

BROADWAY BOOKS and its logo, a letter B bisected on the diagonal, are trademarks of Random House, Inc.

Visit our website at www.broadwaybooks.com

First edition published 2003.

Book design by Mauna Eichner

Cataloging-in-Publication Data is on file with the Library of Congress.

ISBN 0-7679-1382-5

10 9 8 7 6 5 4 3 2 1

# AUTHOR'S NOTE

The events depicted in this book reflect my experiences at Arthur Andersen. The conversations recounted here are based on my best recollections and, wherever possible, those of others present at the time. When describing events or conversations that occurred when I was not present, I have relied on the accounts of several people who were there. Where indicated, names have been changed to protect the privacy of those involved.

Although the interpretations and conclusions in this book are mine and mine alone, the story of Andersen could not have been told without the cooperation of more than fifty former employees, executives, and close associates of the Firm, many of whom are quoted by name in the book and spent hundreds of hours with me or with Jennifer Reingold. I salute their courage, and I thank them, along with those who are not named, for their strong desire to set the record straight. Jennifer and I also relied on historical documents, speeches, newspaper reports, and biographies to re-create the early days of Andersen as well as other key events that occurred after I left the Firm. Citations have been noted extensively.

# CONTENTS

 **FINAL ACCOUNTING**

# The Andersen Way

*The day Arthur Andersen loses the public's trust is the day
we are out of business.*

— STEVE SAMEK, Country Managing Partner,
United States, for Arthur Andersen, on the firm's
Independence and Ethical Standards CD-ROM, 1999

"I DON'T CARE WHAT YOU USED TO CHARGE," barked Robert,
a partner in Andersen's Business Consulting unit, at the stricken
young manager. "You're at Arthur Andersen now."

Robert had asked the manager, a friendly and straightforward
young man who had just joined the Firm, for an estimate to produce a CD-ROM for a large European bank going through a
merger. Although intimidated, the manager responded bravely,
"That's as high as I can legitimately go. That's the price for my top
of the line."

Robert stared at him, disgusted. "We don't do anything for
$50,000." The manager looked as if he might melt into a puddle of
shame. After giving me a pleading glance, he slunk out of the partner's office, knowing that when he returned he had better have a
generously padded price for his piece of the project.

Now it was my turn to endure the wrath of a ravenous Arthur
Andersen consultant stalking fees. Robert, the young manager, and
I were collaborating on a proposal to help the bank coordinate its

compliance manuals and ethics policies and design a brief program to introduce them to employees in the wake of the giant merger. On that day in December 1998, I had already been with Arthur Andersen for more than three years as head of the Ethics and Responsible Business Practices Group, but I had never—and would never—get used to moments like these. I knew I was in for it, too, since I had estimated the fee for my group's portion of the work at $75,000. It was a fair estimate, but not a particularly profitable one for Robert, who as engagement partner on the project would be measured on the total fees.

And I was right. As Robert loomed over me, linebacker-broad shoulders flexing ominously, he reminded me of nothing so much as Zero Mostel's transformation into a rhinoceros in the Ionesco play of that name.

"What's this $75,000?" he shouted, reverting to the machine-gun style of speaking he used to keep anyone from sneaking in a contrary word or thought. "What do you mean, $75,000? This is the big time, young lady." (I didn't take that as a compliment.) "What kind of a consultant are you?"

"A good one, Robert," I managed to squeeze into the ongoing barrage of invective. "And for our piece of the project, that's a high-end estimate." But Robert was having none of it. "You make that $150,000," he ordered. "Back into it."

I did.

Robert put together the final budget, which I never saw, and personally delivered it to the bank's general counsel, who in our two preproposal planning meetings had been very receptive to our ideas and enthusiastic about the project. I shuddered to imagine the con game that was about to be played on him. So, not having heard from Robert, I called him to find out what had happened. "What's with the proposal?" I asked. He told me he had delivered it. "What was the bottom line?" I said, holding my breath. "Six hundred thousand dollars," he said, coolly. I shouldn't have been surprised by this point—I'd been through the game so many times before at the Firm—but for some reason, I was overcome by a wave of revulsion.

"You mean your piece is almost $400,000? For a few first-year-staff xeroxing policies and typing up a manual?"

"This is Arthur Andersen," came his reply. "That's the way we do it around here."

"And what did the general counsel say when he saw that number?"

"Nothing," said Robert, brusquely. "He just stood there. But don't worry. It was just sticker shock. He'll get over it."

He might, but I wouldn't. "I've got sticker shock, too, Robert. Who's going to pay that kind of money for what we're offering?" His answer was simple. "Relax. We're Arthur Andersen. They need us. They'll pay." I hung up the phone.

At that moment, something snapped. Sure, I was angry, but what I felt most profoundly was utter humiliation, for myself and also for the Firm, which was using its good name to overbill and underdeliver. I wasn't a naïf, shocked to get a taste of the real world; I'd been on the Harvard Business School faculty and successfully consulted to Fortune 500 companies for fifteen years before joining this firm with a more than eighty-year reputation for excellence and dignity. But this place was beginning to look more and more like the "bad example" I used to cite to clients. Called *The Firm* by everyone who worked there, Arthur Andersen felt like the real-life version of John Grisham's famous novel. The prestigious name was being used to justify behavior that never would have been tolerated in the past, behavior that was wrong. I resolved to stop acting like a sheep.

●　　●　　●

That experience flashed back to me some three years later, on March 26, 2002, as I watched reports on a support rally for Andersen, which had just been indicted by the U.S. Department of Justice for its involvement with the collapse of Enron Corp., its star client. On that miserable day, even the weather gods scorned the Firm. Sheets of freezing rain landed on uncovered heads, trickled slowly down cold noses, and slid down the now-soggy T-shirts of several hundred employees of Andersen's New York office. It was the fifth day of spring, but one of the coldest, most unforgiving days of the year—and the day Andersen had picked for a last-ditch public gathering to try to save itself from corporate extinction.

Just as everyone began to assemble, the drizzle became a torrent. "I am Arthur Andersen," blared the stark black letters on the bright orange T-shirts. But the expressions on the employees' faces telegraphed a different message: "I am wishing I were anywhere else in the world." They put on a good show all the same, these young accountants, consultants, and tax specialists, because they had to: Their jobs and their careers were at stake.

On this terrible gray day, Andersen employees tried to show the world that their 88-year-old accounting and consulting firm still had some fight in it. They stood there, shivering on the black stone entryway to the Alliance Capital Building on the Avenue of the Americas, chanting their firm's name and holding up hand-scrawled posters whose messages, blurred by raindrops, looked for anyone else to blame.

*"Even Iraq got a trial before execution."*

*"I didn't shred, my kid needs to be fed."*

*"I worked 0 hours at Enron."*

*"DOJ WHAT?"* ("Sucks" was the preferred answer.)

*"It takes a real Jack-Ashcroft to put 28,000 people in the streets."*

*"It wasn't me."*

One thirty-something guy had shown up with his baby. She napped in her pink coat, oblivious to the crowd of clean-cut, earnest young professionals in their soaked clothes, bemoaning the fate of their once-proud firm.

A carefully selected rainbow of Andersen employees and partners, from the midcareer mom to the African immigrant, came to the podium to tell their stories. Each of them struck the same chord: Andersen was a wonderful place to work. It was a company that had provided each of them many opportunities and a great career. The best thing about Andersen was the people. And why was the U.S. government punishing a hallowed institution with 85,000 global employees for the mistakes of a few? After each speech, the designated cheerleader, a peppy young man with glasses and a bullhorn, led the chant: "I am An-der-sen! I am An-der-sen!" No one seemed to be wondering whether the company somehow deserved its fate. Not one person ever mentioned the people who suffered the worst punishment of all in the collapse of Enron—the investing public.

Finally, Lou Salvatore, a small, elegant man with a full head of thick salt-and-pepper hair and a member of the Firm's innermost circle, stepped to the podium, flanked by a young staffer toting an orange Andersen umbrella. The crowd, relieved to see that at least one of the big shots was out there getting drenched too, perked up and started to chant, "Lou! Lou! Lou!" The chant had a wistful quality, like the rallies fans have in a small-town airport for the local basketball team after it loses the state championship.

Salvatore had been working at Arthur Andersen since before most of the people at the rally were born. He had run the New York office and served as Andersen's acting CEO for six months before the appointment of Joseph Berardino in January 2001. He favored elegant suits, was a major campaign contributor to George W. Bush's presidential campaign, and was very active in Catholic community groups. He'd even hired a nun to work full-time in Andersen's New York offices. I knew him well. He had a decent amount of charisma, for an accountant, and good manners, too. But today he was ready for a brawl.

"We're going to fight them until there's no fight left," he shouted into the microphone, which was a little too high for him. "And we're going to vindicate all of you people and all of the other Arthur Andersen people!

"Because," he said, enunciating every word, "we didn't do anything wrong!" A hopeful whoop erupted from the crowd. "And when the fight is over," he continued, "everyone is going to walk away proud, saying 'I was, I am, and I always will be Arthur Andersen.' We'll beat the weather, we'll beat the Justice Department, we'll beat the competition, and everybody will be just fine."

•  •  •

As the rally blared on, Andersen's CEO, Joseph Berardino, sat in his corner office on the twelfth floor, staring out the window at the crowd below. As the head of the worldwide Firm, Berardino had presided over a perfect storm of accounting scandals and management missteps. He had fought his way to the top of the company he had joined right out of Fairfield University—and now, just a year later, it was over. Faced with a criminal indictment, mass client defections, and the possible collapse of the $9.3 billion Firm, he realized that there was no way out, and he announced his resignation. He had failed his firm.

A few hours later, he would appear on CNN's *Moneyline with Lou Dobbs* to tell the world that he was taking the fall—for the good of his company. "What I do know is we have a lot of great people who deserve a career," he said, hooded eyes downcast, shoulders slumped, the picture of self-flagellation. "And if my sacrifice helps just a few of those, I will feel really good about what I've done to-day. I've been trained by my parents and by Jesuits, who taught me in college that the greatest thing you can do is do something for someone else. That's all I'm thinking about right now. Someday, maybe, I'll think about myself."

Berardino would not, however, cop to what the world already knew—that contrary to Salvatore's remarks, Andersen had, indeed, done something wrong. It had become a place where the mad scramble for fees had trumped good judgment. And it was that failure—not a government vendetta—that left hundreds of employees shivering in the rain, begging for their jobs. Less than three months later, Oscar Criner, a computer science professor and foreman of the jury, stood in a tense Houston courtroom and pronounced the Firm guilty of obstruction of justice in the investigation of Enron Corp. The Firm announced it would stop auditing public clients by August 31, effectively ending the existence of one of the world's best-known companies. It was a quick and brutal halt to a business that had prospered for nearly a century.

On October 16, 2002, on a warm fall day in Houston, Andersen partner C. E. Andrews stood quietly in the courtroom as the judge handed down the maximum sentence—a $500,000 fine and five years' probation. Andersen defense attorney Rusty Hardin, dapper in gold tie and tan suit, mustered the appropriate outrage and an-nounced an immediate appeal. "Does it, from a societal standpoint, make sense to destroy an entire company because of what you be-lieve was the conduct of a few?" he asked. "We will go to our grave saying we are not guilty." Leslie Caldwell, director of the Enron Task Force for the Justice Department, had a different take. "The government did not destroy Arthur Andersen," she said stonily. "The management destroyed Arthur Andersen."

•   •   •

Going to work at Arthur Andersen had been like taking a job at IBM. It was a great and venerable American brand that had, over the course of the twentieth century, become a global symbol of strength and solidity. Behind its famous doors was a group of highly trained professionals known everywhere for their reputation for hard work, competence, and a steady hand. "We were the Marine Corps of the accounting profession," said Rich Lowe, a retired Andersen partner. But then, during the 1990s, something changed. In my years working at Arthur Andersen, I came to believe that the white-shoed accounting firm known for its legions of trained, loyal, honest professionals—a place that once had the respect, envy, and admiration of everyone in Corporate America—had lost its way. The accountants and the consultants forgot what it meant to be accountable.

The fall of Arthur Andersen, I believe, was no murder. It was a suicide, set in motion long before there was ever an indictment. Yet while the guilty verdict sealed Andersen's fate, by the time it came it was merely a formality, the last nail in a coffin whose grave had been primed for burial.

Yes, I was part of a corporate behemoth that was successful far beyond what founder Arthur Andersen ever imagined when he opened for business in Chicago in 1913. I lived the power of a global firm in which you could experience the "Andersen Way," whether you were meeting with clients in Singapore or San Diego, in Rome or in Rochester. But I also experienced a culture rife with conflict and an organization consumed by never-ending financial and political pressures. I worked with people so in thrall to the great bull market of the 1990s and the power and wealth of their corporate benefactors that they completely forgot that the true purpose of their job was to protect the investing public. I watched as Arthur Andersen came down from its lofty perch to wrestle in the mud in search of more fees, more power, more political clout, more everything. And when that happened, we all got dirty.

It is Arthur Andersen's lack of accountability that has inspired me to write this book. As an observer of corporate cultures, I believe strongly that the suicide of Arthur Andersen—and the assault on the investing public's trust—could have been avoided had people paid attention to the danger signs flashing everywhere in the late 1990s. This is not a book about the Enron debacle, since Enron, in my view, was simply the final straw for Andersen. Instead, it is a book about what it was like to work at a respected company as its culture began to decay. It is also about what happens when the values of an organization begin to distort your own. I, too, went along with a system that I knew was ultimately unsustainable, and I had to live with the consequences.

# The Making of an Android

*My own mother told me in Norwegian, "Think straight— talk straight." No finer heritage could possibly be passed on from one generation to another. It has been as a firm rock to which I could anchor in a storm. Never has it failed me. . . . This challenge will never fail anyone in a time of trial and temptation.*

—ARTHUR E. ANDERSEN

THE TELEPHONE RANG just before 6:00 P.M. on a beautiful spring evening in April 1995. I was in the Boylston Street office of my consulting firm, Resources for Responsible Management, looking out over Copley Square. To the left stood the elegant Romanesque Trinity Church; directly across the square was the Copley Plaza Hotel with its regal red awnings, and to the right, I could see the handsome Boston Public Library up the street. It was a pretty spectacular location, one that I felt mirrored the success of the firm that my husband, Chuck Powers, and I had opened almost eight years earlier. We consulted primarily to Fortune 500 companies on ethical risk related to strategic, organizational, and environmental change.

I put the phone to my ear and heard the silky yet urgent tones of a man who was about to change my life. It was a headhunter for Ray & Berndtson. "Is this Barbara Toffler?" he asked. "Your name has been suggested as someone who might be right for a position that we have with a consulting firm. It would be an opportunity to set up a new consulting service line in business ethics. Would you be interested in getting more information about the job?" As it happened, we were at a transition point with our company. Chuck had just secured the funding for the start-up of a nonprofit environmental science organization—one based in New Jersey. My longtime associate, Amy, had just had a baby and wanted to spend more time at home, and few of my clients had been located in the Boston area to begin with. We had wondered, just that week, whether it might be time for a change—and suddenly, opportunity rang. "Of course," I said, and gave him my fax number. Ten minutes later, I was looking at a rather sketchy job description in a nameless but "prestigious, well-known" consulting firm.

The position sounded incredibly interesting. Actually, it sounded fabulous. It appeared to be, as I would later explain to anyone who asked, an entrepreneurial opportunity within a resource-rich organization. Wow, I thought, this is like a dream. I could do the same work I've been doing, but with a regular paycheck. (No matter how successful the company, as the head of a small operation, you are always aware of where the buck starts and stops—and the others who are dependent on you.)

The next day, I called the recruiter back. "This sounds very intriguing," I said. "I would like to pursue it, but I don't truthfully feel I could without having the name of the company." He called back a few hours later and said, "The firm is Arthur Andersen." I was taken aback. Wasn't that an accounting firm? "Are you sure you don't mean Andersen Consulting?" I wasn't aware that Arthur Andersen had its own consulting group—nor did I know exactly how Andersen Consulting and Arthur Andersen were linked. Why would an audit firm have a consulting practice, I naively wondered, when they have a large consulting sister firm?

I did know something about Andersen Consulting. In fact, I had conducted a program for its strategy consulting group in 1993 at the Phoenician Hotel in Phoenix. The program looked at some of the situations that could raise ethical concerns for the Firm, using cases I cowrote with Andersen Consulting staff focusing specifically on the pressures faced by high-level managers and young partners. I had been impressed that a consulting group was willing to face some of its "underbelly" realities.

But that was Andersen Consulting. I had been doing consulting for almost 15 years, and I had never heard anything about Arthur Andersen offering consulting services. What I did know about Arthur Andersen was limited, but positive. When I was an assistant professor at Harvard, a consulting client had asked about the then-new Foreign Corrupt Practices Act. The very best piece of explanatory material I could find had been distributed by Arthur Andersen to its clients. It was clear, concise, and knowledgeable, at a time when there was considerable confusion about the Act. To this day I still use the Arthur Andersen description in relevant presentations.

I also remembered the first nonprofit organization that Chuck had started in 1980. Called the Health Effects Institute (HEI), it was an independent entity jointly funded by the Environmental Protection Agency and the then-27 automotive manufacturers to fund research into the health effects of automotive emissions. Because of the political nature of the organization, Chuck and his colleagues needed HEI to be, as an editorial in *The New York Times* stated, "fiercely independent." They chose Archibald Cox—Harvard law professor, former Solicitor General of the United States, and legendary hero of the famous Saturday Night Massacre of Watergate fame—to chair the board. And they chose Arthur Andersen, a name equal to Cox in integrity, as its auditor.

Finally, I recalled that the Firm had invested $5 million to develop, produce, and distribute a case- and video-based business ethics program for undergraduate business majors in U.S. colleges. It had even brought business professors to its St. Charles training facility to teach them how to use the materials. (After I joined Arthur Andersen, I viewed the videotapes and was startled to see Stew Leonard of Stew Leonard's Dairy Store urging young college students to be ethical. "The people that look for shortcuts," he said, "the prisons are filled with them." Leonard later went to jail after being convicted in the largest tax fraud in Connecticut history.)

Arthur Andersen seemed like a place with its priorities straight. Certainly, it had a stellar reputation in audit and accounting—one that had lasted for nearly a century. I told the recruiter I would think about it and get back to him in a few days, while I set out to learn more about what, I soon realized, was an extraordinary organization.

● ● ●

Imagine the scene: Arthur E. Andersen standing ramrod straight in his office, dressed, as usual, in a white shirt and a dark suit, a fresh yellow rose tucked neatly into his lapel. Facing him, fuming, was the longtime president of a large railway company, one of Andersen's first—and most lucrative—clients. While doing the audit for the company, Andersen had noticed that it hadn't properly accounted for maintenance charges that should have been part of operating expenses. He pointed out the error but got no response. Finally, he told the president that if the company didn't clean up its statements, he would mention the inappropriate accounting in his report. Furious, the executive had come all the way to Andersen's office in Chicago to demand that Andersen change his mind and approve the books—or else.

It was a critical moment for the man and his fledgling business. Andersen, DeLany & Co. had been in business for less than a year, and one of its few clients—a well-known company that could destroy Andersen's reputation and torpedo its search for new business—was outraged at its style of accounting. With his red hair and flushed cheeks, Arthur Andersen looked even younger than his 28 years, but he was a stubborn man and a proud man, and he knew he wasn't going to back down. "There's not enough money in the city of Chicago," he proclaimed, "to induce me to change that report!" Andersen lost the business. But months later, that railway company filed for bankruptcy. He had been right.

If you prick the finger of a longtime Arthur Andersen partner, stories like this one flow out like drops of deep red blood. That single maxim, "Think straight, talk straight," was the touchstone of the Firm. Arthur Andersen, partners would say with pride, was a place where integrity mattered more than fees, where standing up for what you believed in was a virtue, where it was better to do the right thing than the easy thing. Andersen and his successor, Leonard Spacek, were portrayed, almost cartoonlike, as heroes of American capitalism, men who stood up for the investing public and men who understood that for a professional services firm, reputation was the only thing that mattered.

Of course, stories like this one tend to be exaggerated when they find their way into corporate lore. Yet even rivals commended the Firm for its intensely loyal culture and willingness to be the conscience of the industry. Throughout its history, the Firm regularly broke lockstep and spoke out against accounting abuses or bad policies. It risked the wrath of its clients, the government, and its rivals to push for what its leaders felt was right. Sometimes, that meant losing lucrative fees. Other times, it meant gaining enemies. But everyone agreed that Arthur Andersen was a place with courage.

•  •  •

To be a young immigrant in Chicago at the turn of the century was to be a part of the most exciting, dynamic city in the world. In an eyeblink, Chicago had transformed itself from a prairie cowtown to the nation's second-largest city. Hundreds of families arrived every day by ship, train, and wagon, ravenous for a new slice of life and eager to grab one of the thousands of low-paying jobs available in the new manufacturing heart of the country. Chicago looked like the future, too, as newly rich industrialists began to build the most innovative and luxurious buildings ever seen. The "Chicago style" transformed American architecture and helped a brand-new, quintessentially American city rise from the ashes of the great Fire of 1871. In its place emerged a city where rules were made to be broken and everything was possible. Music in a cacophony of languages, from Polish to Italian to Greek, flowed through the trash-filled city streets. Saloons and factories, brothels and banks flourished side by side. Chicago brimmed with energy and with chutzpah.

The year 1913 was a time of progress and excitement in American business. Every week brought a new invention or concept that would improve lives. There was the introduction of the electric dishwasher, the first moving automobile assembly line in Highland Park, Michigan, and, of course, the exploding popularity of the Model T. It was also the year of the first federal income tax, which would create a need for specialists able to decipher the new rules. It was the perfect time for 28-year-old Arthur E. Andersen, a first-generation American, to hang out his shingle.

On December 1, 1913, unnoticed among the new gadgets and concepts, Andersen and a colleague from Price Waterhouse, Clarence M. DeLany, took the plunge. They opened for business inside Chicago's bustling Loop in a small office at 111 West Monroe Street. It's a short walk down the street to Andersen's headquarters. When I signed on in 1995 it was a bustling but soulless postmodern box that, by mid-2002, was virtually empty.

From the start, Andersen was a maverick. He wasn't Scottish or English, like so many of the U.S.-based accountants who had been sent abroad to gain a foothold in this booming economy. He was based in Chicago, not New York, as many of the prominent firms were. He thought practical experience was a lot more valuable than a classical education and preferred hard workers from rough-and-tumble backgrounds over highly educated sorts. And he came to believe that American companies deserved a new type of accounting, one that went beyond the numbers to really embrace the business problems of a client. His concept of auditing resembled consulting as much as it did accounting: Andersen advertised not only audits but also "investigations for special purposes, such as to determine the advisability of investment in a new enterprise or the extension of an old business," and "the designing and installing of new systems of financial and cost accounting and organization, or the modernizing of existing systems." Today, as we condemn the fusion of consulting and accounting, it is worth noting that Andersen himself probably wouldn't have seen a conflict—if it was done with integrity.

Arthur Andersen was famous for his moralistic persona, but accountants and integrity were not usually synonymous in those days, particularly in Chicago. This was a city where the accountant who grabbed the headlines was not the straitlaced Andersen but rather

Al Capone's own bookkeeper, Jake "Greasy Thumb" Guzik. Standards to become an accountant were inconsistent at best. Corporate secrecy was the order of the day, since having one's books audited was something one did by choice rather than by government fiat. But Andersen did things differently. He insisted that the accounting be "right," even if the rules permitted a different interpretation, and he never hesitated to challenge anyone on that matter.

Arthur Andersen & Co. grew steadily. But it would take—ironically—the major collapse and bankruptcy of an energy and utility company to put the young, aggressive firm on the map for good. Unlike in the Enron saga, they were the good guys this time. The Insull group of companies was the Enron of its day, and its president, Samuel Insull, was Ken Lay and Andrew Fastow rolled into one. A colorful, bold Brit who as a youth finagled his way into a job as assistant to Thomas Edison, Insull was placed in charge of many of Edison's power companies and later went off on his own to build an enormous web of electrical utilities. By the 1920s, Insull controlled hundreds of power companies—mostly by pyramiding one acquisition onto another. Like Enron, Insull played a wheel-and-deal game that ultimately would collapse: Just before the crash of 1929, he created two investment trusts that helped purchase large stakes in Insull system companies. They were funded by stock offerings and short-term loans backed by his own equity.

Although Insull made it through the crash, by 1932, the value of his equities had fallen so far that they could no longer cover the loans. The bankers, fearing a default and bankruptcy whose reverberations could deal another blow to the economy, looked for a neutral party to step in and straighten things out—and settled on Arthur Andersen. Andersen, with the help of his employees, did his job and more. He kept the companies out of bankruptcy, unwound multiple transactions, and ultimately helped put the utility industry back on its feet. It was a huge job for the still-young company, requiring most of its Chicago staff to work full-time on the project, but it paid off big.

Arthur Andersen & Co. had become a player. But it was government regulation—an attempt to stop the profiteering that had destroyed the savings of millions—that gave the accounting industry its biggest boost. In 1933, the New York Stock Exchange required all Big Board companies to have their numbers audited annually. The same year, Congress passed the Securities Act of 1933, which allowed the Federal Trade Commission to set some basic accounting standards—and also, for the first time, said that a corporation, its officers and directors, the underwriters of a stock, *and* the accountants all could be held liable for problems with the company's financial statements. The next year, Congress created the Securities and Exchange Commission to oversee the financial reporting process for public companies. It was a blessing and a curse for auditors. Suddenly they had huge amounts of business falling into their laps, but for the first time, they could end up on the hook should things go wrong.

As Arthur Andersen's reputation grew, he became a well-known public speaker who used his fame as a bully pulpit to discuss the special responsibility accountants bore. In a 1932 lecture on business ethics, he said:

> If the confidence of the public in the integrity of accountants' reports is shaken, their value is gone. To preserve the integrity of his reports, the accountant must insist upon absolute independence of judgment and action. The necessity of preserving this position of independence indicates certain standards of conduct.

Inside the Firm, he worked hard to create something different—a business with its own standards and principles. Andersen's obsession with consistency would eventually become known as the "One Firm" concept; that no matter where you were in the world, if you were a client of Arthur Andersen, you could expect to receive the same quality of work, the same approach to the work, and the same types of people trained the same way. "We must have, as we have never had before, a united family, whether the offices are within or outside the borders of the United States, and we must be tied together as a continuing organization, making for better service to the outside world," wrote Andersen in a 1946 memo.

Although Andersen was a professor, when it came to learning inside the Firm, he rejected outside help. He saw training as something that would be carried down from partner to first-year, from master to student, from father to son (there weren't any moms and daughters at this time), and something that should continue throughout one's career, with regular lectures and meetings. The "Andersen Way" would be ingrained in each new employee as they signed on with this eccentric man and his growing family. Even then, he was creating a group of insiders that saw itself as something apart from the mainstream, an inner circle that admitted only a select few.

Andersen also distinguished his firm with the creation in 1939 of the "Blueback," a memo that every engagement partner had to write to the management of a company once the audit was completed. Rather than just a letter certifying the numbers, auditors were supposed to note anything they had seen in doing that audit that might be useful to the company, anything from the fact that a plant was a mess to a suggestion that a reorganization of a certain division might save the client some money. Some clients resented the advice, others ignored it, but the reports—bound in blue covers—became a key distinction for the Firm.

After being ill for years, Arthur Andersen died in January 1947. It was a huge blow for an organization whose reputation was so bound up with its namesake. The Firm almost went under—Andersen, always afraid of losing control, had never really designated a successor—but then Leonard Spacek stepped into the void. Spacek was another poor midwestern boy, a short man with a big voice, and he was famous for being the only person who could fight with Andersen and get away with it. "I used to tell him, 'I'm from Iowa and I can always go back there and plow corn,'" Spacek said. Spacek was a tremendous speaker and communicator who made an effort to be more approachable than the aloof Andersen, stopping to chat with first-years in the elevator and reducing Andersen's palatial office to a more appropriate size for the head of a partnership. Although Spacek was a compromise candidate, within a few years he was as firmly entrenched in power as the founder had been.

It was under Spacek's leadership that the firm grew into the most respected—and feared—accounting firm in the world. Revenues nearly tripled between 1947 and 1956, growing to $18 million, of which $4.6 million was net income, and partners increased from 26 to 85. By the time Spacek gave up his operating role to become chairman in 1963, revenues had reached $51 million. While Andersen was famous for having the guts to take on a wayward company, Spacek went so far as to take on an entire industry—and the government, too—in his quest for an accounting system that made sense. "Leonard believed that you could be outspoken within the profession and develop a firm on integrity, and you would be respected by your clients for trying to move the profession forward," said Harvey Kapnick, another former chairman of the Firm, in an interview shortly before his death in August 2002.

Spacek took Andersen's concepts and expanded them dramatically. First, he set out to grow the Firm into a truly global partnership, where a client could expect the same quality of service everywhere in the world. The decision came after Forrest Mars, a major client based in London, told Spacek that the service there—through an affiliate company—was "lousy." After conceding that he'd never been there to check it out, Spacek then went to London, fired the affiliate, and decided that Arthur Andersen would have its own offices, with its own standard practices, anywhere in the world a client needed them. By 1963, Arthur Andersen boasted 55 offices in 27 countries. The offices would be staffed not with American expatriates, but with local nationals who had gone through the exact same training as the Americans. And they would share in a single profit pool, so that everyone had a stake in building new offices and everyone benefited from the existing business, too.

Starting in the 1950s, Spacek became the nagging conscience of an industry that desperately needed reform. Interpretations were inconsistent and rules were woefully outdated, he said, calling the Generally Accepted Accounting Principles (GAAP) "generally antiquated accounting principles." It was nearly impossible, he said, to compare the statements of two companies in the same industry.

I firmly felt that accounting principles should be based upon a principle of accounting that was fair to the consumer, to labor, to management, to the investor and to the public. Now to the public so the public would know that no one is lying, to the consumer because so much of our accounting either in wartime or peacetime was a determining factor of what prices were. The investor, for obvious reasons—he had to make comparisons. If a company was earning $5.19, it should be $5.19, not $10.38 at another company that didn't follow good accounting.

Spacek had a solution: the establishment of what he called a U.S. Court of Accounting Appeals, a higher, independent court that would enforce a uniform code of accounting principles. He got lots of publicity for the idea, but the other firms, who saw his rabble-rousing as a threat to their own power, ultimately shot it down. So Spacek—to the frustration of his Big 8 counterparts—continued the crusade on his own, taking on first the oil industry and then the railroads and the savings-and-loan industry. The railroads, he said, had overvalued their earnings by as much as 50 percent because of arcane old rules set up by the Interstate Commerce Commission that didn't require them to depreciate rails, ties, and other property. To back up the point, Arthur Andersen resigned all of its railroad accounts but two—the companies that agreed to change their accounting. The Firm bolstered its reputation as a company that took a stand, even at the expense of losing a client.

The savings-and-loan crisis, when it came, ensnared almost every one of the Big 8. But Arthur Andersen skated away virtually clean, because it had made the decision, years earlier, to resign all of its clients in the industry. S&Ls for years had taken advantage of a loophole that allowed them to boost earnings by recording the value of deferred taxes. Arthur Andersen accountants thought the rule was misleading and tried to convince their clients to change their accounting. When they refused, Andersen did what it felt it had to: It resigned all of its accounts rather than stand behind accounting that it felt to be wrong.

It all added up to a firm with a reputation that seemed good enough for me. I called back the recruiter and said it would be my pleasure to fly to Chicago for an interview.

•   •   •

I was not genetically predisposed to be an Android—the term others used to describe the vanilla persona of the typical Arthur Andersen employee, plucked out of undergraduate schools not for connections, or even creativity, but for the ability to adapt and to play by rules set long ago. I remember a discussion I'd had when I was teaching at Harvard with Tony Athos, then a professor specializing in organizational behavior. Tony asked me how I would describe myself professionally in one word. It came to me instantly: "debunker."

I was the kind of person who loved to challenge conventional wisdom by turning a situation on its head. When faced with a strong institutional culture, my first instinct was to analyze it—and, sometimes, to rebel against it. I had a reputation for being aggressively outspoken (I called it honesty), to the point that at the end of my first year teaching M.B.A.s at Harvard, my students honored me with a cake and an aerosol can labeled "Bullshit Repellent." Sometimes being a debunker was a good thing, sometimes not. But that was me. So Arthur Andersen was not exactly a place I could have imagined working before I got that fateful phone call.

My whole career path had been unorthodox, to say the least. Yes, I had been on the faculty of Harvard Business School for eight years and built a successful consulting firm, but I took a rather circuitous route to get there. A black-tights-and-turtleneck-clad Smith College dropout, I had spent a few years hanging out in Greenwich Village, smoking and drinking coffee at the Café Figaro, and working in the theater before going back to get my B.A. at Columbia. I was 31 years old when I began my Ph.D. studies in organizational behavior at the Yale Graduate School's Department of Administrative Sciences. My dissertation examined the interaction between a person and the organization that hires him, and the type of occupational role that that person ends up playing. I found myself fascinated by the crossroads of behavior and culture. Why did people behave in a certain way in one organization, when in another environment they might act differently? I concluded that unlike the traditional view of organizational socialization—which says that an institution inculcates its norms and values into the individual—the individual has some impact on the organization, as well. It wasn't simply a one-way street. But I had not yet met an Arthur Andersen Android.

After two years teaching at Boston University's Graduate School of Management, I landed at the Harvard Business School as an assistant professor of business administration in the area of organizational behavior. Although it wasn't my official field, I decided to write a book on business ethics. Contrary to the traditional ivory tower theoretical discourse, my book, *Tough Choices: Managers Talk Ethics,* used a Studs Terkel–like interview approach to look at real businesspeople facing real ethical dilemmas. The book won recognition as one of the first to draw attention to real-life ethics from a business point of view, not a religious or philosophical one.

I didn't get tenure at Harvard, but I spent an incredible eight years there. I refined my views on ethics, and I learned how to interact within one of the strongest organizational cultures on the planet. At Harvard, it is assumed that you must mold yourself, Jell-O–like, to the institution. It was a tough, invigorating experience, and a good practice run for Arthur Andersen. Next, I drew on my Harvard experiences and relationships and teamed up with my husband, Chuck Powers, a former Yale professor and vice president of Cummins Engine Co., to launch Resources for Responsible Management (RRM) in 1987. Our company coincided nicely with a growing interest in the topic that had been building since the 1970s. Several companies began to design and deliver business ethics programs, and some recognized how their cultures affected behavior and did assessments to identify and rectify their vulnerabilities.

In 1991, the world of business ethics changed dramatically—awakening, once again, the debunker in me. That November, the U.S. Sentencing Commission issued guidelines for sentencing corporations convicted of federal offenses (Federal Sentencing Guidelines for Organizations, or FSGO). The FSGO required extremely high fines for companies whose employees committed misdeeds while doing their jobs. But there was a catch: If a convicted organization had in place seven "mitigating factors," any penalty would be significantly reduced. Collectively, these factors were referred to as "an effective ethics program" and included having an ethics officer, policies and procedures, and a reporting mechanism such as a hot line or ombudsperson. The FSGO guidelines were well intended but, like many regulations, had loopholes. Now a company no longer had to worry about the way it conducted its business, the risks employees faced in doing their jobs, or the integrity of their decisions. While I liked the focus on ethics, I worried that the guidelines were like a "get out of jail free" card for Corporate America. From my perspective, they relieved corporations of some of their ethical responsibilities and substituted what I sometimes called "mindless legal compliance." I wanted to fight back, and, in 1995, I believed that Arthur Andersen offered me that opportunity.

●　●　●

I arrived at Arthur Andersen's Chicago office in May 1995 for my first interview and found myself bobbing along in a sea of golf shirts. The Firm didn't have casual dress—ties were de rigueur—but the day had been devoted to a series of workshops, so the dress code had been relaxed. The funny thing about the casual outfit was that everyone wore the exact same thing. I wondered if there had been some edict announced over the paging system: "Monday is golf-shirt day—collars required." This was, I immediately sensed, a place with a distinct culture.

I met with only a few people that day, including Dean Fischer, the partner running some of the Firm's new consulting services and my boss-to-be. Fischer, a buttoned-up midwesterner with an overgrown crew cut, looked like a Boy Scout but talked a savvy game. I was told he had a quick and fierce temper, but I saw no sign of it that day. Dean seemed really enthusiastic about having me on board, and he asked me a lot about my clients, the fees my firm charged, and our revenues. We had a brief discussion about title, and we agreed that if I was offered the job, it would be as national partner—a position with much of the authority of an equity partner but with fixed compensation and no voting rights. Equity partners, by contrast, owned a piece of the Firm and made the management decisions. It sounded fine to me.

When I told Dean that I wasn't interested in the job if it wasn't in New York (my husband had also been offered a job in the area), he said okay—with a catch. "This is a firm with a very distinct, incredibly complex culture," he said. "We have a terrible history with experienced hires. I don't think this firm is going to grow if we can't bring in people like you. I would really like to break this cycle. If you're really going to be successful here, I would like you to commit to staying in Chicago for six months to a year." He looked me straight in the eye and said, "I am going to stick to you like glue. I will teach you the Firm. Otherwise you'll never succeed."

That day I also met with Gary Beu, head of human resources in Chicago. Gary was a friendly, outgoing fellow in his early forties with a slightly receding hairline. We hit it off immediately. In the eight months I spent in Chicago, he became my friend, mentor, crying towel, and complaint department. Gary mentioned that Arthur Andersen was beginning to have a problem with turnover despite spending millions on training, and that it was gaining a reputation as a place that trained all the best employees in every *other* accounting firm. Gary also mentioned how tough it was for new people to fit in. There had been many failures with experienced hires, particularly with "luminaries," AA's word for outsiders with established careers like me.

Many people in the group I would be joining, the CRCO, or Central Region Consulting Organization, had started their careers as accountants, joining Arthur Andersen right out of college (including Dean and Gary) and only later becoming consultants. Although I found out that Arthur Andersen had its own hotshot Business Consulting Group, I wouldn't be part of that but, instead, would be part of the CRCO, a motley mix of consulting services tied tightly to audit. It was a part of the Firm that was suddenly getting a lot of attention, and the hope was that my work could further help this group take off.

The strangest thing about that day was that neither Dean nor anyone else asked me exactly what it was that I did or what it meant to work with a client on business ethics. Although I repeatedly emphasized that there were a number of ways the corporate world viewed ethics and that we should talk about the Firm's expectations, no one seemed to be interested. It bothered me, but I liked the feel of the place and the people I met, and I suddenly desperately wanted this opportunity to work out. So, I think, did Dean, in the same way two people on a first date decide, before they really know each other, that they've met "the one." I went back once or twice more after that to firm up details, but the deal was essentially done. I would start at Arthur Andersen's Chicago office in October 1995.

*Teach your children well*
—CROSBY, STILLS, NASH & YOUNG, 1970

Dean and Gary, both lifelong Arthur Andersen loyalists, knew something that I didn't—that the Firm's intense focus on its own people really applied only to those who started as youngsters. Joining Arthur Andersen wasn't an ad hoc decision, as it was at so many other companies. Even in the mid-1990s, when corporate loyalty was supposed to have gone the way of the dinosaur, it was a firm that hunted for those who were receptive to the rules of this venerable place and who wanted to make a career there. The precedent had come straight from Arthur E. Andersen himself, who was by all accounts obsessed with getting the right people.

While the concept had been refined over the years, adding psychology and science to Andersen's own nose for a good hire, it remained essentially the same until the day I started there. That was both wonderful and terrible: The Firm's deep commitment to training and recruiting was its greatest strength, but it was also, in a way, its Achilles' heel. By the mid-1990s, a decline in accounting majors, a booming economy in other areas, and an internal emphasis on consulting meant that more and more people with experience were hired—people like me. In contrast to the Androids, we were hired for our years of expertise, our skills, our contacts, our opinions. Yet Arthur Andersen's culture was founded squarely on the idea of shaping people to the Firm, not vice versa. It created two classes of citizens, leading to confusion and conflict.

The "One Firm" concept was the glue behind every major move, particularly this one. To have the same high quality of service everywhere in the world, the people, too, had to be of standard quality. They would be inducted into the secret rituals and procedures that constituted the Arthur Andersen Way, but the most important part of the process was first identifying the best and brightest and then molding them, like raw clay, into a new form: Arthur Andersen Man. And it was Man: The first woman partner at Arthur Andersen, M. Virginia Nabors, was not named until 1976, and by 1998, women made up just 7.5 percent of partners, according to *Bowman's Accounting Report*.

The seduction process began long before a student graduated from college, usually with the offer of an internship. By the 1990s, the Firm was even running programs for high school students. It usually sent relatively recent graduates to a college's initial recruiting meetings, and students were amazed to see their acquaintances transformed from the collegiate slobs they once had been into young professionals. They dressed smartly, in perfectly pressed suits, white shirts, and ties, carried themselves well, and somehow looked as if they'd arrived, although they were still in their early twenties. "They looked the best, they dressed the best, they talked the best, their hair was trimmed, they were always well kept," said one former auditor who was recruited out of Notre Dame in the early 1980s. "It looked like Hollywood to me."

Arthur Andersen offered something special: a way of life. For accounting students, particularly those who were the first in their family to attend college—a type the Firm targeted for its hunger and drive—getting a job there meant making it. They all knew that their chances of making partner were slim, and that they were in for a rigorous, exhausting few years as the "grunts." But there was that big fat brass ring at the end. Even if they didn't make partner, the opportunities for an Arthur Andersen–trained accountant were many and choice. We would "tell them that they should find other employment because their future was limited," said Spacek in an oral history, "but . . . help them get into good jobs because they were what I call our 'fifth column.' When they got into the businesses, they remembered their alma mater, that's all." The point was to maintain goodwill, so that even the people who didn't make it remembered their experience fondly and would go out of their way to steer business to the good old Firm.

With a standout reputation for integrity, Arthur Andersen was upfront about its values, and used that to its advantage. Said one former employee: "I went in with this pie-in-the-sky vision: If I have to be an accountant, I might as well be one who's going to try to do good. What always struck me about AA was that integrity and honesty were the most important things. And that we will be the watchdog." In 1973, the Firm became the first to issue an annual report, and received broad praise in 1974 for the creation of a Public Review Board, a group of ombudsman types whose job was to monitor the Firm's internal systems.

To get a job at Arthur Andersen, you had to have the requisite GPA and extracurricular activities. But you also had to have the right stuff. The Firm used few formal recruiters, preferring to rely on its own staff, managers, and partners, whose enthusiasm and pride came from the heart. It used the first interview to ferret out certain types of personalities and behaviors. By the mid-1980s, this had developed into a process called Critical Behavior Interviewing, which every single recruiter used. There were two categories of personality traits. Those in Group A were called "innate" behaviors, while those in Group B were dubbed "learned" behaviors. There were nine characteristics—four innate, including initiative and integrity, and five learned, such as time management and attention to detail. Students were regularly asked how they'd handled an ethical dilemma or a situation in which their integrity was questioned. No strong response to that meant no job.

To make it to the next round, you had to have all four qualities in the innate behavior group and as many as possible in the second group. Recruiters checked off "does have," "may have," or "did not see," and if you didn't score well in the "does have" category, you were out of luck. As a result, on-campus interviews were a little bit different from the other firms'. "Deloitte would ask you about debt defeasance," said a former employee, "and they [AA] were like, 'tell me about band.'" All over the world, recruiters were given the same card with the nine characteristics on it. Skills could be taught at Arthur Andersen, but you still had to have the nature. The Firm would handle the nurture.

The second interview usually took place in the local office where you hoped to work. As with most big companies, you'd meet with people from the group with which you might be working, but there were few queries about accounting skills; the assumption was that the skills were there, or if not, that the candidate was smart enough to learn them. The real issue, again, was personality: Is this someone with whom I'd like to entertain a client? Is this a guy I can work with? Is this a good guy? If the answer was yes, the partners would talk while the recruit was at lunch and he'd get the offer when he returned. If he didn't overdo the free drinks and get soused, that is.

●　●　●

Now it was time to build an Android. Training was considered a sacred part of the Firm even when Arthur Andersen started it in 1913. It was part of what the Firm was, who belonged there, and how things were done. Training and development was an investment—a costly one, averaging an incredible 6 percent or more of the Firm's total fees every year. However, training was seen as a critical advantage and the only way to ensure that its people would take the same approach to a problem in every office.

New hires typically would spend their first week in their home office, then attend a training program for two weeks before formally beginning their job. In the 1960s, many sessions were held at the Knickerbocker Hotel in Chicago for consultants, and Northwestern University's downtown campus for auditors. Eventually, the Knickerbocker became the Playboy Hotel, the numbers of trainees became unwieldy, and these white-bread professionals decided they needed their own space. In 1970, then-CEO Harvey Kapnick bought St. Dominic College, a small women's college in St. Charles, Illinois, a prosperous agricultural hamlet of some 42,000 people thirty-five miles from Chicago. Included in the $4 million deal were dorms, academic buildings, and fifty-five acres of bucolic woods. Renamed the Center for Professional Education and commonly called St. Charles, it transformed regular people into Androids.

The metamorphosis from mild-mannered college graduate to competent, efficient Android began when you landed at O'Hare or Midway Airport on a Sunday night en route to Arthur Andersen's famed St. Charles campus. You might have been arriving from Philadelphia or Biloxi, Mexico City, or even Beijing. You might have grown up in a small town or a huge city, been an athlete or a bookworm, had money or clawed your way through college. You might have been designated an accountant or a consultant or a tax specialist. But as you looked around at your fellow "green beans" arriving from all over the globe, you realized you all had something in common. You'd been carefully selected by the crack team of Arthur Andersen recruiters, who had systematically weeded out those who wouldn't fit into this powerful culture. And you were here to start not a job but, it was hoped, a career that would take you to many different countries and offices. You'd work like a dog for several years, but it might pay off. In twelve years or so, a few of you would make partner, with annual compensation starting at around $400,000 or higher by the late 1990s. Most of the rest of you would be gone—probably not by your choice but by Arthur Andersen's. It was up or out.

Before you started your training at St. Charles, you'd spend a week in your new office, where you'd learn some basic how-tos, as well as soak up some of the in-house culture. "The first day I reported to the office [in 1951], the office manager gave me a tour and then said, 'Here is where you hang your hats,'" recalled Eugene Delves, a former partner. "Then he gave us each five bucks and told us to go to Edwards' Hats and buy a hat. You had to wear a felt hat from Labor Day until Memorial Day, and a straw hat after. Every fall we would all go. [Edwards] would look at me and say, 'Six and seven-eighths long oval. You get a black one this year.'" The hat requirement was phased out in the 1960s, but the requirement of dressing to look older—like the client—wasn't. Office managers would routinely advance new hires money to buy the proper suits, if necessary. "It reminded me of Catholic school," said one former manager. "We always got laughed at for wearing our uniforms. It was the same thing at Arthur Andersen. In a group of young people you could spot the Arthur Andersen people." Androids were different, and every new experience confirmed it. It was an exclusive club.

Another Arthur Andersen quirk was the requirement that you take lunch out of the office. When I arrived in 1995, it wasn't a hard-and-fast rule anymore, but the idea of brown-bagging it in the office still was frowned upon. You were supposed to eat out, in professional establishments, looking like the professional you were. "The culture was that you were a businessperson in the business community and you should be seen having lunch out," said one manager. "It was a big burden for the kids: A fast-food restaurant is not where professionals eat." Again, it was a place with different customs and rules. Although I had always been the type to work through lunch, I adjusted to this one quickly—and gained several pounds during my first year at the Firm.

After learning the ropes, the newbies headed for St. Charles, where everything was predetermined, from the schedule of your day, to the group you were assigned to, to the size of your room (6 feet by 14 feet, with a desk, a bed, a shower, a toilet, a sink, a closet—and, by the mid-1980s, a window). There was no phone and no television. "They were not supposed to stay in their rooms," said Richard Nerad, who began as an auditor but soon joined the consulting side and eventually became managing partner of the Professional Education Division. "They were supposed to get out and talk to people." Even the partners stayed in the Spartan rooms, ignoring the hierarchy for a time. This gave green beans a way to begin to build connections with partners who might become your champions, shield you from internal politics, and help you succeed. It was how you learned to like and to trust the partner—something that later became an absolute requirement for success at the Firm.

The St. Charles tour of duty started with an hour of orientation in which the core values of the Firm—integrity, stewardship, and training—were laid out. There would be brief lectures on how to behave in public and a bit on the dress code. Into the 1990s, men were still required to wear dark suits, white shirts, and power ties, and women wore skirts, closed-toe shoes, and, for a time, rosettes or small ties. Tips on how to handle yourself at a cocktail party—even how to hold hors d'oeuvres—were freely shared.

Although eventually the Center brought in many professional educators and developers to study the best methods of inculcating the Andersen Way, they almost never taught the classes, leaving that to partners, managers, and even people at lower levels. There was no shirking one's duties, either. For many years, the unit commit-tee, the all-powerful group of partners that determined a partner's compensation, noted how much time one had logged at St. Charles. The partner "professors," too, were subject to the strict rules of training, even before St. Charles. Gresham Brebach, a for-mer consulting partner, remembered how he was not allowed to leave The Knickerbocker even though his wife was about to give birth. "I said, 'Jesus, I've got to see my daughter,' and [his boss] says, 'Well, Gresh, you can't. I'll send her flowers.'" Brebach stayed. He had no choice.

After orientation, you'd get down to work—an exhausting, stressful, two-week program for the auditors and a three-week ses-sion for the consultants. The auditors would spend most of their time with an audit case—for many years, a mid-sized manufacturing company and later, a chain of hair salons—while the consultants went through intensive programming training. Over the years, the courses had several different names (the audit training course was called FAST, for Firm-wide Audit Staff Training, and later ABA WST for Assurance and Business Advisory Services Worldwide Staff Train-ing). But the core principles were the same. "You go through this miniaudit from start to finish," said one former manager. "They teach how to do it the AA way, which was the only way, and there was no deviation, the point being that they do it the exact same way in Paris. If you were looking for a certain file, you know exactly where to go, you can open up the schedule, and there it is, by God."

After a long day in the classroom, there were usually a few hours of homework. There was also time scheduled every day for group-oriented athletics, such as softball, basketball, or volleyball, and you were leaned on heavily to participate. Then it was time to eat, again with one's group of 25 to 30 fellow green beans. Nerad said a special effort was made to make the food exceptional—the kind of food befitting an Arthur Andersen professional. "Most of them hadn't eaten that well since they were home with Mother," he said. "We deliberately did not want them to complain about the food."

The day wasn't over yet. After dinner, you were expected to hang out at the bar with the other students, as well as the partners. "It was designed to be you work hard and you play hard," said Brebach. "If I was teaching a class, I would go to the bar. For the first-year staff, to sit down and have beers with the partners was a big thing. There was no class system, there was no status. Partners would buy. It was a great way to build camaraderie." It was also a great way to learn what was considered acceptable behavior and what wasn't. Those who didn't behave or were late for scheduled classes or activities faced group teasing or, sometimes, humiliation. Basic socializing techniques were always at work: Help others. Don't stand out. Be professional. Be part of the group. "It was a blast," said Jonathan Goldsmith, who attended St. Charles in 2000 and who now runs andersenalumni.net, a Web site for Andersen alums. "I wouldn't even think twice about not participating. I would think you would feel out of it if you didn't do those things."

By the end of your time at St. Charles, you had bonded with your colleagues through a combination of sleep deprivation, hangovers, and, of course, a sense of accomplishment. The message was that you had achieved something special as a group that you couldn't have done as an individual. "St. Charles created a wonderful glue for everyone around the world," said Bob Lorenz, a former audit partner. "To most of us that saw it develop and grow, it was a source of great pride." It was all done to create a unique mixture of tough love and camaraderie, to mark these young souls with knowledge and values that were supposed to last their entire careers. "We got a common terminology and a common language," said Nerad. "We not only got to know one another but used the same terms. When somebody said something specific, we could see a whole concept. When they talked about a B-2 schedule, nobody had to describe it to them." It was good to be an Android.

But it was also about leverage. Arthur Andersen, like other professional service firms, made its money by using young, low-paid staff to do the majority of its work. It was a risky proposition; if you couldn't trust those people to do the right thing, the entire model would collapse. But if you put them all into a laboratory and ensured that they would emerge more similar than different, you had something special. "It was our intent to create a group that was very interchangeable," said former partner Victor Millar. "One of our selling points was if we had a partner who got hit by a truck, we had ten others who could do the same. We were Androids and we were proud of that. We understood the problem of groupthink, but on the other side, it allows you to build a very, very profitable model."

Over time, the consulting group would make the most out of St. Charles, requiring every single new hire from every single location all over the world to go through the same training. For cost reasons, the audit side began to run the training schools at two other sites starting in the early 1980s—Eindhoven, in the Netherlands, and Segovia, Spain—but nearly everyone from the United States and many other countries still made the trek to the wooded setting that was St. Charles. Some former partners say that the decision not to bring all of the international hires in for audit training later created fissures between the Americans and the non-Americans.

By 2001, St. Charles had a 500-member permanent staff, which developed more than 400 different courses. It was one of the world's largest training centers, with some 68,000 people coming through the doors every year. It also became something of a mecca for other companies, which would hire the St. Charles professionals and rent the space for their own training. After several expansions and renovations, St. Charles became a village unto itself, with dining and training facilities for more than 1,800 people at a time. There was a souvenir store, a hair salon, a shoe repair shop, game rooms, dry cleaning, and a bar on site (built after Androids got into trouble at some of the town bars years earlier). It was like starting college all over again, yet this was supposed to be the real world. Later, when the Firm broke apart, Arthur Andersen retained the right to St. Charles, and Andersen Consulting (now Accenture) leased part of the campus, paying around $50 million per year. After September 11, much of Andersen's training was put on hold, and after the Enron scandal hit, the professional staff was fired en masse. All those years of training and education fell into the same black hole that consumed the entire company.

•   •   •

As the first day of my new life approached, Chuck and I decided to make a minivacation out of my move from Boston to Chicago. We loaded up the Saab with my clothes and my files, picked out an eclectic assortment of music—Bette Midler, Ella Fitzgerald, and some sixties folk—and hit the road. It was an adventure, and while I-87 may not have had the glamour of the Pacific Coast Highway, and I was no pioneer making the trek over the Donner Pass, I reveled in the "something new" that lay ahead. I had been doing the same kind of work for a long time. The idea of having a national stage and big-company funding for my ethics work seemed too good to be true. Resources! Respect! And then, of course, there was the money. As an entrepreneur, I had done pretty well, but never as well as I would at Arthur Andersen. I felt reenergized in a way I hadn't for years. To get to have a new adventure at this stage of my career felt like such a bonus. Even a night in a Utica motel took on a charm of its own.

That bubble of elation burst when I walked into the Monroe Street headquarters of Arthur Andersen on October 1, 1995. No, it actually began to deflate the night we arrived. At that time Arthur Andersen kept several corporate apartments for employees in Chicago on short-term assignments. On an earlier visit I had been shown apartments in three buildings but told that, as a partner, I probably wanted to be in the Randolph Street building that sat on the shore of Lake Michigan. The other buildings, I was told, were more for managers and youngsters. When I was shown my apartment on that earlier trip, I had asked if it was possible to get one that looked out over the lake. Unfortunately, I was told, the apartments looking over the lake were only for equity partners.

And so the hierarchy began to assert itself. As a national partner, I was entitled to a city view. I was also told that I would get a bed, dresser, sofa, table, and a few chairs—but no credenza and no plant. Credenzas and plants were for equity partners. My first night I realized that there was something else that national partners didn't get—window shades or curtains. My beautiful city view, seen through large picture windows, was a mass of twinkling night lights that kept the bedroom bright as day. I found myself sleepless in Chicago.

The next day, I visited the housing office to request window coverings. The housing rep looked at me with surprise. "Arthur Andersen does not provide window coverings," she said. "Okay, so I'll put my own up," I said, only to be told that no holes could be made in walls or ceilings. "No one's ever complained before," said the rep. Right away, I sensed a difference between myself and the Androids. As it turned out, I spent months fighting for a damn window curtain and never got one. (I did finally hang a suction-ended closet pole over which I draped a drop cloth for darkness and a sheet for color. Shades of my college days.) It wasn't that the Firm was disorganized or cheap. It was just not "the way things are done around here."

This story may seem insignificant, but it's not. It is the perfect illustration of what made Arthur Andersen Arthur Andersen—the hierarchical culture in which for so long there was no deviation from the norm, however silly the norm may be. For most of its existence, this was not a place where independent activities were tolerated or encouraged. It was a culture in which everyone followed the rules and the leader. When the rules and leaders stood for decency and integrity, the lockstep culture was the key to competence and respectability. But when the game and the leaders changed direction, the culture of conformity led to disaster. At Arthur Andersen, I would face for the first time in my life a situation that challenged the conclusions of my dissertation. This was a culture so strong that most individuals were helpless to change things. By the time I got to the Firm in 1995, it was, to me, a place where people had begun to talk and think more crooked than straight.

None of that, however, was going through my mind as I tossed and turned in anticipation of my first day. As I walked into the

1960s-era black and white building housing most of Arthur Andersen's Chicago employees, I felt ready to make a difference. I spent the morning filling out a sheaf of paperwork. Finally, after lunch, I was called into the office of Dean Fischer, my new boss. The second I stepped through his doorway, I could feel the tension. I understood immediately that something was wrong.

"Sit down. We have to talk," he said, his face reddening. No hi, no welcome, no nothing. This wasn't the jovial guy who had talked me into coming to Arthur Andersen. "I'm not heading this group anymore," he said, his voice oozing bitterness. "I've stepped down." My heart just sank. "So who do I report to?" I asked. "I don't know," he snapped, "but it's not me."

I tried to remain calm. "You said you were going to stick to me like glue for the first two months. What happened?"

Dean wouldn't say much, other than he had had a run-in with his boss. He said—and I noted the irony—that it was over an ethical issue.

"But you're the person that wanted this position," I said, flustered. "You're the person that brought me in. Nobody else is going to have any idea who I am and what I do."

Dean was already checked out. "I don't know," he said, looking as upset as I felt. "I just don't know. You'll have to wait and see."

And with that, the conversation was over. It was Day One and I was already embroiled in some kind of internal political battle. Now what? I didn't have a laptop, I didn't have a curtain, and I didn't have a boss. I had studied enough corporate cultures to know that without a mentor or a person to be my protector, it was going to be rough.

Not long after I started at the Firm, I got a call from Pete Bott, one of the Andersen Consulting partners who had hired me for that session at the Phoenician Hotel a few years earlier. "Congratulations," he said. "I think it's marvelous that they brought you in." As we talked, I realized that he assumed I had been brought in to do internal work at Arthur Andersen, something similar to that workshop. I explained that I thought that was interesting, too, but that I had joined Arthur Andersen to sell services. "Well, I think that's good too," he said, sounding disappointed, "but I would like to see you focusing internally because we could all use it." This partner was an Andersen lifer who knew the place inside and out. It struck me as kind of an interesting statement to make at the time, but I didn't ask him any questions. I just tucked it away in the back of my mind, not to be recovered until much later on.

# The Cult in Culture

*Because of our tradition, everyone here knows who he is
and what God expects him to do.*

— Tevye, in *Fiddler on the Roof*

Until 2000, when Arthur Andersen changed its symbol to a meaningless red-orange blob in a desperate attempt to grab some New Economy buzz, the Firm's global icon was a most famous set of doors. They weren't just any doors, mind you: They were a set of two stern, strong, weighty wooden doors, and they were the gateway to every one of the Arthur Andersen offices in 84 different countries.

The doors first came into being in the 1940s, when the Firm moved to opulent headquarters on the top two floors of 120 South LaSalle Street in Chicago. Originally called the State Bank Building, it was built in 1928 and featured an incredible art deco glass ceiling on the second floor that takes your breath away even today. It was a headquarters worthy of a firm that had arrived. And Arthur Andersen's son-in-law, Vilas Johnson, decided that the Firm needed an entranceway deserving of its growing reputation. He selected two mahogany doors, with three indented panels on each, and printed the name of the Firm across both of them in gold lettering. Glass doors were becoming popular, but Johnson rejected them. "These are not billboards," he said. "These are the doors to a Firm of professionals." Being professional wasn't cheap—the doors cost $1,000—but Johnson somehow hid the real price from his boss, Arthur Andersen, and told him they cost $200. "If [Arthur Andersen] had known the true cost of the doors," joked Leonard Spacek in his oral history, "we probably would have had a barroom set of doors."

It was Spacek who realized the symbolic power of the doors, and he seized on them at a time when the Firm was struggling to find an idea it could rally behind. "They came in and they would put [logos] on stands around me in my office, and I said, 'Take them all out, they all look like Alcoholics Anonymous to me.' All the other firms were putting in big glass doors. I was walking out of our office and waiting for the elevators," Spacek said. "I looked around at the doors and said, 'Let's use those doors.' To me, those doors represented confidentiality, privacy, security and orderliness. And it struck me that those thoughts epitomized the common vision I wanted all of our people to share."

The doors symbolized the Firm on presentations, on annual reports, on stationery, on binders, on T-shirts, on tote bags. They were substantial, like the Firm. They were closed and you couldn't see through them, an image that projected confidentiality. They were like the old bank buildings, constructed specifically to give the impression that your money was safe inside. But in Arthur Andersen's case, they were meant to assure the client—and the public—that what was going on behind the doors was both private and beyond reproach. The doors announced, "Trust us." And for decades, people did.

The doors proved a simple but wonderful way to promote the One Firm concept at Arthur Andersen to both clients and employees. When I traveled to our offices in Jakarta, or Oklahoma City, or Tokyo, they were the first things I saw, whether in a turn-of-the-century edifice or a modern skyscraper. The comforting familiarity implied that the treatment you'd get once inside would be the same, too. Eventually, the original doors were moved to St. Charles, where they were displayed proudly to all the incoming new hires. By passing through those doors, you would begin a new way of life.

Yet if those doors symbolized strength and confidentiality, they also symbolized something more foreboding to me—a place that was secretive, hidden, closed. Only those behind the doors knew exactly what was going on, and, by the time I got to Arthur Andersen, what was going on was a lot more about chaos and confusion than calm competence. Once I got a glimpse of this inner sanctum, I realized that there were many more metaphorical doors behind those doors, and that only some people knew how to open them.

I had studied organizational culture for much of my professional life, yet only now did it occur to me that both "cult" and "culture" come from the same root. At Andersen, people didn't seem as if they belonged to a cult in the sense of worshiping an out-of-the-mainstream charismatic leader. There were no charismatic leaders at Andersen. But their behavior—their overarching commitment to the Firm and what it stood for—and the Firm's efforts to shape that behavior were, to me and to many others, cultlike. I found myself surrounded by Androids who did many things because that was the way they were done. It would never occur to them to question any practice, despite the cosmic changes taking place both inside and outside the Firm. Yet suddenly there also were many new people joining from elsewhere as consulting became the growth engine of the Firm. The stolid, trustworthy, proudly boring way of the accountants began to lose its appeal as auditing revenues plateaued. And the stability and respectability of Arthur Andersen was losing its pull as the booming economy gave young business majors many different career options. Slowly, a mighty culture was disintegrating into a soulless cult behind those doors, and I stumbled right into the middle of it.

● ● ●

With Dean out of the picture, my first few months at Arthur Andersen were difficult and frustrating. Everywhere I turned, I met a faceless bureaucracy telling me "We don't do things that way here at Arthur Andersen." I was lucky to find Bill Ryder, a senior manager and auditor-turned-consultant who was intrigued by my practice and asked to join me during my first week. Bill had been with the Firm for 11 years and knew Arthur Andersen inside and out. He was a godsend, telling me what to say and what not to say, how to get what I needed or wanted without offending, and which form went with what. Although I was technically his boss, he clearly was my mentor when it came to understanding the tangled web of alliances and policies that was Arthur Andersen.

When it came to setting up an ethics practice without an equity partner to stand behind us, Bill and I were at an enormous disadvantage. Arthur Andersen was a meritocracy, but it was also a place where patronage was priceless. From the very first days at St. Charles, youngsters were told to seek out a mentor, someone who was going places, someone to whom you could hitch your star. There was no formal mentoring program, although when I came to the Firm, Gary Beu was working hard to establish one, but everyone knew they needed someone pulling for them from above. The concept was wonderful in that it bonded senior-level Androids to the young kids. But there was another aspect: It created a level of loyalty and career dependency in the developing managers that made it difficult for them to challenge a questionable decision down the road. How could you question someone who could "make" you, or, if not, discard you like so much trash? In any case, we had no one. Dean had been replaced by a partner named Clem Eibl, who seemed uncomfortable in his new position and not at all sure what my group was supposed to do.

Business and management consulting—whether in a powerhouse strategy firm like McKinsey or a boutique firm like my own RRM—has a distinct culture. It is a culture shaped by people selling somewhat abstract services where experience is supposed to produce the judgment and wisdom necessary for success. It is a culture also shaped by the consultants' ability to convince the potential client of the value of their services. And it is a culture that acknowledges the power of interventions, the enormous successes, and, at times, the failures that can occur. It is a culture characterized by ambiguity, complexity, and, if successful, intellectual acuity. Yes, it has charlatans, but also many very talented people.

One thing I understood was that while my group was part of a consulting organization—the CRCO, or Central Region Consulting Organization—the organization itself was fully an extension of the audit culture. Although I was a consultant, I was not part of either of the two major consulting groups affiliated with the Andersen name. The first, Andersen Consulting, was by now a separate organization with its own offices, fee structures, and management, although it still contributed up to 15 percent of its profits every year to AA. The second was the Business Consulting Group, a technology and human resources group spawned by Arthur Andersen to sell the same kinds of extremely profitable installations and services that AC was selling, but to small and mid-size clients. AC had been such an amazing success that its profitability was now outstripping that of the audit division, and that had created deep fissures between the two. The Business Consulting Group appeared designed to mirror AC and its amazing success. Whatever the motivation, the various units caused much confusion, both inside and outside the Firm. Many of us frequently received mail addressed to Arthur Andersen Consulting, the senders apparently hoping that someone inside could sort it out.

All of my delusions about being looked at as an asset to the Firm disappeared quickly during my first few months in Chicago. How could I be an asset? I couldn't figure out how to fit in or how to do any of the things that had become almost second nature to me in my previous ten years of consulting. It didn't matter what I had thought or done or how I had acted before. As a fellow new hire later put it, "It is Year Zero with the Khmer Rouge. You have just been born." We, the experienced hires, were brought in at different times, with a multiplicity of ideas and backgrounds, and were expected to adapt to the Firm.

There were so many arcane ways of doing things. Bill took me to open an account at First Chicago Bank—you weren't supposed to stick with your own bank, but rather work with the Firm's representative at the Firm's bank, which was, of course, an audit client. I was advised that most partners put a portion of their compensation into a particular investment fund. As a partner, no taxes were withheld from your bimonthly compensation, so it was essential that we put a sufficient amount aside to pay taxes. I opted for a straight money market account, and the bank's Arthur Andersen representative seemed shocked that I wouldn't simply take the Firm's word that the recommended fund was the best choice.

It was made clear to me that partners joined downtown clubs where they frequently met with clients and each other for breakfast and lunch. I chose the Union League Club, a favorite gathering place for several AA clients. The Club was just what it sounds like—a formal, tradition-bound institution that required business attire for everyone except overnight guests on their way to or from the elevator. Next, I learned to lunch out every day at Vivere, the Italian Village's ground-floor dining room, where an Android was seated at every table. Yet whatever I absorbed of the Arthur Andersen culture came through osmosis. Outside of the first day, when I received half a day of introduction to benefits, dress code, office hours, and how to fill out a time report, there was no way to learn what everyone else already knew about the place. I also received a voluminous maroon "Independence and Ethics" binder, with no discussion of its contents. It went right on my shelf, where it collected dust, as, from what I could tell, did everyone else's equally bulky maroon binder.

The Firm did have a program for new experienced hires, called Transitions, meant to ease the shock of coming into a place with such a powerful culture. Held a few times a year, it had started just before I got there, as a response to the growing numbers of experienced people being hired and their enormous attrition rate (as much as 70 percent annually). It was a three-day, fourteen-hour-a-day session held at St. Charles. I was supposed to go, but I never could make it (you were not supposed to forgo client work to attend), and when the senior manager in my group, Natalie Green Giles, told me what went on, I lost any desire whatsoever to be there. "The assumption was that you had to be taught everything," said Natalie. "I called it Stepford in the Biosphere."

Although the idea was a good one—the Firm knew that people needed some sort of introduction to this place—people coming in with experience weren't nearly as open to the Andersen Way as college graduates were. Natalie and many others found the approach condescending and off-putting. The format was a series of lectures, followed by a dinner social hour. There was also an opportunity for journal-writing about the things you were leaving behind by coming to Arthur Andersen. "It was total indoctrination," Natalie said.

People were divided into groups and urged to compete. During the day, bits of trivia about the Firm—"AA was the first tenured accounting professor at Northwestern," etc.—were flashed, almost subliminally, on screens, and you were supposed to take notes. At the social hour, there was a quiz show. Those who had retained the most info won prizes like tote bags, while those who answered incorrectly were embarrassed with a loud buzz. To convey how important it was to fit in, Transitions featured a skit in which six CLMs, or "career-limiting moves," were spelled out. They were:

1. overcustomizing your office

2. not getting results

3. being low-energy

4. making yourself unreachable

5. sugarcoating the truth

6. trying to do it all alone

"They were delivered with a sense of humor," said Natalie, "but the underlying messages were sincere." Translation: Give your life to the Firm—and don't stand out.

Transitions or not, it was patently obvious who had grown up with the Firm and who was merely an interloper. It was absolutely impossible to know how to fill out most of the endless forms unless you'd been doing it since you were 22 years old. For someone like me, it would take 15 minutes to fill out my time sheet. It took me months to understand that the different categories of time use— for the things you were doing when not engaged in billable work— were essentially a code. If you understood how to use the categories, you could make yourself look better. Many of us newcomers seriously hurt our official productivity by tossing most of our nonbillable hours into a general admin category, as opposed to sorting out what was personal development, or marketing, or mentoring others. We simply didn't know what went where. But for someone who'd studied the Gospel according to Arthur, it was bing, bing, bing—literally a two-minute operation.

It was the mid-1990s, but the legacy of Andersen and Spacek still roamed the halls like stern ghosts, issuing dictates that weren't really followed anymore but still managed to bind together those in the know. Some aspects were small, more about image than anything else. Shortly after I started, I asked Clem Eibl and a few other partners if the Firm would be sending out announcements about my joining the partnership (as most law firms and other partnerships do). It always seemed to me a great marketing device, and we always did it at RRM when a new consultant joined us. They looked at me as if I were from the moon. The Firm just didn't do that, in part because there had been so few outsiders, but mostly because the individual had little recognition at Arthur Andersen. Finally, Bill and I ordered printed announcements and sent them out ourselves.

Then there was, of course, the dress code, which was starting to break down (in January 2000 the Firm would succumb to business casual). Yet still in 1995, you could be sent home for wearing the wrong thing or mocked endlessly for having any sort of individual style. I was never punished for committing any sartorial sins, but one of the women in my group did cross the line when she took the unpardonable action of wearing open-toed shoes (and we're not talking about strappy Manolo Blahnik spikes here, but rather a pair of conservative Arche black suede shoes with rubber soles, strictly for comfort). Bill, appalled, told me to take her aside and tell her never to wear them again. "You must be out of your mind," I said. "No way!" Another time, a female intern working with our group wore pants to a client meeting. Bill, my "voice of Arthur Andersen," was horrified. "This is absolutely not the way she should be going to a client," he said.

Then there was the Mountain Man, a Ph.D. in economics from Caltech who also had been recruited by Dean. Like me, he had been brought in to use his prior contacts and experience to sell consulting services. Dean had introduced me to him on one of my early visits to Chicago, essentially to show that if he could adapt to the firm, anyone could.

He apparently had been a wild-haired, bushy-bearded, sandal-wearing, California hippie. But when I met him he was shorn of his locks, clean-shaven, and dressed in a muted striped shirt and tie.

He was also wearing shoes with laces, which he told me had been one of his greatest adjustments. Dean had decorated a couple of beer bottles with homemade labels bearing a sketch of this economist's "before" look and the words "Mountain Man Brew." But, of course, going from hippie to yuppie in a flash by wearing shoelaces and exposing your chin did not mean successful adaptation. To fit in at Arthur Andersen, you needed to change your soul—and Mountain Man was never able to do that. He lasted little more than a year before, as I understand it, he was criticized for "eating time"—spending more time working on a client's project than had been allotted or could be billed. He may have needed to do that to make the project work, but eating time was not the way to win favor at Arthur Andersen.

Many of Arthur Andersen's cultural norms were based on good ideas but seemed to me to have morphed into being more about control than anything. Take the principle of public service and charity contributions. Arthur Andersen had always been a place that prided itself on its commitment to charity and to public service. In the years of Leonard Spacek, the Firm began to match staff contributions, another creative move for a private partnership. Partners, in particular, were also expected to become paragons of their community, serving on boards and attaching their names to good works as often as possible. It was strictly a business decision, said Spacek. "We weren't trying to be the leaders of the social or charitable groups," he said. "My idea was to try to help somebody else be the top man and thus obligate him or her to us and the Firm. Thus, in effect, I said, we get our brownie points with obligation."

Starting in the 1970s, charity had become mandatory for every partner at Arthur Andersen; the partner contributed 2 percent, and the Firm's foundation would add the next 2 percent. "It was one of the most controversial issues during my tenure," said Harvey Kapnick in the Firm's official history. Partners could choose where their money went, but at Arthur Andersen, as at many U.S. institutions, the big drive was for the United Way (and yes, Arthur Andersen was the United Way's auditor). I requested an alternative charity for my donation, since the United Way had recently been involved in some ethical issues of its own. But what really bothered me was the amount I was told I was expected to contribute. My husband and I actually do contribute that amount or more to charities of our choice. Now I was being told what I was to support, and with how much, so the Firm could be recognized for a magnanimous donation. I bit my tongue, wrote the check, and once again wondered what netherworld I'd stepped into.

In other areas the rules remained, but only as an empty shell. One example was the upkeep of the office. In the days of old, offices were kept spotless, for the same reason as everything else: to project the proper image in front of the client. Spacek had been so obsessed with this issue that he wrote, in 1954, a famous memo (referred to internally as the "Walk Briskly" memo) after he saw a pack of young Androids joking and laughing on their way out for coffee.

> It is exceedingly embarrassing to find men with their feet on desks or chairs, leaning back in chairs, reading newspapers, or two or three in an office laughing and apparently gossiping or otherwise not appearing to be occupied. Everyone should make it a habit to be busy all the time. . . . When walking in the halls, walk briskly. Under no circumstances should anyone read a paper in the office. As a matter of fact, newspapers should not even be on desks.

Granted, this kind of top-down control wouldn't have been accepted anywhere in 1995, but partners still talked about these types of things in vague hopes that they could recapture that discipline. On the ninth floor of Arthur Andersen's flagship Monroe Street office, where I worked, the young consulting staff members sat at cubicles in the middle of the floor, while the partners had offices on the perimeter. Forget about newspapers: The whole place was truly a god-awful mess. Looking back at the Firm's trial and the issue of whether Andersen shredded documents to avoid a subpoena, I have to say that if the other offices were as disorganized as Chicago was in 1995, they wouldn't have known where to start. Papers were stacked everywhere—on cabinets, on the floor, in corrugated boxes on top of filing cabinets, and on every available desk space in the middle of the office. There were special places where the formal client files were kept, and they stayed relatively orderly, but any of the work papers used to conduct an audit or run a consulting project were scattered all over the place.

Confidentiality? Hardly. Professionalism? I don't think so. In addition to the papers, there were shoes and boots on the floor, jackets and sweaters on chairs, file cabinets, and other surfaces, and—to add to the fraternity house ambience—platters of wilted lettuce, dried-out sandwiches, and congealed pizza scavenged from postmeeting conference rooms nestled cheek by jowl with stacked work papers (you were supposed to eat lunch out, but breakfast and snacks were a different story).

The place looked awful, and Clem Eibl raged about it endlessly, but no one listened. I suppose an excuse for the mess might be that people were working too hard to attend to housekeeping matters, but my sense is that attitudes had definitely changed. "If anybody ever walked in here," I remember him saying, "they would never hire us. If they thought this is the mess that their papers were going to be kept in, they would have every reason to walk out the door." It was the same with the auditors in the New York office when I moved there in 1996.

It's worth noting that in the four years I worked at Arthur Andersen, no one ever once told me that I should get rid of documents or shred anything at all. I did periodically clean up and dump things out, but not because I was supposed to adhere to any document-retention policy. In fact, Firm offices provided archive storage space, and I was encouraged to use it rather than throw *anything* away. The jury that convicted Arthur Andersen discounted the shredding, but to me it would have been quite an unusual day if, in Chicago or in New York, people had suddenly begun to shred like mad.

• • •

I remember from my days in the theater business that in the musical *Fiddler on the Roof,* the three daughters of Tevye, caught between the tradition of Anatevka and the modernity of the world outside their village, or shtetl, make choices that send their lives in different directions and begin to unravel the Traditions that have for so long guided their lives. The oldest stays with her community but challenges the tradition of arranged marriages by marrying Motl the Tailor instead of her parents' choice, Lazar Wolf the Butcher. The second daughter follows the Jewish radical she loves to far-off Siberia. And the third shatters Tradition—and her family—by marrying a Cossack and staying in Russia even as her Jewish parents are forced to leave.

In a way, being at Arthur Andersen in the 1990s was like being catapulted back into the Anatevka shtetl. The way things had always been, and the expectations that had guided unquestioning behavior, were suddenly no more—and the implications for the Firm were dramatic. The business of auditing large public companies had been carved up: There were few huge new clients to land, and mergers were reducing competition and fees even further. In the mid-1990s, some partners were asked to leave because they weren't pulling their weight. No longer did making partner mean you could put your feet up and ride out the rest of your career in a golf cart. "There was a period of time that the partners were a paranoid bunch," said former partner Bob Lorenz. "They were much less secure, and much more concerned that they made it to retirement." Now auditors were being forced to hustle for business, and it wasn't a natural fit. "Entrepreneurial [behavior] was not encouraged," said Steve Leiter, a former audit partner. "That changed in the late 1980s and early 1990s, when you kind of ran out of the revenue base."

For everyone working at Arthur Andersen—and possibly everyone in the business world—the decade of the 1990s was different. On one hand, the opportunities were vast. Capitalism had vanquished all other economic systems, and the U.S. economy roared along like a hungry beast. On the other hand, the last vestiges of paternalism were disappearing. Layoffs became normal. Competition was cutthroat. And money was being made hand over fist. Public companies—Arthur Andersen's biggest clients—were beginning to reward their top executives with unimaginable sums, thanks to their passionate embrace of the stock option and the market's equally passionate response to them. The Androids wanted to bask in that glow as well. Why shouldn't they be the equals of their illustrious clients? While they couldn't make the tens of millions their clients did, partners were now making $200,000, $400,000, $600,000 annually, with top partners topping $1,000,000—princely sums for the sons and daughters of postal workers and shopkeepers. To be an auditor, the best reputation was no longer enough: You had to have the best reputation, a client-driven attitude, *and* the best price. For Arthur Andersen, which had long prided itself on its principles, it was a rude shock to discover that few of their clients seemed to care about them.

Like the residents of Anatevka, some auditors were sticking to their traditions, trying to continue to serve their long-standing clients with the same attention to detail and the insistence that the client keep immaculate books. As one retired partner said to me recently, "In the old days, the client didn't tell us what to do. We told the client what was right. And if they didn't listen to us, we dropped them. In those days, being dropped by your auditor was a scary business; it usually meant that your stock price would drop as well. Not anymore. Now if the auditor tells the client something it doesn't like, the client drops the auditor—and that can mean a few million dollars a year right down the drain." Those traditionalists also resisted the pressure to sell consulting services.

Others changed their stripes, reinventing themselves as consulting salespeople and using their client relationships to get a foot in the door. Still others seemed to take the most aggressive approach—turning a blind eye to accounting standards in order to earn the goodwill and trust of the client, and squeezing the consultants into meetings as often as possible in hopes of getting more overall business. It was this last group that seemed to me to be the most highly valued at the Arthur Andersen of the mid- to late 1990s.

It was natural that consulting seemed to be the future of the Firm. Andersen Consulting had taken the industry by storm to become the largest single consulting firm in the country, and its growth catapulted Arthur Andersen to the top of the Big Six. As public companies put in costly new computer systems and looked for any edge they could find, they were willing to pay these new merchants of technological advice just about anything they asked for. But consultants didn't act like auditors, and although auditors had already learned that as Andersen Consulting built its own unique strong culture, they still tried to graft their rules and approaches onto their own growing consulting units, including mine, which later became BRCA (Business Risk Consulting and Assurance Services Group).

The styles and approaches of auditors and consultants were different in so many ways. First, an annual audit for publicly held companies is a legal requirement. An accredited public accounting firm must perform that audit, and fees for an audit are budgeted annually. Consulting, for the most part, is discretionary spending. That meant that the audit culture was all about annuity clients. Since an audit must be done every year, the goal is about making sure the client will stick with you for the next audit, and the next. Consulting was about one-off projects. If you did a great job you'd hope for more work from the client, but the nature of most consulting projects was to analyze a problem, recommend a solution, and put it in place. Success, theoretically, should happen when the client doesn't need the consultant anymore. So you had to make as much money as quickly as possible, knowing that the source might well disappear later.

But in the consulting culture growing within Arthur Andersen, the annuity mentality remained a driver. So audit partners pushed their colleagues and their young charges—specifically managers—to try to turn consulting jobs into annuity jobs. The perfect type of consulting engagement at Arthur Andersen, I discovered, was delivered by a unit of BRCA, a group called Business Process Risk Consulting, which provided internal audit services to companies wanting to outsource their own internal accounting. The obvious conflict of interest notwithstanding (where are the checks and balances, one must ask, if an auditor is allowed to do not only the external, but also the *internal* audit for one client?), internal auditing was regular work.

If a consulting project had to end, then the point was to find another reason to stay once you were there, morphing from the discretionary to the necessary. Like the famous Roach Motel, consultants were taught to check in, but never check out. I watched with awe, and some trepidation, as Bill transformed the scope of work for two of our early clients, one a health care company and the other a securities firm, from specific project engagements to long-term commitments with ongoing monthly "next steps." In both cases, the anxieties of the client contact person (in each case new in the position) were carefully massaged to create a growing dependency.

Traditionally, consultants had been rainmakers and auditors were supposed to be watchdogs. Now the auditors, guardians of the public trust, were becoming consulting shills. Their culture of upstanding respectability was disintegrating, but many audit partners tried to hold on to the symbols of the past while trying to keep pace with the new world outside their doors. Some saw themselves as gatekeepers, guarding the incursion of consultants into their clients' offices. Others tried to control the actual activities of consultants working with their clients, becoming mediators and interpreters. It made for a very volatile brew inside Arthur Andersen.

Another key difference was the fact that auditing was a specific process, with consistent regulations and training. Arthur Andersen's emphasis on one unified approach worked well with auditing, but not so well with consulting (although the programming-oriented consulting that Andersen Consulting specialized in used the same concept). There were no specific requirements to become a consultant, no certificate of proof that you had mastered something or passed the CPA exam. In consulting, the range of approaches was vast. The type of consulting that my colleagues and I did was customized to the specific situation. After all, you couldn't provide litigation support in the same way for two clients, one facing a fraud lawsuit and the other a sexual harassment accusation, and you couldn't use a boilerplate approach for an ethically sticky situation or to explore a client's unique vulnerabilities. The auditors I worked with couldn't understand this. And why should they? They had been brought up in a tradition of consistency and standardized methodologies and rules, and they were flummoxed at the fluidity of our discipline and the added cost of customized work.

Finally, auditing was entirely about leverage: using low-paid, inexperienced people to do the lion's share of the work, using the somewhat higher-paid managers to supervise them, and bringing in the top-earning partners only when major judgment calls or decisions were needed. This process worked in the audit and accounting field because the skills to be learned each year were discrete, and performance-evaluation forms could measure those specific achievements. Like Tevye, everyone knew who he was and what the accounting profession—if not God—expected him to do. But Arthur Andersen had created too many partners making too much money—1,835 by 1996—and now the ratio of partners to staff had become too big, putting added financial pressure on the numbers. Said Bob Lorenz: "The reality was there wasn't enough money for all of the partners."

Revenues continued to grow—to $4.6 billion in 1996 for Arthur Andersen (not including Andersen Consulting, which added another $5.3 billion)—but the profits were being further and further stretched. The leverage model was straining under the weight of so many partners, and to rescue it the Firm tried to replicate that model with those of us in consulting. But many kinds of consulting required expertise, and trying to send low-paid, inexperienced young people to do the job of experts was dangerous for everyone involved. (The exceptions were large fraud investigations and the production of technology manuals, where hordes of low-level people spent weeks or months photocopying bills and receipts or copying pages of technical instructions.)

This reminded me of an experience I had in the early 1970s, before I started graduate school. I was living with my husband and children in New Haven at a time when divorce was in style and "groups" were all the rage—from Esalen to women's liberation groups to T-groups. An entrepreneurial psychiatrist in the community, Mark, capitalized on this new culture by starting the Center for the Person in Transition to conduct group sessions for people going through separations or divorces or who were recently widowed. I came on as executive director, which meant that I would handle all of the administrative duties. Mark soon asked me to do the intake for the groups, and to lead two of them—despite the fact that I had no training and no experience other than a few undergraduate psychology courses.

I didn't have a clue how to run a group therapy session. Since there was no end point (people didn't sign up for a specific number of sessions, they just joined a group), my job, essentially, was to build a dependency so that the client kept on coming and coming, and never felt strong enough—or well enough—to leave. Over time people came to trust me, although they shouldn't have, and I found myself making comments that affected these people's lives. It all came to a head one day when a young woman who was recently separated from her husband came in to see about joining a group. Her name sounded familiar, but I couldn't place it. She began to tell me what had led to her failing marriage, and as she talked, I remembered the news coverage of the horrifying events. Her five-year-old daughter had been abducted as she walked home from school and was found murdered several days later. Here was this frightened, needy woman coming to me for help. And here I was, an absolute sham, pretending that I was in a position to provide that help.

I had enough wits about me to pick up the phone and call a psychiatrist friend at the Yale Child Study Center and ask if I could send her right over. I got her into a cab, shoved a handful of bills into the driver's hand, and directed him to the Center. Then I went back inside and walked into Mark's office. "We have to talk," I said. "You and I are doing something terribly unethical. We are harming people who come to us in need. I will stay long enough to turn the office and the books over to you or someone you appoint, and then I am out of here." I subsequently decided to go to graduate school, and vowed to myself that I would never pretend to be able to do anything I was not educated or trained to do.

Now here I was at Arthur Andersen, having a nightmare déjà vu as I watched some of the younger people in my group and in other groups do their best to "help" clients who had come to Arthur Andersen in need of assistance. Just as I had sold and delivered "mental health" with no qualifications, these consultants who just a few years or months before had been college undergraduates were selling "business health." They knew as much about business—or about derivatives or fraud or whatever—as I knew about therapy. Anyone could call herself a therapist. And anyone could call himself a consultant.

We were supposedly still the guardians of the public trust, but no one ever mentioned that. Everyone did, however, talk about making money all the time. On my second day at Arthur Andersen, I was surprised, and delighted, to be asked to go with a group of consultants to a law firm representing a major client that was being sued for a faulty product. Many of the consultants in our office worked for the litigation support group, a consulting service that helped companies facing legal issues, usually working with their outside counsel. When they heard there was an ethics person around, visions of revenue-generating sugarplums danced in their heads. As five of us trooped down Clark Street, one of my colleagues gave me a brief rundown of the case, which concerned a customer's injury and whether or not it was the company's responsibility. Could I put together an ethical argument on the company's behalf? It was a natural request, I suppose, but I certainly did not believe my job was to justify other companies' bad ethics. I was there to help them *improve* their business practices.

I told them that I could make such an argument, but that I could just as easily make an argument supporting the opposing view. That was one of the reasons, I explained, why I would never serve as an expert witness. My colleagues were stunned. Expert testimony brought in big bucks. But if they thought I was crazy, I was also silently questioning where they were coming from. What, I wondered, was an independent audit firm doing making money by advising clients on how to beat a product liability problem? Weren't they supposed to be neutral when it came to the court cases and other things that might have a direct impact on a company's numbers? (I did later learn that much of Arthur Andersen's PAC money went to candidates who favored tort reform.) Uncomfortable as I was, I marched right along with them into the luxurious offices of one of Chicago's top law firms and constructed an ethical defense for the lawyer's client. I did add that I would not testify in court to what I had just said, and I gave them a quick view of what an ethics expert for the plaintiff might say. It was a disconcerting end to my first client meeting.

We in the CRCO were an odd lot. Running the show was Gary Holdren, who had jump-started the group in 1986 in response to a request from a legal client for help with one of its clients, Drexel Burnham Lambert, the investment bank that was at the time under SEC investigation for insider trading. The law firm had asked Arthur Andersen to step in as an outside monitor of sorts to ensure that Drexel didn't destroy or alter any documents. "You could think of Andersen as an insurance policy that Drexel didn't do anything crazy," said Holdren, now president of Huron Consulting Group.

As ironic as it may seem today, it was a tribute to Andersen's reputation that the Firm was viewed as a trusted corporate watchdog. As part of the project, the lawyers needed hundreds of grunts to copy and date-stamp millions of sheets of paper. "Almost everyone in the Firm who was a first- or second-year went out there," said a former manager who spent several weeks in Los Angeles. "There were so many people needed. If you were free in Phoenix, you'd be sent to L.A., because we had 'chargeability' out there. At one point, there were sixty people in the garage with photocopiers, stamps, and paper clips, copying everything in the entire firm." What was supposed to be a short project went on for about two years, with the group bringing in an amazing $50 million in fees, said Gary.

It wasn't exactly what you would call value-added services, but it provided huge amounts of billable hours in a leverage model, and Gary saw the potential for big money. He called the work "Litigation Services," and that was the first of what evolved into a host of consulting groups. Eventually, there were several different groups, including Corporate Recovery, Government Contracts, Litigation Support, Business Fraud Risk Services, Environmental Services, Derivatives and Treasury Management, Computer Risk Management, Contract Audit Services, and a few others. Because Arthur Andersen's U.S. boss, Dick Measelle, saw this area as something of a skunk works, it evolved constantly. Service lines were quickly added once it was clear whether or not there was any potential.

Although we were all in the CRCO, there wasn't a lot of interaction inside the office. Consulting partners seemed to be running their own fiefdoms, with little knowledge or regard for what it was their fellow partners were doing next door. The most significant amount of time we spent together was when an audit partner, trying to depart from Tradition, herded us together as part of a "team" effort to pitch services to a client. Rarely, if ever, was there any coordination as we marched, a predatory pack, down the blustery Chicago streets in search of fresh blood. Sometimes we stalked huge companies with no Arthur Andersen connections, later referred to as "Elephant Targets." More frequently, we tried to convert current audit clients into companies that would use us not only for audits but also for a host of other consulting services.

In my first few months in Chicago, I was trotted out to client after client, often with a mixed group of auditors and consultants. Sometimes we tried to cobble together a strategy on the way over, but more often than not the strategy became a hope that if we threw everything up against the wall, something might stick. Typically, the auditor—the keeper of the sacrosanct *relationship*—would set up the meeting with the client, then would call as many consultants as he could to come in and strut their stuff. As we all filed into a room together, I inevitably felt like one of the Seven Dwarfs. Yet unlike Snow White's hearty crew, we didn't exactly whistle while we worked. The system managed to pit us against each other, since if the consultant who spoke before me managed to attract the interest of the client, that might mean he had no time or budget left to consider my wares. As a result, we would frequently interrupt one another and even undermine our colleagues in hopes of getting a few minutes of the client's attention. And since we had no common training bond or intellectual approach, we often contradicted one another.

I remember one meeting at a telecommunications company where four of us sat across the desk from a tall, distinguished executive. Like a line of trained dogs, we sat up on our haunches, paws raised in eager-to-please performance, waiting to be thrown a biscuit from this gentleman. The audit partner introduced each of us, then laid out his construction of the client's "problems" that he was proposing we address. One of our "team," a member of the Fraud practice, rushed in with a proposal to create a telephone survey on ethical behavior for the client. I thought it would be a useless, mindless, money-gouging activity, based on nothing more than using youngsters to generate revenue. I did not want to be associated with this proposal, but I couldn't shout out "That's absurd." Nor, I decided, could I just sit there and let incompetence hold sway. So I spoke up, politely expressing my concerns about the proposed idea and offering some alternatives. Now the audit partner and the "team" were the ones who looked horrified. I had made my own colleagues look bad. (Probably they would say that I was just trying to grab the attention of the client.) On the trek back to the office, I was given a brief lecture on the meaning of "One Firm, seamless service." Suffice it to say, we didn't quite meet the definition of a team. The client was not impressed. No services were sold that day.

That scene was replayed several times. In a pitch to the CFO and general counsel of a huge consumer goods client, the partner who came with me ditched the presentation we had prepared and announced that if hired, he would be directing me to conduct a plan of his design, which I believed to be of little value but high revenue. Again I "corrected" him in front of the client—and again was lectured on the trudge back to West Monroe. No one ever challenged my ideas; they just said that I was not their kind of team player. I wondered why I'd been hired as an expert, then not allowed to use my expertise.

In fact, for all the desperate energy expended, the CRCO's consulting services were a tough sell. Clients would tolerate the meetings, but most of them said "No" to the audit partner before we were out the door. It was somehow as embarrassing when we finagled our way into a deal as it was when we were politely ushered out. Part of this was personal: I had never been much of a cold caller and hated the hard sell. At no point did I have the time to really sit down with a client and learn about its needs and then make a thoughtful presentation that really addressed them. Soon, I found myself giving pitches for stuff I didn't even believe in. I began to feel that in many cases we were blatantly trying to shove services down people's throats, offering things that I for one didn't think were essential. The goal, it seemed, was simply to make money. Eventually, the thrill of victory would begin to feel almost as bad as the agony of defeat.

•   •   •

I stayed in the Chicago office for eight months. Even before I moved to New York, bringing Bill Ryder with me, I had come to the conclusion that Arthur Andersen's view on ethics consulting—and on all of its consulting—was very different from my own. We were told we were supposed to develop commoditizable methodologies that could be delivered by lower-level people who got relatively low salaries but who could bill at stunningly high rates. My whole career—and the careers of many of the other luminaries brought in—had been all about expert custom client work. That was how we had succeeded. Now we were expected to boil everything down to preset "analysis" and a set of simple prescribed remedies—remedies so simple that a young person with little more than a college degree and one or two on-the-job training assignments could be sent out to minister to the corporations of the world.

All of this crystallized for me shortly before I left Chicago. Dean was no longer my boss but was still in the office, and he asked me to attend a meeting in Chicago with a friend of his from a D.C. law firm. After quick introductions, Dean told me they wanted me to work with them to develop a standardized computer-based training program in business ethics. The idea was to design a one-size-fits-all program and market it to companies that had to meet the Federal Sentencing Guidelines for Organizations. The company would purchase enough CDs for each employee to have one. Then the employee could take the CD home, take care of the company's ethics requirement at any time, and sign off on completion of the program right online. What a convenient way to get the government off your back! Surely, U.S. corporations would be willing to pay big bucks for such a goody.

I could have been more politic in my response. But that wasn't my style. With blood pounding in my head, I shot back, "Dean, this is exactly the kind of ethics consulting that I had told you was worthless during my discussions with you. This is simply a loophole. You and I talked about helping companies improve their cultures." I continued, almost shouting, "If you want a rote program to teach people simple policy statements, go get yourself a computer technician. But if you want something to help individuals deal with ethical dilemmas that will help their companies avoid disaster, you can't do it with this."

Dean turned bright red and almost began to shake, he was so angry. "We're a business," he shouted. "And this is good business. We could sell it to every one of our clients." On one hand, he was right. This was a business opportunity; who the hell was I to turn it down? Certainly, many companies believed computer-based training was a perfectly acceptable way to teach anything from word processing to leadership. To Dean, like many Arthur Andersen partners I would interact with, ethics was just another service. And if we could develop a handy-dandy solve-your-problem product, what a windfall this would be. Unfortunately for me, I was clinging to principle, which previously had served me well financially, and to what I believed made good business sense in the long term. I was still holding on to my dissertation's key idea that I wouldn't have to sacrifice my beliefs. I'd make *them* accept mine.

•  •  •

Ultimately, I came to realize that my inability to fit in wasn't entirely personal. Other "luminaries" came to me with similar experiences and frustrations. "If a person had a problem," said Mary Gottschalk, a director in the Firm's Global Derivatives and Treasury Risk Management Practice from 1995 to 1997, "that was prima facie evidence that that person didn't fit here at AA." I had delivered programs at GE's extraordinary Crotonville educational center, at Chase Manhattan Bank, and at Aetna in the days when they all had some of the most outstanding training and education curricula in the corporate community. None of them felt like indoctrination centers. The jargon constantly used by the Andersen lifers felt exclusionary and confusing.

And the Androids' self-identification with the Firm was truly amazing to me. It reminded me of a concept in psychology called the local/cosmopolitan orientation. Some individuals—cosmopolitans—identify themselves by what it is they do: "I'm an artist," "I'm a banker." Others choose the local identification, the organization—and that's how everyone was at Arthur Andersen. For the local, the feeling is

"Without the institution, I'm nothing." The loyalty of the partners was something akin to that of a military unit. Instead of "my country, right or wrong," it became "my company, right or wrong." No one ever said, "I am an accountant." Said Steve Leiter, a former partner: "I said I'm a partner at Arthur Andersen. Otherwise, I'm Steve."

There was simply too much similarity of thought, too much acceptance that the way things were done was the best simply *because that's the way we do it,"* to see that this culture was turning in on itself. The robotic approach was not simply about the green eyeshades and dexterity with numbers. It was also about class, ethnicity, and gender. Women, despite some high-profile attempts to make them a more visible part of the senior leadership, were still largely an afterthought in positions of power when I arrived. Yes, there were women partners, but there weren't many of them, and the upper echelons of management were entirely made up of white males. Few minorities or non-Americans had made it into the inner circle, either.

It wasn't because of the machinations of some powerful graybeard, either. Arthur Andersen was at its base a democracy, with each equity partner getting one vote on the most important issues. Yet even in the late 1990s, the process of making equity partner was as much a ritual of the old boys' network as it had ever been, probably because the voters tended to think the same way about just about everything. The meetings took place in a local office, and the equity partners of an office would collectively decide who in their ranks would be elevated into the Firm's most exclusive club. Partners were allowed to argue the merits of one or the other, but ultimately the final vote, which was taken after the meeting, almost always rubber-stamped an already agreed-upon decision.

During a few of these meetings in New York, it became clear to me that the Firm had a long way to go when it came to treating women equally. By the time potential partners were brought up for discussion at these meetings, their promotion was essentially a fait accompli, but partners were still allowed to raise objections. At one partner meeting in New York, a male human resources executive was promoted, although almost all of us felt he didn't deserve it. A senior partner explained that the candidate had said that not being partner prevented him from performing his job as well as he could. There were a lot of grumblings, but the partners acquiesced. In a meeting several months later, a woman, also the director of a staff function, came up for promotion. Like the man, she wasn't particularly well thought of by the office. I, for one, didn't think either of them deserved partnership.

In no way, however, did this woman deserve the reputational shredding she got because of her gender. She did indeed get the nod, but for quite a different reason than the man. The story that filtered out of the meeting was that a high-ranking partner gave a speech in which he acknowledged her shortcomings but said that he had decided to promote her to partner because the Firm needed more women partners. To humiliate this woman and then to promote her anyway, making her a token in the eyes of every partner in the New York office, was truly unforgivable. Another female partner and longtime Android was so furious that she wrote a blistering note to all of the partners in the office excoriating them for their behavior and decrying the ongoing sexism in the Firm. A male partner sent us all a reply the next day stating that there was no sexism at Arthur Andersen, just a commitment to promoting only people who met the Firm's high standards. Eventually the note-writer resigned. I think I had a pretty good idea why they had trouble getting good women partners at Arthur Andersen.

Another meeting, held around the same time, demonstrated a similar attitude toward minorities. If there were few women in visible jobs, there were even fewer minorities. One African-American partner recalls attending a partner meeting where he was the only African-American present (there was one more African-American partner in the office, but he didn't attend). He watched as a senior woman stood up and challenged the office managing partner. "It's wonderful that there are more women going up for partner, but the numbers are still terrible," she said. And what about minority partners, she wanted to know, whose numbers were still worse?

"The high point for me," said the minority partner, "was when one of the partners jumped up and said, 'We need to be careful here that we don't start trying to hire or promote people to partnership that aren't really qualified. We do have our standards.'" No one said a word to challenge him. "I'm looking around this room," said the partner, "and thinking, do you really think that this is affirmative action gone wild at Arthur Andersen? I'm the only black person in the room. What's he talking about?" In recounting this meeting to me, my colleague joked that he'd called a meeting of all the black partners to complain. "I've reserved a table for two," he said.

To me, it seemed patently obvious that Arthur Andersen was decades behind the rest of Corporate America when it came to addressing these issues. It was more about ignorance and the lack of new blood than it was about overt discrimination, but again, it pointed to a group of people hidebound by Tradition at a time when the world had changed around them.

• • •

At Andersen, Tradition dictated that we serve the client well but also that we stand up to the client when it does something wrong. Yet in the new world, clients had become too valuable to defy. The distortion of the Tradition now meant you could best serve the client— and therefore, keep the client—by keeping it happy. This created a natural tension and mistrust between auditors and consultants, particularly when working with powerful, high-paying clients, referred to as the Crown Jewels. We consultants were supposed to grow the Firm's revenues—and the auditors knew that—but at the same time the auditors were deathly afraid that we would do something to upset the client, which might cost them the account.

I usually felt like the awkward adolescent whose male cousin had been forced by his mother to take her to the prom. The audit partner seemed to be thinking, "Oh God, please don't make a fool of yourself—and me," and I'm thinking, "No matter what I do or say, he's going to think I've screwed up." Meanwhile, of course, the client seemed to be thinking, "We pay them so damn much already. If they think we need this additional service, it ought to be part of the audit." I knew that the client often didn't want me there, and I knew that the auditor felt compelled to have me there, but at the same time resented it. It was an absurd dance. The auditor was desperate to protect his own relationship with the client. The client didn't want the auditor angry at him, either—what if the auditor turned on him? And we, the consultants, just needed to book some business or we were out of a job. The worst possible sin you could commit at Arthur Andersen, I learned the hard way, was to upset the client—even if they desperately needed to hear the bad news.

In the late summer of 1997, I got a call from the head of internal audit of an Arthur Andersen Crown Jewel. The head auditor had gotten my name from a colleague of mine in the business ethics field and had called directly, rather than go through the auditor on the account. He told me that there had been some ongoing ethical concerns at the company, and that he had revised several of the internal audit procedures in response to them. He wanted to talk about developing a case-based program to encourage people to support the new procedures.

By this time I knew the drill, and immediately called the audit engagement partner to make sure he was in the loop. The engagement partner was a long, tall westerner, complete with string tie and drawl, whom I'll call Tex. Tex was young—probably not yet 40—and for him this was a B-I-G client. Like other engagement partners, Tex had very little true responsibility for the nuts and bolts of the audit itself. He was simply too expensive to do the audit, so it fell to more junior members of his staff. If there was a conflict or a question, the staffers were supposed to come to him and he would make major decisions, much as David Duncan did with Enron, but for the most part the engagement partner's job was to massage the relationship with the top executives of the client.

I called Tex, who told me about the basic issues with the client. The most important detail he gave me was that this was a $10 million client. BE CAREFUL! I wasn't to work with the head of internal audit on my own, he said. Instead, he would set up a meeting with the CFO to talk about the request for assistance. However, this time we weren't foisting services on a client with no real needs; it seemed as if the client needed real help.

Tex and I met with the CFO in the spacious old mansion that served as the client's headquarters. Tex's purpose in being there was ostensibly to make the introduction, but his true purpose, as far as I could see, was to watch over me like a hawk. It was always the same: As I made my pitch, the audit partner would inevitably interrupt and "clarify" things that I said in more soothing terms, even if what we were discussing was a serious ethical concern. It was hard to build a relationship with the client, because even if you were all in the same room, your words were being filtered through the mouth of the engagement partner. I always felt I was being treated like a child in those meetings. It was irritating, but I guess I could understand Tex's nervousness. On a project with revenues as high as these, the engagement partner's full-time job was to work with the client, and in many cases this intimate relationship represented his past, present, and future at the Firm. If anything happened to damage it, he would get the blame.

We met in the elegant office of the CFO, dapper in his white-collared, blue-striped shirt and investment-banker suspenders. Present as well were the general counsel and, by teleconference, the head of internal audit and the head of training. Ultimately, we decided that my group would develop a training video for the company's internal finance people that would raise some of the potential problems in a series of vignettes. The video would have an accompanying facilitators guide to be used internally for manager-led workshops. I left that day feeling pleased that we had gotten the engagement, but uneasy because I didn't feel I had the inside scoop on the client. I felt too constrained by Tex and what he had told me to probe any deeper. Later, I asked Tex if I might meet with the CEO to talk about the issues, but he said no.

For a lot of reasons—many of which I take responsibility for—the video project was a total and utter disaster. First, it turned out that not everyone in the company thought it was such a good idea to delve into the dirty laundry. They preferred a "rah-rah!" PR video instead. And, second, although I didn't know it at the time, internal politics at this company meant that if one faction supported a project, the other would shout it down. Then came the constant monitoring of our work by the audit side. Tex, who was based relatively far away, couldn't keep close tabs on us, so another Firm manager from a closer office was assigned to play baby-sitter and, we were told, to be available in case an audit question that we didn't understand came up. He came to every meeting just to watch and schmooze, charging the client for his time. The client was justifiably enraged, suggesting that we were trying to overbill them with extra people. Indeed, we were. But the auditors felt we needed a hall monitor, constantly reminding us that this was a $10 million client.

Then there were our own problems, primarily relating to quality. When we did video projects at my own company, I had done virtually everything from data-gathering and interviewing to writing all the vignettes and participating in casting and directing. At $450 an hour, I now was too expensive to actually do the project, so people in my group who had never interviewed for or written cases were doing so. It was grotesque: How could a reputable firm have completely inexperienced people delivering a service? But if I was to do the work, then I couldn't be out selling, selling, selling. I was "overseeing" the project, but how do you oversee creativity? The vignettes didn't work. In the meantime, the internal audit executive had begun to confide in me his worries about his company. I realized that things were worse than I had been led to believe.

The CEO took a look at the finished video and he exploded. He was furious that the video was about problems rather than being promotional, that it was shot on company property, that it was a downer rather than an upper. Apparently, he'd had a clear idea of what he wanted, but I was unaware of this because I was never allowed to meet with him. Tex was livid that we had angered the client. I was mortified that Andersen's Tradition and structure had forced me to deliver low-quality service, and my group was angry at me that I hadn't given them enough guidance. We were paid almost a quarter of a million dollars, but the client never used the video. In my view, the worst thing of all was that we hadn't come close to solving the client's problem.

At that point I did what I thought was the only ethical thing to do—but something that from Arthur Andersen's perspective was the equivalent of pulling the pin on a grenade. I wrote a note to the CFO saying that the problems originally raised had not been addressed. "As far as I am concerned," I wrote, "you are sitting with the same vulnerabilities now that you had when we started this project." I cc'ed Tex on the note, but I didn't show it to him first, knowing that he would go ballistic. But I thought it was my obligation.

Needless to say, Tex did indeed go ballistic. For him, I was the consultant from hell. As soon as he received the note, he called, spitting venom. My recollection of the conversation goes like this: "How could you have sent something like that without showing it to me first? This is a ten-million-dollar audit client! How dare you put anything like this in writing? We never put anything like this in writing! How dare you tell the client there is a problem? If there is something to be told to the client, you tell me and I will talk to the client." I apologized, but honestly, I wasn't that sorry. I simply thought the client should know, and I didn't have any reason to believe that he would ever hear this from anyone else. I did get a nice note back from the CFO, but the partner and I never spoke again. I had made him look bad and I had committed the cardinal sin of displeasing his prize client and threatening his livelihood.

●　　●　　●

At Arthur Andersen, Tradition also dictated obedience to the partner. If upsetting the client was a bad thing, so was questioning your superior. It simply was not tolerated. In my group, this wasn't an issue, since virtually everyone had been brought in from the outside. But elsewhere, it seemed to have been a hard-and-fast rule for decades.

I was sitting at my desk one day in 1997 when the phone rang. It was a retired partner, who had been asked to give a speech about some of the ethical problems in business today. I didn't know him, but he had heard about me and thought I might be able to give him some suggestions. "Let me tell you what I think is a very, very difficult problem," I said. "It's the problem of a young person who believes that he or she has seen something wrong and is trying to raise the problem to a superior." I then gave an example or two, but the partner interrupted me. "So what you're saying is that a big ethical problem today," he said, "is the problem of insubordination. That these young people think they know better than their bosses." The comment took my breath away. Maybe I wasn't being clear, I thought. "No," I said, "the problem is that young people see things that are wrong. It may be their bosses that are doing wrong, it may be other people in the company, it may be something going on in a client relationship that they are concerned about—and it's very difficult for them to find a way to raise that problem without putting their career at risk." The line went absolutely silent for several seconds. Finally, the retired partner said, "Thank you very much," and hung up the phone. Most executives, whether they believed it or not, would instantly agree and say that in their case, of course, "my door is always open." But for a longtime Android, the idea of challenging the partner was downright unthinkable.

I had learned that for myself. When I moved to New York in June 1996, I first reported to a partner named John Kelly, who was head of Metro New York Audit. He seemed to take an interest in our group and noted that new businesses needed to be carefully nurtured. Although he was an old-school Arthur Andersen type, we got along terrifically. At the end of the fiscal year 1997 (August), we sat down to determine the group's target for the next year. In our first full year, we'd made just over $800,000—not enough to make a dent in the company, but we'd met our target and it seemed a good start for a new business. After some discussion, John and I agreed to set our group's fiscal year 1998 target at $1.8 million before planned fee adjustments, or official discounts, and $1.3 million net, based on an analysis that Natalie and I had worked on for weeks. I was nervous about meeting the target, but I thought we could do it. We had John to champion us inside the Firm now, and we were building business.

That all changed a few months later, when John abruptly moved back to his office in New Jersey. I never understood what had happened, but once again, I had a new boss. His name was Joe Berardino, and he had been head of the Metro New York Commercial Practice. Now he was taking on leadership of Metro New York Audit, and soon afterward, in April 1998, he would be promoted to head the entire North American Audit Group. It was a big job, although if anyone had told me he'd end up running the Firm one day, I doubt I would have believed him. Outwardly, at least, Joe didn't fit the Android mold. He was a tall, dark man with wrinkled suits who always seemed to need a shave. He seemed pleasant and met with our group a few times. He was said to be an outstanding client man and had been top dog on some of the area's most prestigious clients. Initially, we were excited to work with him.

It turned out that what Berardino seemed to be more interested in than anything else, as far as I could tell, was cash. In late November, Joe called me into his office, then on the fourteenth floor of the midtown New York building, ostensibly for an official meet-and-greet now that he was my new boss. We talked about the targets John and I had agreed on, and he cut me off immediately. "I'm changing it," he said flatly. He didn't want to see our projections or our targeted clients or anything. He just pulled a number out of the air and announced, "Your target will be $2.8 million [gross]." I was speechless—but not for long. I looked him straight in the eye and said, "That's impossible. We can't do it." He stared at me, shocked that I would dare to challenge his edict. "No one has ever said that to me before," he spat.

"Well," I said, "I just did." He came back with "If you need more work, hire more people." Berardino was suggesting the classic auditor strategy for making money: hire more low-paid people for the group. It was the auditors' Field of Dreams: Hire them and the work will come. But we didn't fit an audit model, of course. You couldn't put 22-year-olds in charge of a company's most sensitive problems. "Then sign off on my hiring a couple of senior managers who have contacts and can bring in work," I countered. "No way," he said. Now I was mad—and scared. There was no way we could do $2.8 million, I thought. But somehow we'd have to. This was Arthur Andersen, and you simply did not question the boss.

# Cain and Abel Andersen

*It was corporate warfare. In this case, the rebels won.*
— PAUL VOLCKER, speaking at Baruch College's
2002 Financial Reporting Conference, May 2, 2002

I N MY YEARS OF CONSULTING, one important thing I've learned
is that most people do not want to do unethical things. Usually,
unethical or illegal behavior happens when decent people are put
under unbearable pressure to do their jobs and meet ambitious
goals without the resources to get the job done right. In the 1990s,
"perform or get purged" became the mantra of the day. At Arthur
Andersen, that mantra took on a special touch of evil. Once a firm
defined by what its employees had in common, it became a place
where enemies lurked everywhere—inside and out.

By the mid-1990s, the single greatest threat to the Firm was Andersen Consulting, the global consulting group spawned by Arthur
Andersen and nurtured through its infancy. Although almost from
the start, Arthur Andersen had a systems practice that helped companies organize their financial and accounting systems, it had only
sporadic success until the 1950s, when a small collection of computer geeks peered into the future and saw something no one else
did. Starting in the 1970s, the upstarts came into their own, like
teenagers certain that their parents said nothing worth listening to,
and a rift opened within this once-unified group.

This growing split was one of the key elements transforming the Firm's tight-knit, proud culture into one filled with paranoia, jealousy, and rage. During my tenure at Arthur Andersen, the conflict led to obsessive behavior on the part of equity partners who couldn't get over what they saw as treachery by their brethren on adjoining floors. It was a huge distraction at a critical time for the Firm, and took up valuable time and energy that might have been used to ferret out client wrongdoing, to save a souring culture, and to build on its world-class reputation to become the Firm of the twenty-first century.

When did it all begin? Well, it depends on whom you ask. As in any nasty divorce, both parties have a story that starts with betrayal and ends with self-defense. No one disputes, however, that it was success—not failure—that caused the two groups to cleave so dramatically. The Systems Group, also known as the Industrial Engineering Group, had existed, on and off, almost from the birth of the Firm. It first gained some traction after World War II, when Spacek hired two former Navy men and best friends, John Higgins and Joe Glickauf, to work on designing payroll systems. The development of the first computer at the University of Pennsylvania passed unnoticed through the minds of most people, but the news hit Glickauf like a bullet. He went to Philadelphia to study the contraption, than hightailed it back to Chicago, where he met with Spacek and convinced him that something revolutionary was going on—something in which Arthur Andersen absolutely had to be involved. Spacek said that if Glickauf could convince the partners to invest in this thing, he could lead the way.

Imagine the utter confusion of a group of audit partners at the Drake Hotel one weekend in January 1951, as their colleague unveiled a gadget that would, he promised, change the world. Glickauf, so excited he stuttered in his haste to get the words out, showed the partners a small computer that he had designed, dubbed the "Glickiac." It was full of lightbulbs, tubes, and wires, and he explained that it would make obsolete everything then known about processing business information. Glickauf begged the partners to support the resources needed for the Firm to understand this new field. Perhaps because Spacek had primed the pump, they agreed to invest in this new technology. Spacek was creating a skunk works, and by 1953 had funded a computer training school for a select group of young auditors.

In early 1953, General Electric called, looking for help. The company was building a new state-of-the-art plant at Appliance Park near Louisville, and it wanted to install a computer. "We found that everywhere we went to learn about computers, Arthur Andersen & Co. had been there ahead of us," said a GE executive. They asked AA to do a feasibility study on which computer to use—the Univac I or a new offering from IBM. Eventually, the Firm recommended the Univac, and General Electric then asked it to install the system. Presto! A new industry—computer consulting and installation—was born. With a new name—the Administrative Services Division—gross fees in 1956 were $1.8 million, double the previous year's. Although revenues soon fell off for a few years, Spacek never cut funding despite sniping from some partners that this was "Spacek's Folly." "It was an expensive thing and it all happened at once," Spacek said in 1989. "I must say, though, that I will forever be grateful to the partners. I allocated one-third of all of our income to what I called the extracurricular things [also including expansion overseas]. It was a lot of money to the partners."

Although the consultants weren't officially auditors, they were still, like every Arthur Andersen employee, required to spend two full years in the audit practice before moving to another group, be it tax or consulting. Since computers were so new, the experts at Arthur Andersen were self-taught.

One was Victor Millar. A son of a California oil drilling foreman who spent summers on the rigs, he arrived at U.C. Berkeley intending to be a petroleum engineer and ended up with an M.B.A. in accounting. Millar admired the elegant simplicity of the Arthur Andersen accounting model, where the auditors followed the same procedures everywhere around the world, and he decided to try to do something similar with the consulting group. Shortly after being made partner in 1968, Millar, who ran only the computer unit at the time, decided to develop some common methodologies and standards for the consulting practice. He helped streamline the various groups into one unit right around the time that Arthur

Andersen's new leader, Harvey Kapnick, bought the St. Charles campus. Eventually, the Firm required that every Administrative Services employee get computer training. Millar was creating a parallel organization to Arthur Andersen, but one that shared its commitment to "one firm" with strict standards and cultures for everyone who walked through those famous wooden doors. Later that decade, when Millar took over as head of consulting, he renamed the group the Management Information Consulting Division.

The lockstep march would soon start to change—ironically, because of a decision on the auditing side. In about 1964, according to Millar, the firm decided to stop requiring consultants to work as auditors for two years. This happened not because it was seen as a waste of time—it wasn't—but because the audit business was growing so quickly that a war for talent broke out. Becoming an auditor in the 1960s was considered a ticket to a stable lifestyle and an honorable profession. No, you wouldn't get rich, but you'd always have work, you'd be comfortable if you made partner, and you'd have the respect of your peers and your community. That meant that accounting students were hugely in demand, so much so that Andersen asked its consulting group to stop recruiting accounting majors, because it was stealing talent that was desperately needed on the other side. In the late 1960s, the company stopped asking consultants to get auditing training altogether. It was a drag on resources for people who were certain to leave the practice.

Several former or retired partners say this was the first step in developing a generation of future leaders who had none of the deep bonds forged with auditors. "The real bitterness emerged," Millar remembered, "when we began pulling in people [into the leadership circle] with no work background and no personal relationships with the auditors." George Shaheen, later the head of Andersen Consulting, who would get the credit—and the blame—for making the moves that led to the Andersen divorce, was in one of the first classes of Arthur Andersen hires without the audit requirement.

As Administrative Services continued to grow, becoming the only computer consultant with the clout to challenge IBM, the audit business faced some serious challenges. Much as it did in the late 1990s, a huge mergers and acquisitions boom and many new public companies meant lots of work for auditors in the late 1960s. When it ended quickly and brutally, the entire accounting profession hit a brick wall, since by this time the remaining public companies had already been divvied up among the Big 8. Partnerships like Arthur Andersen's saw their finely honed leverage model come under pressure. The less mature consulting model, which had fewer partners and more worker bees, looked better in comparison. At the same time, the demand for computers had exploded.

Complicating matters was the fact that, much as it did in 2002, several public company failures, such as that of Penn Central Railroad, led to a wave of litigation against auditors. Next came Watergate and the discovery that several companies had managed to make illegal political contributions while their auditors either didn't know or didn't care. In 1970, there were 71 lawsuits naming public accountants as defendants in the United States. Just two years later, there were 200. The cost of insurance skyrocketed, raising the costs for the entire Firm. For a few years, it was virtually impossible for any of the Big 8 to acquire insurance.

It was in the mid-1970s—the actual year remains in dispute—that the consulting group began to contribute more profit per person than the auditing side. "It was less that we had achieved our type of growth and more that parts of the audit business had dried up," says Millar. The partnership as a whole would not really be aware of the shift for several years, but an era had ended. The auditing business would never regain its former glory, and the consulting business was about to hit warp speed. By 1978, consulting contributed 21 percent of the company's $546 million in total income.

It fell on Harvey Kapnick, the AA CEO from 1970 to 1979, to preside over this power shift. He may have been the only one who truly understood what it meant. An impeccably dressed, buttoned-up man whose short stature led some partners to call him "The Little Napoleon," Kapnick had run the Cleveland office for eight years, and was the youngest Andersen employee ever to make partner, at 30.

Kapnick's elevation was seen as a return to the strong leader. Walter Oliphant had run the Firm from 1963 to 1970 but still left the big decisions to Spacek, who had become chairman. Unlike Oliphant, a kind and conciliatory sort, Kapnick wasn't one to be pushed around easily. He was built like a fighter and didn't hesitate to act like one. Kapnick led the firm on an incredible tear, with employees doubling from 9,000 to 18,000 during his tenure. He also helped Arthur Andersen cement its image as a firm of integrity by creating a Public Review Board staffed by outsiders to oversee the Firm. Kapnick also made Arthur Andersen the first accounting firm to put out an annual report and to disclose at least part of its finances. "A public accounting firm has a significant responsibility to the private sector of our economy, not only to clients but also to investors, creditors and the public," he proclaimed in 1974.

During Kapnick's tenure, the Firm decided in 1977 to create a new structure to encompass all of the various international offices around the world. Called the Arthur Andersen Worldwide Organization, it was established under a Swiss umbrella organization, Arthur Andersen & Co. Société Cooperative, which coordinated the various national member firms, all of which were members of both groups. Each member firm and its partners would agree to certain standards and principles that would help Andersen maintain its "One Firm" concept. The compensation would be shared among all of the member firms, and the Swiss umbrella would not provide any separate professional services of its own.

Then Kapnick made a series of moves that some call visionary, and others deride as a naked play for power. All agree, however, that it polarized the Firm and cost Kapnick his job. In the late 1970s, the SEC and Congress, responding to the strings of audit failures and a resurgence in interest in business ethics, grew concerned about the potential for conflicts between an audit business, whose job it was to assure the public that a company's books were clean, and an adjoining consulting practice that made money off those same companies. Could an auditor's independent judgment be affected by the fact that his firm's profits—and therefore, his own compensation— might depend on getting consulting fees from that same client? It was, as we now know far too well, a very valid question—and it drew the same response from most of the Big 8 that it would two decades later: Absolutely not! For Andersen, which now received far more of its total revenues than any other firm from consulting, the scrutiny had an ominous tilt to it. And as the largest accounting firm, it was Arthur Andersen that Congress turned to for answers.

In the late 1970s, Kapnick was called to Washington to testify before the Senate Subcommittee on Reports, Accounting and Management on the issue of whether consulting and auditing should be separated. Around the same time, the Securities and Exchange Commission issued a release, No. 264, that seemed to indicate that the Commission disapproved of auditors' growing consulting businesses. "The growing array of nonaudit services offered by some independent public accountants—and the growing importance of management advisory services to the revenues, profits, and competitive position of accounting firms—are a cause for legitimate concern as to the impact of these activities on auditor independence, objectivity, and professionalism," it read. Kapnick interpreted it as a scary harbinger of more regulation to come.

Kapnick returned from Washington full of concern about the way the winds were blowing. In a series of meetings, he told Andersen's board that the political mood had shifted. It was just a matter of time, he said, before the government forced auditing firms to split off from consulting firms. It would be better if Arthur Andersen did it first, before it was done to the Firm. "If we were going to be forced into separation," he said, "why not do it on our own terms?" Kapnick then laid out a bold vision of a new global consulting firm that would provide all kinds of services, including investment banking, but not auditing. It was exciting and glamorous—but not everyone knew that Kapnick intended to run both firms himself, and also to use the debate as a forum to extend his own term.

Before the split was brought to the partners for a vote, Kapnick had several meetings with top partners where he discussed how serious the pressure was from the SEC. Eugene Delves recalled that at one meeting, a partner who had been with Kapnick in Washington spoke up, saying that Kapnick's fears were exaggerated, and was rebuked sharply by Kapnick. Clearly, there was more than one interpretation of events.

All of that blew into the open at a worldwide partners meeting in September 1979, when, for the first time in Andersen's history, a leader was openly contradicted. In the master ballroom of the hotel, Kapnick presented his plan to more than a thousand partners assembled at tables in front of the stage. His compact form seemed to burst out of his tailored suit as he held forth passionately about his new plan. "Let's turn one great firm into two great firms," he proclaimed. "Let's take the advantage away from the government and act appropriately." "He made it sound as if action had to be taken and we had to anticipate this hammer coming down," remembered another former partner.

Just before getting into the discussion of the proposed split, Kapnick casually mentioned that the first item on the agenda would be a vote on extending his term. This was quite unusual, since typically at such junctures there was time allotted for discussion and debate—and some partners interpreted this, taken in context with the exciting new plan, as a bald-faced power play. Kapnick finished his speech and asked for questions from the partners, each of whom had a telephone at his seat, as well as an Arthur Andersen leather portfolio embossed with his initials and the year he made partner. On the rare occasions when they called in from the phone, their comments were broadcast across the ballroom. Suddenly, the voice of W. C. Brian Peoples, a New York audit partner known as a true blue Android and a straight shooter, crackled through the speakers.

"Harvey, it is inappropriate to extend your term of office without giving the partners a chance to consider your performance," Peoples said. The tension in the room shot up, and a murmur ran through the crowd. "It was like throwing a match into the tinderbox," recalled Duane Kullberg, then vice chairman of the audit practice. "What are you trying to do, Brian?" retorted Kapnick, annoyed. "Do you want a secret ballot?" Peoples said yes, he did. So the meeting broke up into small groups to debate Kapnick's performance. He did manage to win reelection, but by then the momentum he'd gained on splitting up the Firm had changed. Many partners were already concerned that Kapnick's plan could rob the Firm of its future, and Peoples's challenge created still more doubt.

Later that day, the partners decisively voted down his proposal to split the Firm. This was a partnership, and the partner in charge had lost the trust of his colleagues.

But Kapnick didn't give up. "I had become convinced that there would be some way these things had to become separated. The cultures were so different and so opposite," said Kapnick shortly before his death in August 2002. The other partners thought the debate should be over—that the Firm had voted it down—and they believed that an audit firm without a consulting practice would be at a major disadvantage vis-à-vis its competitors, especially with the audit slowdown. "We had something that was unique in the audit business," says Kullberg. "We didn't want to see it go. We still hadn't realized all of the fruits of that investment." A powerful group of partners wanted Kapnick out, but a coup would require a vote of all of the partners. Instead, it met secretly in New York and decided to send Kullberg, two other audit partners, and Millar, who had just been named head of consulting, to Chicago to confront Kapnick in his office on October 8, 1979. The group got right down to business, handing him a written statement saying that Kapnick had lost the support of the partnership and didn't have the commitment to keep the Firm together.

Icy and dismissive, Kapnick shot them down as soon as they got the words out. "I absolutely am not going to resign," Kapnick said flatly, "and you should all go away and think about what you're doing." Then the true battle began.

Kapnick immediately sent out a worldwide telex announcing that he had been asked to resign, but wouldn't, and called for a meeting of all partners in December. However, the partners quickly built a coalition strong enough to force Kapnick's hand, scheduling an earlier partners meeting in Houston at which he was likely to be voted out. Faced with no choice, Kapnick announced his resignation and early retirement on October 14, 1979.

In hindsight, it appears that Kapnick had the right idea. But his tactics got the best of him—and the Firm—as well. "He may have been a visionary," said Millar, "but people felt misled. His approach to getting it done was not a good one." As Peoples and others suspected, the drive to split auditing and consulting fell by the political wayside, in part thanks to the election of Ronald Reagan, and for years there was no more discussion of separating the two groups. SEC Release 264 was rescinded. It was back to business—but the interests of both sides were beginning to diverge for good.

• • •

A political scientist at the University of Pennsylvania, Alvin Z. Rubinstein, had a theory about Soviet leadership during the Cold War. Bald leaders, who were almost always reformers, were inevitably followed by hairy ones, who would clamp down and stay the course. Lenin, Khrushchev, and Gorbachev were in the former group; Stalin and Brezhnev were in the latter. At Arthur Andersen, it wasn't so easy to ascribe leadership qualities to hair. (For one thing, hats were mandatory until the late 1960s.) But it is true that radicals and conservatives tended to follow each other.

Certainly, the next managing partner, Duane Kullberg, was nothing like Kapnick. He would try—unsuccessfully—to ease the growing rift between the consulting and auditing wings of the Firm. Kullberg was conservative and competent, an auditor of Scandinavian origin from Minneapolis who looked like an aging James Dean. As a result of the Kapnick debacle, the Firm decided to limit the power of the CEO by adding more checks and balances and by creating a nominating committee, which would consult partners and carefully interview dozens of candidates for the job. In the end, however, the secret power meetings still catapulted one name—and one name only—before the partners for a vote. Kullberg was named Andersen's CEO in February of 1980 and immediately set about uniting the various factions. He quickly put through a fee increase, which earned him instant partner support.

For most of the decade, Andersen returned to its roots as a stable, prestigious place to work. There was, however, a growing frustration with the way the audit partner controlled the terms of most engagements. Consulting partners on both local and national levels, no matter how high up in the organization, still had to report directly to auditors. "The consulting partner was always number two," said Millar. Auditors, on the other hand, were terrified that consultants would upset the delicate relationship with the client that they had worked so hard to build. They mistrusted them and wanted to look over their shoulder at all times. "The cohesiveness was unsustainable," said one high-ranking former partner at Andersen Consulting. "We were like a teenager who wants his own set of keys."

In the 1980s, auditing revenues continued to grow, although at a slowing pace. The Supreme Court's 1978 reversal of a decision prohibiting advertising by lawyers led the American Institute of CPAs, the accounting trade group, to lift its own ban on advertising by accounting firms. The result was a series of costly, aggressive advertising campaigns by Arthur Andersen and its rivals. In the meantime, Andersen's consulting group became the envy of the professional services world. No one seriously considered splitting the Firm again—after all, the external threats had dissipated in the more pro-business Reagan administration—and Kullberg was more or less able to handle the consultants' request for more power within the Firm. "There were issues, but they were gradually being worked through," said Brebach.

Slowly, the consultants gained a few more seats on the Arthur Andersen board and on the various committees that held power. And Kullberg began to work on making sure that consultants, who were bringing in a lot more revenue per person, were receiving more units (the earnings system by which partners were paid) to reflect that. "Kullberg's view was to just be patient," said Brebach. In 1986 Kullberg, who liked task forces, created a group to determine the future direction of the company, called the Mix of Services Committee. Dominated by auditors, it naturally concluded that auditing should remain the main seat of power, with the other groups—consulting and tax—continuing to report directly to auditors. This infuriated Brebach, who would be named to the top consulting slot in 1987. It also helped convince Victor Millar to leave Arthur Andersen in 1986, shocking many partners who saw him as an Android of the first order. Millar supported Kullberg, but he also wanted to be the boss, and Kullberg had decided to run for a second four-year term. "I was fifty at this point and recognized that I wanted to run something," Millar said. "I also saw the incredible litigation risk in the audit practice."

Millar said that most consulting partners were still committed to Arthur Andersen, but a growing minority of people were starting to resent the fact that they were bringing in so much more to the Firm. "People rising to the top, like [Brebach], had not had that experience working with auditors. By now everyone was focused on the difference in profitability. I felt it was going to break off." At the same time, audit partners felt more strongly than ever that the consultants had transformed into a bunch of ungrateful upstarts who had no appreciation for the sacrifices their colleagues had made for them. The accountants had financed the unit from birth, giving up their own profits as an investment for the Firm itself. They had given up a lot of control, they thought. And they also had come to rely on the money: By 1988, consulting's growth rate was 33 percent to audit's 14 percent. "There was a crossover," said Millar. "It was like the hitching of a race horse and a farm horse to the same trailer."

In December 1986, Millar left to head the new consulting unit at advertising highflier Saatchi & Saatchi, a brash, cash-rich company that hired him to buy and build the world's largest consulting group. Millar makes no bones about the fact that Andersen's consulting group was at the top of his shopping list. A few months later, Kullberg and Millar—who had parted on good terms—met for breakfast, and Millar made an offer to buy the consulting practice. Millar had valued the group at roughly $1 billion—about five times the group's earnings, and almost exactly what Arthur Andersen would receive some fourteen years later in arbitration. Kullberg never responded, and when Millar followed up, Kullberg said the board wasn't interested. Then, in 1987, came a meeting in London, attended by several top consulting partners, in which the group decided to change its name to Andersen Consulting. They were doing it for branding reasons, they said, since their name, the Management Information Consulting Division, didn't exactly slip off the tongue.

But the auditors saw a cabal of Benedict Arnolds at work. Wondered Kullberg: "What's the next shoe to drop?" So in late 1987, the board, still auditor-dominated, decided to add a noncompete clause to the partnership agreement saying that if any partner left the firm, he couldn't work in the same industry for one year. Chief Operating Officer Larry Weinbach, widely considered the bad cop to Kullberg's good cop, explained it as only natural. "We knew we couldn't stop people from leaving the Firm," he was quoted as saying at the time. "But if they did, we wanted to make sure they didn't take clients or proprietary information with them."

As Brebach and a group of colleagues read the agreement in a small conference room in New York, the clause leapt off the page. "It popped up like a neon light," said Brebach. "I knew it was there for a purpose, which was to inhibit the consulting partners from doing anything on their own. It was never even talked about before. It was a threat." Brebach, infuriated, pushed back from the table. Something had to be done, he thought.

What was done, however, would set in motion a conflict that would end, more than a decade later, in the professional service firm's equivalent of nuclear war. Brebach first hired law firm Kirkland & Ellis to look at the noncompete clause to see whether it was enforceable. Then, in April 1988, he organized a secret meeting, with a dozen top consulting deputies, to figure out what to do. It was held in a private room in the basement of the "21" Club, New York's tony bastion of WASPy power players. The group discussed whether to accept the noncompete clause—which the lawyers told them was ironclad—and if it didn't, what other options it had, ranging from outright divorce to a financial separation to doing nothing at all. Another topic the lawyers brought up—the growing litigation risk from bad audits, due to the fact that plaintiffs were increasingly naming auditors in their corporate lawsuits—worried many in the group. After all, a suit against the auditors was a suit against the consultants. All their money was commingled in one large pot.

Brebach then took a step that still haunts him today. He had asked an acquaintance at Morgan Stanley to put a valuation on an independent consulting practice with more than $1 billion in revenues. He handed out a memo to everyone at the meeting listing that estimate, plus all the alternatives. "We had a list like any good consultants," recalled Brebach. "I made the mistake of handing out the sheets and not collecting them." One partner who was at the meeting said no final decisions were made, other than to confront Kullberg and COO Weinbach about the noncompete clause, which happened shortly afterward. "It was a good, pragmatic discussion," he said. "Some people wanted to run out of the door right then, and others felt this wasn't the time."

•　•　•

What Brebach didn't know was that one of his "21" Club partners had already told Kullberg about the meeting and showed him the three-page memo. So, when he got a call from Kullberg saying that he would like to meet with him in New York, he thought he might hear that he had won. And for a second, on that Monday morning, that's what he heard. "I want to congratulate you on your success," said Kullberg. "We're taking the noncompete out." Brebach was elated. "Terrific move," he said.

While Brebach insists that Weinbach uttered the following words and Kullberg is equally certain that he himself said them, no one disputes the events themselves. "Not so fast," one of the men said, stony-faced. He pulled out his copy of the "21" Club agenda and laid it on the table in front of him. "Do you recognize this?" Brebach colored a deep red and said nothing. "Gresh, my understanding is that you organized this meeting," said the partner. "I hereby relieve you of your duties as head of the North America consulting practice." Brebach had betrayed the partnership and the "One Firm" concept. He was out.

Brebach froze. He knew he had taken a risk, but he never imagined he'd be ratted out. "This is really rash behavior," he sputtered. "This is way out of line. You're going to rue the day you did this. This is not going to go down well!"

Brebach's ouster brought the simmering tensions at Arthur Andersen to a rolling boil. "Gresh was doing the right thing," said one former partner who was at the "21" meeting. "He was taking on the right issues, but everything was in-your-face. There was no strategy. I think he should have been fired," not for holding the meeting, but for being careless, he said. "You don't leave a trail of paper." It's unlikely that Brebach's folly had anything to do with the Firm's decision, many years later, to rewrite the Firm's document-destruction policy and shred the Enron papers. But the irony is hard to ignore.

> *They used to say if you wanted to know what it felt like to be a black person sitting in the back of the bus, go be a consultant at Arthur Andersen.*
> —A FORMER ANDERSEN CONSULTING PARTNER

That is an outrageous comment, especially since almost no one at Arthur Andersen, particularly a partner, had any idea what it felt like to be a black person at all. But I've included this quote because it demonstrates just how intense the feelings became during the 1990s, when the relationship between AC and AA deteriorated into outright disdain.

Millar and Brebach joined forces, starting a new company and convincing some Andersen Consulting partners to jump ship. Arthur Andersen promptly sued them, and the two countersued, claiming that Arthur Andersen was trying to do whatever it took to make sure that the new firm, ICG, a unit of Saatchi & Saatchi, never got a client. The suit was settled in 1989, but the anger remained and those who dared to defect were seen as traitors. Even Eugene Delves, a longtime partner and part of the original group of four that worked on the General Electric computer project, felt the chill of being "excommunicated" when he joined Saatchi & Saatchi. Furious at his leaving, the Firm erased Delves's face from a picture of the four prominently displayed at St. Charles, as if he had never helped to build the business that was bankrolling the company. Only after his son, an Andersen Consulting partner, raised hell was the picture restored.

With each new dispute, the Firm's vaunted culture took another body blow. To Kullberg's credit, he knew that Arthur Andersen's problems were bigger than Brebach. Already, he had created a "Change Management Task Force," made up of fifteen partners of different ages, countries, and practice areas, with a facilitator trying to break through the communication barriers. After a full week of meetings that went nowhere, Kullberg told the group members that they could either go back and get the job done, or he would announce to the partners that they had failed. The group went back to work, meeting for almost three agonizing weeks, and finally hammered out an agreement backing the creation of Andersen Consulting as a separate business unit with its own profit pool.

It seemed, to the auditors, like a bold move that would finally put an end to the endless bellyaching of the consultants. In the reorganization, audit and tax stayed together. Each group would have its own profit pool, with one key caveat: The group that earned less would have the right to a subsidy of up to 15 percent of the other group's earnings. It was, by then, almost always a one-way subsidy. By the end of 1988, the year the company celebrated its seventy-fifth anniversary, Andersen Consulting contributed 40 percent of the firm's $2.8 billion in worldwide revenues, up from 33 percent just two years earlier, and a disproportionate share of the Firm's profits. The partnership approved the new plan in January 1989, which also included a new seat for AC on the board of Andersen Worldwide, bringing AC's total to seven of twenty-four.

There was another major change: AC consultants now would report directly to other consulting partners—not to auditors. Consultants considered this a huge victory, since they felt constantly hamstrung by audit partners. The auditors signed off on this one. But when the auditors later launched their own technology consulting group, Business Consulting—and expanded risk consulting, my unit—they made sure that they would never lose such control again. They were still fighting the last war. And we all paid the price for that.

Arthur Andersen's technology consulting group, say many people on both sides of the transom, was not originally intended to compete with Andersen Consulting. Rather, it seemed a good way for the company to pick up some technology-related business among smaller market companies, which AC wasn't particularly interested in. "In the mid-1980s," said Brebach, "the projects were getting larger and larger and we [AC] didn't want to do that kind of work, but we had some people who were good at it. So I said, 'Why don't you all go over there and start a consulting practice for them?'" In 1990, the deal was formalized in what was called the Florida Accords. Arthur

Andersen would stick to clients of $175 million or less in revenues for technology-related consulting. It was already working on expanding what later became risk consulting, the audit-connected services that would include my group. And AC would focus on the large-company systems business. It was all so neat.

In late 1989, the partners approved the restructuring plan. Exhausted, Kullberg announced that he was going to resign and take early retirement two years before the end of his term. The effort to make peace had worn him out, and his constituents were still not satisfied. Despite the problems his resignation telegraphed, Kullberg put on a brave face. "We are Arthur Andersen, we grew up in the system, and there is a consensus among partners that we will make this work," he said at the time.

Not everyone had grown up in that system, but partners who still held control had. So the Arthur Andersen board of wizards went behind the curtain again—and again, they chose a leader best known for being the opposite of the previous one. After three days of deliberations, they chose Lawrence A. Weinbach as their new chief. Weinbach, then 49, was a brilliant accountant and a lifelong Android who had gained internal fame as an M & A expert. A silver-haired, trim man who had worked his way up from a hardscrabble childhood in Waterbury, Connecticut, Weinbach brimmed with confidence. This job seemed like just one more title to add to his collection. He spent most of his career on the East Coast, running the Hartford office, the New York audit group, and then the New York metropolitan area before he was named chief operating officer in 1987.

Since the AC folks considered Weinbach an auditing hardliner, they viewed his election as a slap in the face. He was also an American, which infuriated many of the worldwide partners, who were eager to see someone from one of the scores of international offices at the helm of "One Firm." In an interview with *The New York Times* just after being named to the post, Weinbach set the tone. "Consensus is good, but there are times when it slows you down," he said.

Under Weinbach's rule, the two groups increasingly operated as entirely separate companies. In the New York offices on the Avenue of the Americas, the groups moved to different floors, so the only interaction we had with AC people was in the elevators.

You could always tell who was who. For one thing, the Andersen Consulting people dressed better. They just seemed hipper and richer. The same was true of the offices. You didn't need to be a psychic to see which way the money was flowing. You just had to peer out the elevator door.

Every Arthur Andersen floor had a forest-green carpet leading to those ubiquitous doors. By the time I got to New York, that green carpet had become frayed and sad. It evoked another era, that of bankers' lamps, cigars, and suspenders. But on the AC floors, blond wood and frosted glass conveyed another image—one of modernity and growth. It was a jarring contrast to the stolid secrecy of AA. "If you mistakenly went to the wrong floor, you said, 'Wow, nice offices!'" said a partner who worked in the New York office in the late 1990s. "Then you went back to your own floor and it was like a rabbit warren—a bunch of rat holes with a ratty carpet. It was ugly!"

The two groups now had separate brands, recruiting processes, and pay scales. They both continued to grow: AA at an 11 percent pace, AC at a 26 percent pace in 1996. They still shared the St. Charles training center, but never interacted there. The only place they had regular contact was on the board of Andersen Worldwide, where the leadership change hadn't done much to usher in the era of peace and love. Just before Weinbach was elected CEO, George Shaheen and Richard Measelle were elevated to run Andersen Consulting and Arthur Andersen, respectively. Dick Measelle was a short, self-contained man with sandy hair who did not seem to me to be a dynamic leader. He had, however, thought long and hard about changes the organization needed to make, although little resulted from his suggestions.

Measelle had been getting a lot of flak for the money he was spending to create the "School of the Future," a technology-based school in Oakland that he hoped could be a new model for education. He was also criticized for his interest in softer management concepts, such as his idea to bring in a corporate anthropologist to examine the Firm's culture. When I spoke to Measelle after Dean told me that I was on my own, he said, "Well, you don't want to report to me. They think I'm a visionary, and that's not going to help you." Visionary, I learned, was not a good thing to be labeled at Arthur Andersen.

George Shaheen was Measelle's antithesis—and would end up as Weinbach's nemesis. He, too, had been with the firm for almost two decades, since he came out of Bradley University in Illinois with an M.B.A., but had never been an auditor. Shaheen had a strong midwestern accent, but that was about the only thing that pegged him as a typical Arthur Andersen partner. He was always outspoken about where he saw the future—and needless to say, it was not in auditing as it then existed. *Fortune* described him as "tan, trim and impatient," and that about summed it up, if you threw in the occasional stream of profanity.

Although Shaheen had originally been considered a team player, his apparent disdain for Arthur Andersen and his fire-up-the-troops style of leadership at AC won him loads of friends and piles of enemies. No one was on the fence about George. A natty dresser who loved to model the latest in briefcases, Shaheen didn't suffer fools—gladly or otherwise—and acted more like a CEO than a member of a partnership. "He was not the developing or nurturing kind of guy," said Brebach. "But he was well liked and was not difficult to get along with, not arrogant. He changed over time." By the time Shaheen took charge at AC, some people—mostly auditors—thought arrogant was his middle name. That was quite a statement from an organization that took pride in its own haughty reputation.

But Shaheen had a lot more than hot air behind him, including an incredibly loyal cadre of consultants. Under his tenure, Shaheen led Andersen Consulting to its most profitable and fastest-growing period ever. AC became the single largest consulting firm in the world, thanks largely to its model—borrowed in part from Arthur Andersen—of using energetic young "green beans" to staff massive technology consulting projects. They worked constantly and intensely, traveling the world and rarely seeing their families. Of course, they were paid well for it: There were 20 "professionals," or nonpartners, for every partner at AC in the early 1990s, compared to just over half that for Arthur Andersen. A growing pie could now be split among fewer people—but the consultants still had to pay up to 15 percent of their profits to their former friends on the other side of the tracks.

In 1994, just before I got to Arthur Andersen, several key events took place. For the first time ever, AC's revenues virtually matched those of Arthur Andersen. It was already, as we know, much more profitable. What's more, the technology consultants, who had always hated the auditors' overbearing attitude, no longer needed to borrow leads and introductions from audit clients. It was like an abusive relationship, in a way: The auditors needed the consultants' money and sparkle, but resented it at the same time. And the consultants now saw the auditors as the ultimate downers. They were going places, and they didn't need any hangers-on in green eyeshades.

The one part of Arthur Andersen's business that was posting great margins was its own consulting group. There was so much systems and technology work out there that it seemed not that big a deal for the Firm to move beyond the Florida Accords into larger businesses. Arthur Andersen's technology unit was then renamed the Business Consulting Group. And for a time, even the ultracompetitive Shaheen said in public that there seemed to be enough business to go around. There was simply too much money to be made with the Fortune 500 companies in areas such as SAP and systems overhauls. Later, of course, there was the explosion of the Internet and Y2K. Still, for a group of people whose entire career was based on trust, it had become a scarce commodity around the office. Said one former AC partner: "I knew that a fish in a small pond with a tributary will find the big pond as soon as it gets going. As soon as they got their sea legs, they would go after our clients."

Suddenly, people who saw one another only in the elevator were running into one another outside the office of a CFO, where they had come to pitch for the same business. At the same time the transfer payments from AC to AA accelerated, to the point that the Firm estimated a $170 million payout from AC to AA for fiscal 1997, boosting per-partner income by $200 per earnings unit. From the AA side, the pie seemed large enough for everyone. And for Dick Measelle, it was this expansion, along with the fast growth of Arthur Andersen's own consulting group, that would support its stellar—but stagnating—audit business. "We don't want to be *just* auditors,"

Measelle would often say. "We want to be the Trusted Business Advisors." Measelle felt that the Firm had no choice but to push forward on consulting, because if it didn't, it would lose business—both auditing and consulting—to the rest of the now Big 6, which were aggressively pushing their own consultants. I liked Measelle—he was the one whose "vision" brought me in, after all—but he wasn't particularly popular with the old-time auditors. They felt that by moving away from the core business, he was acknowledging what seemed like an inferiority complex. The wife of one high-level Arthur Andersen executive put it best. She cracked, "All of these guys have to fly first class and stay in the best hotels. Because they're just accountants."

By the mid-1990s, the sniping had worsened dramatically. In yet another effort to patch things up, Weinbach put together a committee made up of five people from each unit to work things out. Nothing came of it. Then, in 1994, he tried to unite the firm under his "Andersen 21" concept (it was about the twenty-first century, not that "21" club meeting), but again, both sides dug in. The eighteen-month project was a disaster from the start. Dispute resolution experts from Harvard came regularly to put the two sides through problem-solving exercises. The groups met twice a month—sometimes more—but nothing worked. "It went on and on," said one very high-ranking partner in the group. "It required half my time and it was at the expense of half the things I needed to get done at the time."

In the summer of 1996, Weinbach offered a surprise split-the-baby solution that would move Arthur Andersen's Business Consulting unit to AC. This was a shock to Measelle and Shaheen, who had gotten Weinbach's permission to hold secret talks about a deal that would allow AC to exit the Firm at a certain price. The auditors naturally hated the idea, and AC turned him down because they felt that it would distract them from their larger client projects, according to one former high-level AC partner. Measelle has a different explanation. "The fact that Shaheen turned down the offer of Business Consulting by Weinbach indicated that the real agenda of AC was and had always been to exit the Firm," he asserted.

Finally, said many former partners from both sides, Weinbach simply gave up. Rather than try to crack heads until something happened, he decided he, too, had had it. In February 1997, he said he would resign by August, rather than run for another four-year term. In short order, he was named CEO of Unisys Corp.

•  •  •

The Palais des Congrès was a cavernous space, one of the only places in Paris that could accommodate the nearly 2,800 partners of Andersen Worldwide. It was the annual partners meeting, but it was anything but business as usual. Although Weinbach presided over the meeting, he was clearly a lame duck. And for the first time ever, the board of directors could not work its magic and come up with the one man guaranteed to win the Andersen plebiscite. I wasn't at this meeting, since it was for equity partners only, but here's my understanding of what happened, which I developed from talks with many of them.

Before the April 1997 meeting, Andersen's 12-person nominating committee, made up of six AC and six AA partners, had submitted Shaheen's name to the board of partners as the replacement for Weinbach. The board, which was two-thirds auditors, had to approve it by a two-thirds majority in order to make him the sole candidate for the partner vote—but it refused, despite the fact that there was no strong candidate from the auditing side either (Measelle had dropped out of the running amid plans to retire, re-marry, and move to London). The board also knew that the second name the commission had chosen—Jim Wadia, an Indian-born tax specialist who ran the London office and who was relatively unknown—wouldn't sit well with the consulting partners, although his selection might help ease the brutal global tensions felt by Andersen Worldwide's non-American partners.

Stalemated, the board decided to let the two men make their case before the partnership and then decide. Shaheen went first—and pulled no punches. In his 20-minute speech, Shaheen said that the audit function hadn't changed much since the nineteenth century. To create a twenty-first-century firm, the audit function should be completely reconceived using technology, with large data centers allowing Arthur Andersen to do what he called a "real-time audit" instead of reporting on what had happened six months before.

What he was really saying, thought many of the audit partners, was that audit was dying, and that consulting was the future of the Firm. Yet some of the audit partners supported Shaheen. They felt he was the only one who was saying what everyone else was thinking—that it was time for radical action. The Band-Aids of the last decade had healed nothing.

Next, Wadia took the stage and played the peace card. With his soft voice and British cordiality, he was the perfect anti-Shaheen. While he did support the idea of giving the consulting side more power in the future, he also called for a one-year hiatus before making any changes at all. Stay the course, he said soothingly. It will work out. After both speeches, the men took questions from the audience, and—shades of Kapnick—one questioner almost ended Shaheen's campaign in a heartbeat.

If you lose the election, said the partner, will you support the one who is elected? Wadia nodded eagerly and gave the expected answer: Absolutely. But Shaheen, who was never much of a politician, paused, then said slowly, "I don't know if I can make that commitment." His comment rocked the house. Shaheen later said he was only being honest. But his words seemed to confirm what many feared about him—that he wasn't, and would never be, a team player. "One partner doesn't own the place," said an audit partner who was there. "We all do. Shaheen gave the impression he considered partners to be his employees."

The next day, the board met but remained split. "There was only one problem," said one partner. "There wasn't anyone acceptable to Andersen Consulting but Shaheen, and there wasn't anyone acceptable to Arthur Andersen who was George Shaheen." After a full day of deadlocked discussions and trial balloons, with emissaries from the board scurrying back and forth between Shaheen's and Wadia's hotels, it came down to a few possibilities. One, arranged in a meeting between Wadia, Weinbach, Shaheen, and another board member, was a deal in which Shaheen would run the worldwide Firm while Wadia headed up Arthur Andersen. Both Wadia and Shaheen agreed, contingent, of course, on the board's approval, and made plans for a joint meeting the next morning to start the "lovefest," as one partner termed it. But the Arthur

Andersen board members had in the meantime floated another proposal, which had Shaheen as the candidate to run Andersen Worldwide on the condition that an Arthur Andersen partner be named CFO and another one COO as a way of checking his power. It seemed like a workable compromise when it was presented to the full board of Andersen Worldwide—but when an emissary showed up at Shaheen's hotel with the proposal, he said no, believing that he had a different deal. "Everyone in the room was shocked that he turned it down," said a former board member. The Arthur Andersen folks rejected the first deal, and then Weinbach decided to end the standoff by voting in favor of Wadia. "You're going to put the firm at risk!" shouted Shaheen when Weinbach called to tell him what he had done.

In May 1997, Wadia's name was put forward to the partners, and for the first time in Andersen's 84-year history, the single candidate lost. He received only 51 percent of the votes, less than the two-thirds required. Stung, the board backtracked and put Shaheen's name forward. Just over a month later, Shaheen, too, lost the election, gaining just 63 percent of the total. Adding to the humiliation was the fact that the rift had now spilled beyond those closed doors and into the public domain. How can a company be your "Trusted Business Advisor" if it can't get its own house in order? "Nobody ever conceived that this could happen," said Weinbach at the time. "I wish this process was over."

But it wasn't. Wadia was named head of Arthur Andersen, replacing Measelle, and Shaheen stayed on as head of AC. Board Chairman W. Robert Grafton, an audit partner from Washington, was named the interim CEO of Andersen Worldwide and did little to fill the void. "On a scale of one to ten," said one partner, "Weinbach was a seven in terms of his ability to project leadership. Grafton was a two."

In the next few months, Shaheen got his ducks lined up. First, he asked Weinbach for permission to get a legal opinion on who owned Andersen Consulting. The lawyers told him that the consulting partners owned AC but had certain obligations to the Firm as a whole. He then called a meeting of all Andersen Consulting partners in December in San Francisco to decide whether or not to file for divorce. When Wadia and Grafton found out about it, they angrily insisted on coming to speak as well. In his speech, Wadia acknowledged AC's grievances and offered an independent board within the Firm, also offering to freeze the onerous transfer payments at about $180 million, adjusted for inflation, per year. But he was clear on the fact that AC and AA should stay together, and for the consulting partners it only reaffirmed their belief that they would never get what they thought they deserved. "Wadia basically told us to eat shit and enjoy it," one partner said.

That was all the AC partners needed to hear. The next day, December 17, 1997, the consulting partners voted unanimously (with one abstention) to break off from Arthur Andersen. That same day, Shaheen filed for arbitration with the International Chamber of Commerce as required by the Andersen Worldwide partnership agreement. He claimed that Arthur Andersen's direct competition with AC in the technology area nullified the onerous 1977 agreement, part of the creation of the Société Cooperative, that required any Andersen unit that left to pay a price of 1.5 times its current revenues. By the time the arbitration decision came down, that could have meant $14.6 billion. A few months later, Andersen Worldwide, headed by Grafton, tried to halt the process by setting up a "partner protection committee," made up of only accounting partners, to protect the interests of Andersen Worldwide and Arthur Andersen. It was war.

For those of us who had come into the Firm after the two units were largely separate, it was hard to understand the fury with which the audit partners reacted to the move and to Shaheen in general. We had never worked with Andersen Consulting partners. We hadn't joined the Firm together and worked together on auditing projects. We had so much trouble getting along with each other that we couldn't fathom the meaning of this whole other bitter battle. But for every Android in the Firm, what had happened was more than a business dispute. It was the ultimate act of disloyalty—the rejection of everything a partnership stood for. Andersen had always been a place that kept its dirty laundry behind those wooden doors. Its brand was based on one united front—and the consultants had violated that honor code.

After Shaheen's move, outright hostility replaced cold politesse. In the New York office, every elevator trip was an unpleasant experience. You could tell by which floor someone punched whether they were with you or against you. It was a pretty tense way to start the day. One Arthur Andersen consulting partner, who started just before the arbitration was filed, told me about a horrible faux pas he made. "At my first lunch," he remembered, "I said, 'There's something I don't quite understand. With all this consolidation going on across financial services organizations these days, why don't AA and AC just merge? They could become one organization to provide integrated, seamless services to the client.'" The table went silent in mute shock. "My boss looked at me like I just stepped off Mars," he said.

The conflict affected the way all of us did our jobs. Lou Salvatore, then New York office managing partner, who would later become the interim CEO of Arthur Andersen, was on the negotiating committee that had tried to work out a settlement. It's fair to say that for Lou, a born and bred Arthur Andersen partner, George Shaheen was the Antichrist. At every partner meeting I went to, which was about once every six weeks, Lou would start the meeting, no matter what its official purpose, with an update on where things stood. Then he would get enraged and emotional. In a heartbeat, these meetings would change from a report on new business to an emotional diatribe about what George said and what George did. It would be the first thing he would bring up, the last thing he would bring up, and he would bring it up in between as well. George Shaheen haunted Salvatore and the other top leaders at Arthur Andersen in a way that turned the arbitration into an obsessive personal vendetta.

Some interactions were downright silly. Steve Leiter, a former AA partner, remembered an altercation at Madison Square Garden, where the two groups still shared a luxury box. During a concert, Leiter took a seat near the front of the box. "This guy comes up and goes, you're in my seat," he said. "I said, 'I'm sitting here, so it must be my seat.'" Macho posturing ensued until the other guy pulled rank. "I'm an Andersen Consulting partner," he blustered. Retorted Leiter: "I'm an Arthur Andersen partner, and I can kick your ass."

As Leiter remembers it, the consulting partner backed down. "This wouldn't have happened with Arthur Andersen people," he said, pointing out that they all knew each other well, for one thing.

The battle was fast becoming a game of legal strategy: AC parried first by supporting the clause in the partnership agreement that specified one arbitrator rather than, as AA thought logical, three. Most people thought the lawyers at Simpson, Thacher & Bartlett had lost their marbles. Why risk your entire business on the decision of one person? The AC folks also gambled by insisting that the arbitrator come from a country where neither office had a legal presence. With two of the largest firms in the world at war, that didn't leave much—only a random selection of woefully underdeveloped Third World countries such as Burkina Faso and Iraq. Said Jim Quinn, the lead litigator at Weil, Gotshal & Manges and the head of Arthur Andersen's arbitration team: "I'll never forget that when we got the list of countries, one was Togo—and the capital of Togo was Timbuktu. So we kept saying we could actually go to Timbuktu for that arbitration. It was absolutely unbelievable."

Quinn took the position that relying on one adjudicator from these places would be absurd and that it should be a group of people from North America and Europe, since they knew the businesses best. AC, on the other hand, reasoned that if it was going to take a chance, why not go to an educated person from a country with an entirely different monetary scale? "We went to places like Nigeria and interviewed people," said one member of the AC team. "They don't think in billions." The assumption, even from the consulting side, was that AC would have to pay a price for its freedom. But how much? Ultimately, in March 1998, both sides accepted Guillermo Gamba, a Harvard-trained lawyer from Colombia, as the sole arbitrator. He had arbitrated only one other ICC case—a restaurant franchise conflict. Now he was responsible for solving one of the biggest corporate disputes on the planet. Both sides would file their positions with Gamba, who would take time for fact-checking and then start the clock on a six-month decision schedule.

*Andersen v. Andersen* got uglier and uglier. It certainly seemed, for a time, that Arthur Andersen had the advantage. In the summer of 1998, Andersen Consulting changed its logo to simply AC, omitting any mention of the word *Andersen* in most of its public documents. I noticed it one morning on my way to the office. Suddenly, it was AC, not Andersen Consulting, that worked downstairs from us—a sign, some of us thought, that AC was acknowledging a future loss of the Andersen name and more. But I wondered if we were just being outflanked again, and if AC simply was grabbing the strategic advantage by rebranding on its own terms. If AC was going to lose, why did it seem so damn smart?

Then, in September 1999, just before I left the Firm, we all got a true shock. George Shaheen, the public face of all those ungrateful wretches, announced that he was quitting after 33 years to join Webvan, an online grocery start-up that was about to go public. The press interpreted Shaheen's move as a sign that everyone—even an executive at one of the world's most successful companies—was bolting for the New Economy. Most outsiders saw his move as a get-rich-quick ploy, since he could have become a billionaire if Webvan had a successful IPO. But inside the Firm, some AA partners saw it as just another sign that AC had no case. After all, if AC were to win the arbitration, it would certainly file for an IPO, making millions for the top executives. It looked to some of my colleagues as if the rats were leaving a sinking ship. Others, of course, secretly admired Shaheen for doing what we all wanted to do—take a shot at making billions. "People always said George wanted to be a jillionaire," said Quinn. "Still, everyone was just dumbfounded."

Certainly Jim Wadia, Mr. Congeniality, took every opportunity to smooth the way should Andersen Consulting, its bellicose general off to fight New Economy wars, opt to reconcile. But it didn't. So Wadia, who spent most of his time on the arbitration process, upped the stakes, asking for $14.6 billion based on AC's growth projections and the 1.5 multiple revenue penalty. He traveled the world, visiting local AA offices and projecting serene confidence that the arbitration would go our way. He put out regular voice mails to the office managing partners (in our case, Salvatore), who forwarded them on to the rest of us, rallying the troops and telling us that the struggle would soon be over. It certainly seemed that way: Just a few weeks before the settlement, AC offered a last-minute deal—a pay-off of around $2 billion (the transfer payments, along with less than $1 billion more) in exchange for its freedom and the right to keep its name. Wadia, full of misplaced pride and having created expectations of a windfall, knew it was below what his board had agreed upon as a possible price. So he turned the deal down flat.

But Gamba's decision would make Wadia and all of his partners look foolish. On August 7, 2000, a warm Monday morning in Paris, he handed down his ruling while most of France was on its annual holiday. As Quinn sat in a conference room, flanked by several partners and lawyers, including Wadia, Salvatore, and Berardino, a colleague read from the decision over a speakerphone. The first words he read sounded encouraging: Arthur Andersen's consulting unit had not violated any of the contracts. "We were thinking this is pretty good," said Quinn. "Then he read the third or fourth paragraph, which said that Andersen Worldwide had violated its obligations, and I immediately knew that we lost. We all just sort of shook our heads." The energy left the room like the air in a punctured balloon.

Gamba went on to pin the ultimate blame on Andersen Worldwide during Weinbach's tenure for letting the conflict spiral out of control. In short, it was all about dysfunctional leadership. "Andersen Worldwide failed to take any course of action when the scope of service conflict surfaced," he wrote in his ruling. Gamba gave Arthur Andersen the right to the Andersen name—and let AC leave with a bill of just $1 billion, most of which had already been set aside for transfer payments, despite the fact that Andersen Consulting had an estimated market value of $25 billion at the time. It was a devastating blow to Arthur Andersen. In the end, what the Firm got was about what Victor Millar had planned to offer for the consulting group back in 1987, when it was less than one-fifth its current size. "We got the wrong arbitrator," said Quinn. "I don't think it's any more complicated than that. Anyone who knows anything about this type of arbitration says 'Boy, you got screwed.'"

Discredited and humiliated, Wadia resigned immediately—he had agreed previously with the board to do so if he lost—leaving yet another gaping hole in the leadership structure. "Jim Wadia was a brilliant man," said Art Bowman, editor of *Bowman's Accounting*

*Report* and a longtime Andersen observer, "but he led them down the path of destruction. It was not so much an aggression as a self-assuredness that they were going to prevail, and there was no strategy for what would happen if they lost." The end of the revenue-sharing agreement would mean an instant $100,000 haircut per partner for all AA partners, who had received more than $300 million in transfer payments from AC in 1999. But they had lost more than that, since a $2 billion award could have meant more than $1 million per partner, and a $14.6 billion award—the amount AA felt it was entitled to—would have brought each partner a $7.8 million pot of gold.

It would have been an almost inconceivable windfall for a group of hard workers from modest origins, many of whom had joined the firm in search of nothing more than a steady job and a stable career. Assured of a big win, some had already spent big. "Some of them had already bought the new house and the new yacht," remembered one New York partner. "There was a full expectation that we would win. It had been fanned by the leadership."

Worst of all, Arthur Andersen's audit practice was by 1999 the smallest audit business in the Big 5, with the slowest rate of growth (12.6 percent). Rivals such as Ernst & Young and KPMG were monetizing its consulting groups, making billions by selling them or spinning them off. Andersen was left with a plateauing audit business, a small tax business, and a fast-growing but still relatively small consulting business, even as the SEC, under Chairman Arthur Levitt, began making noises about the conflicts between auditing and consulting. The pressure was unbearable. Losing clients—no matter what they did—was not really an option.

In the fall of 2001, Eugene Delves, who had left the Firm in 1986, placed a phone call to Joseph Berardino, Andersen's new chief executive. Berardino didn't know him, but he listened as Delves told him that December 2001 marked the fiftieth anniversary of that fateful partners meeting that convinced Arthur Andersen to invest in computers. "Arthur Andersen should do something to commemorate that, before Accenture does," Delves said. Accenture was the new name for AC, which had reinvented itself to the point that it didn't even mention Arthur Andersen in the corporate history on its own Web site. Berardino thought it was a tremendous idea and agreed to help plan a celebration. But it never happened. A few months later, Berardino was gone and so was the Firm. Accenture, for its part, skated away clean from the avalanche of litigation, breathing an enormous sigh of relief that it had lost just one thing in the battle—that doomed name.

# Billing Our Brains Out

*Italians hate Yugoslavs, South Africans hate the Dutch,*
*And I don't like Anybody very much.*

— "THE MERRY MINUET," SHELDON HARNICK

*One Firm.* As I sat silently in the car on the way to Denver International Airport in the fall of 1996, I imagined Arthur E. Andersen rolling over in his grave. A more appropriate description of the place, I thought, would be "One Firm whose members hate each other's guts." I was on the way back from a meeting with a multinational audit client that had brought us in because it was concerned about some possible corruption at an overseas site. It was clear that the company needed help, and our group was ready to provide it. But as another Arthur Andersen consultant from a different group and I rode together to the airport, we weren't excitedly discussing the possibilities for the project. Our minds were whirring madly: Each of us, it seemed, was entirely focused on how to cut the other one out of the deal.

At Arthur Andersen, it was verboten to upset the client. But no such restrictions were placed on our upsetting each other in mad pursuit of our fees. In this case, there was a possibility of bringing in about $175,000. Unfortunately, it couldn't really be shared: Arthur Andersen's illogical fee-measurement system not only didn't reward a group effort at all, it actually worked to the disadvantage of anyone who helped bring in business but didn't end up running the project itself. The young Androids called it, with acidic accuracy, the "Fee Fuck."

To understand this contorted concept, it helps to understand Arthur Andersen's version of *The Matrix*, which was as impenetrable to me as the film version was to Keanu Reeves. The matrix concept had come into fashion in the business world in the 1970s as a management system that recognized everyone's interests and encouraged and supported collaborative efforts. In a matrix, most individuals reported to two or more bosses, often a function leader and a project leader. For example, an engineer designing a new computer would report to the head of engineering, but would also report to the computer project manager. The matrix might also include a corporate and divisional structure in which, let's say, a human resources manager would report to both his division's VP and his corporate VP. Ostensibly, this structure was supposed to coordinate functional and project lines to enhance productivity, profitability, and communications. The "mechanisms" for the matrix coordination were the people who sat at each "node" of the matrix, reporting to two or more others.

The concept was elegant. In practice, the stress could be unbearable. Pleasing two or more bosses with different, and often competing, goals ripped the hearts out of some of the most conscientious employees. Over time, for many corporations, the matrix fad faded. But not at Arthur Andersen, where a formal matrix was put into place around 1997, after Jim Wadia took over. Before that, however, the Firm had an informal matrix when it came to the way a partner was credited with fees.

Traditionally, audit clients were served by audit partners, managers, and staff of the office in the geographic area of the client. Audit partners and senior managers, who oversaw most of the staff, were measured on what were called "generated fees" and "supervised fees." Generated fees followed the person. No matter the office in which the job was set up, or the service line overseeing the job, the fees went to the office of the individual doing the work, as that individual's generated fees. So the fees for any work performed by me or any member of my group, anywhere in the world,

came to the Metro New York office. However, if I used, and therefore supervised, anyone from another office on a project, the home
office of that individual received the fees. So if I contracted for a $2
million job in Europe and worked with a team from the European
office, the Metro New York office received fees only for the hours I
worked. The European office received the team members' fees although I had supervised their time and work. As a result, using personnel from offices other than a partner's home base was severely
frowned upon, and could have a significant negative impact on
compensation.

Supervised fees, which reflected the fees of everyone on a partner's project, regardless of where the partner was based, were measured but had little true impact on a partner's units, the mechanism used to determine annual compensation (total earnings
would be divided by units, and each partner's units were doled out
individually). So that hypothetical European job would indeed
record $2 million in supervised fees for me, but in the Arthur An-
dersen system, that would count, when it came to review time, for
nothing—no benefit to my office, and none to me. And if a partner brought business into the Firm, but neither performed any of
the actual work, nor supervised work conducted in his office, that
partner got no formal credit whatsoever.

In the world of audit, this peculiarity wasn't as critical as it
became in consulting, since an audit was usually conducted by
people from one geographic office. The exceptions occurred when
an audit required a unique expertise available in only one or two
offices. For example, a diamond mining expert based in South
Africa might be needed on a mining company audit in Nevada.
The expert would be flown in to help out and part of the audit fees
would then go back to the South African office. When it happened,
it usually made sense, and it helped the Firm as a whole. Sure, the
local audit group would record a little less revenue, but they would
have a more effective audit and a happier client.

The rise to prominence of consulting put pressure on the system in three ways. First, people were doing project-oriented work
that might be in several offices of a client, not one location. So
there were more people from more parts of Arthur Andersen

involved at one time in the same project. Second, as new consulting groups were created, they were usually established in one or a very few offices. If a client needed a service but it didn't exist in that region, another office was brought in. And if a service was successful, expertise from outside the region had to be brought in to other sites to recruit and train people to consult out of those regions, and to solicit business. But the fee system, I found out the hard way, didn't change to accommodate these new realities.

It was only in the late 1980s, as Arthur Andersen was trying to build up its consulting in response to Andersen Consulting's growing independence, that the Fee Fuck appeared in full Technicolor. It happened in the new litigation services group, which by the mid-1990s was bringing in some $100 million in fees annually. Now, certainly, creating a new group was looked upon as a good thing within Arthur Andersen—especially if that group almost immediately landed a multimillion-dollar engagement. But the system didn't really work to the benefit of the litigation services group, and there was the rub: Gary Holdren, the group's founding partner, wasn't getting credit for all of that new business. He got kudos, sure, but all those all-nighters at the copy machine by young Androids in Los Angeles did almost nothing for him or for his unit in the eyes of the Firm. That's because most of the minions working on Gary's project had nothing to do with either his business line—consulting—or his office—Chicago. They were low-level auditors from different offices who had free time and were shipped out to Los Angeles, where they could rack up lots of hours. While new ideas and groups were applauded, dollars were what counted. And the dollars had to be in your own office's bucket.

In this instance, the young Androids' fees went right back into the coffers of the Phoenix or the San Francisco or the Cincinnati or whatever local office that they came from. This meant that partners in those offices got fee credit, while Gary's bottom line reflected *only* the fees brought in by him and the peons that had gone to L.A. from Chicago. Yes, he had done a great thing for Arthur Andersen. But he, or anyone who headed up a similar project, would be measured ultimately not on his "fees supervised," which covered the entire scope of the project, but on his "fees generated," which was probably a few hundred thousand bucks. Both fees supervised and fees generated were measured, but supervised fees applied only to him—and not to his office or his group—and counted for virtually nothing.

Gary, needless to say, was irked. So, being an intelligent guy, he eventually came up with a way around the problem. He somehow convinced the other Arthur Andersen partners to allow him to create a new midwest consulting group that would supersede the current billing system—conveniently allowing the fees to accrue to him, while in some cases stripping the partners in those offices of their income streams. "This was so fucked up, it was double Fee Fuck," said a former manager in the Chicago office. The rule was clear: "One Firm" didn't apply when it came to sharing fees. During my tenure at Arthur Andersen, the reality was that our ethics group and I were judged solely on the revenue we brought into our office—with no credit for anything originated or supervised anywhere else.

In the end, it was all about the bucks. Yes, performance reviews included many factors, but no one paid attention to them. Either you brought in the money or you wouldn't be around for too long. Every penny counted when you came up for a promotion. And if you had made partner, the fees were important because they determined how many more partner units—the equivalent of shares in the Firm—you would get at review time. The four cornerstones of success at Arthur Andersen—People Management, Quality, Thought Leadership, and Financial Performance—were referred to colloquially as "three pebbles and a boulder." The boulder was financial performance. The rest, it seemed, was a joke.

The Gary Holdren experience was not the first struggle for fees, but it was the one that got everyone's attention. As consulting became more important to the Firm, the system was exposed as a zero-sum game in which the only way you could win was by screwing your fellow partner.

While I was at Arthur Andersen, the fight for fees defined my existence. It happened to me constantly: I would bring in business in another part of the world, or guide a project in another office, and never get any credit or revenue. In fact, I would then get in trouble for having wasted time with another office—even if my work led to millions in new business. That happened in Tokyo, where, in 1998 and 1999, I helped several banks develop programs in compliance and business ethics. Here I was the engagement partner (the partner heading the project), helping another Andersen group set up these programs. Under my leadership, the Tokyo group built a $3-million-plus practice in banking compliance. I was shocked to discover that this wasn't a good thing, and that almost none of that $3 million in revenue accrued to me. Only my generated fees and those of a manager from our group were accorded to my account. Instead of having beaten my target, I failed to make my numbers.

Ultimately, Andersen Consulting, under George Shaheen, would reorganize its matrix, orienting around industry lines rather than geographic ones. But Arthur Andersen would both start a formal matrix and leave the fee-measurement system in place, believing that the internal competition was good for business. It *was* good for business in the sense that we all felt the heat constantly. But we spent so much time warring with one another that the client's needs were often forgotten altogether.

Eventually, I learned to try to screw someone else before they screwed me. The struggle to win fees for your office and your group—and *not* someone else's—came to define the Firm. Arthur Andersen became a place where people spent a great deal of time in bloody internecine battles that could have been better spent working with clients, pursuing new business, or mentoring young employees. Auditors fought consultants: New York fought Chicago and they both fought Paris; Ethics fought Fraud; Business Consulting fought our consulting group; and Andersen Consulting fought everyone else. To me, it's a remarkable tribute to what remained of Andersen's once-honorable system—and the fortune of a raging bull market—that we continued to make any money at all in this brutally cutthroat environment.

* * *

As I sat in that car on the way to the Denver airport, I inwardly cursed the system that was turning this tantalizing opportunity into an intramural fistfight. A major audit client had approached Steve Silver, head of the Fraud Group in Chicago, about potential fraud in a Southeast Asian subsidiary. He asked me to join him at one of the early meetings, thinking, appropriately, that at least part of the problem might be cultural and that our group might have something to complement his proposed program to train people to detect and prevent fraud. He would soon regret it. During our meeting with the client's head of internal audit, it became clear that what we were looking at was not a bunch of "fraudsters," in Steve's words, but rather a major cultural phenomenon. Although it is unlawful to give or take bribes in the country where the problem was occurring, bribery had become so much a cultural practice that some considered it a career achievement to get into a position where you were the recipient of such payments. This company wanted to know how to communicate—and enforce—the concept that this was not an acceptable way to do business.

The client wanted an assessment of the causes of the problem rather than finding and investigating individuals who had committed fraud. "If you're going to focus on the problem as bad people," I said during the meeting, "you're never going to get this solved." The head of internal audit agreed. He wanted to hire us—and clearly didn't care about Arthur Andersen's internal politics—but then added the words that make every professional services person cringe: "This is the amount of money that I'm going to pay. You people figure out how to divide it up, but that's it."

And so it began. Steve was the one who had set up the meeting, and had flown to Denver fully expecting to be getting business out of it. But if the consulting work went to my group, he would get nothing, even though he brought the business in. Sure, someone might pat him on the back for being a team player, but he was already a partner and he wasn't going to get one single extra unit if he didn't have big fees attached to this project. It was a Catch-22: Steve was helping the Firm—if it made more money, so did he, as a partner whose ultimate pay was a percentage of the Firm's profits—but in regard to the measure that really counted, he was coming up empty.

We could, of course, each take a piece of the pie—my group could do the assessment and recommendation, and the fraud group could deliver a fraud-prevention program. But that presented another set of problems. Steve, and the Chicago office, still wouldn't get as much fee credit as he would if his people were doing the whole project (with me providing some guidance and getting the fees only for the hours I actually worked).

Unfortunately, there were many more moving parts. The head audit office for this client was Denver—and the head of audit in that office, naturally, wanted his audit senior manager to work on this consulting project. Then there was a partner in Arthur Andersen's Business Consulting Group in Asia, the one who somehow discovered the problem and notified the client. He, too, wanted a piece of the action. It was a warring cast of what seemed like thousands—four different city offices, Audit, Fraud, Ethics, Business Consulting—all trying to impose the you-know-what on someone else.

●   ●   ●

On my end, I was looking at what appeared to be a great, interesting project that dealt exactly with our expertise. Given the Firm's obsession with audit control of audit clients, I was already going to lose some fees to Denver—since the audit senior manager was clearly going to be on board to watch over us. Likewise, I'd lose if any of the fees were booked to any Arthur Andersen employees in Asia who helped on the project, or if Steve wedged his way back in. Adding to the Kafkaesque nature of the situation was the fact that someone had to be the engagement partner, the head honcho, on the project. Steve thought he should be engagement partner, since he brought the work in. Denver thought its audit partner should head the project—despite the fact that he had just taken over the account because the previous partner had been rotated out after seven years, as required by the SEC. And I thought I should lead the engagement, because we had the knowledge and experience to do the work.

As Steve and I rode to the airport together (he was going to Chicago, I was going to New York), I don't think either of us was planning a strategy to solve the client's problem. Rather, we were jostling for position. Steve made the first move. "All right," he said, "I am going to be the engagement partner on this." Over my dead body, I thought. "That doesn't make sense, Steve," I said, "because the work that's being done is being done by my group. You don't understand the kind of work that we do. And if you're the engagement partner, then you and the Chicago office get the bulk of the fees. I'll get fees for the hours I put in, and if I have another person working on it we'll get fees for that, but my office won't get these fees and my office is doing the work. So this is not fair." Steve was furious. "But I'm the one who made the connection," he spat. Nothing was resolved, but Steve and I would later have several violent phone arguments, going in circles like dogs chasing their tails.

We spent hours arguing. "You should get credit for putting us together, but not the money," I would say. And Steve, quite accurately, would say, "But I don't get credit for it unless I get the money." At the same time, I was desperate. I was learning the hard way that my attempts to help other offices and their clients had harmed me internally because I hadn't scored anything for the office. We were a new service line and I had been trying to get going. So now I was as out for blood as everybody else. Ultimately, we worked out a Solomonic compromise. John, my boss at the time in New York, suggested that the new audit partner in Denver become the engagement partner and that he in turn divide the fees according to the work that was done. Normally I would have had a big problem with this, but I trusted him, so it seemed the best option.

But that was only Stage One. The resolution of the internal battles for this engagement ultimately took about eight months. Finally, in June 1997, I went with two of the client's lawyers to Southeast Asia to conduct discussions about the U.S. Foreign Corrupt Practices Act with nationals and expats. When we started planning this project in 1996, we had assumed Bill Ryder would accompany me. However, by the time it was a "go," Bill had quit (fed up with the game, he decided to pursue his dream of being an actor). So I had to find another senior or experienced manager to take on the job as a second listener or note taker. No one in my small group was available, so I found a manager from Business Consulting who had the necessary experience in human resources. But soon I would pay the price for getting another group involved.

We finally made it to our destination, but the game still wasn't over. When it came to bringing in fees, the creativity of Arthur Andersen partners around the world was truly impressive. My colleague and I had lunch at the Fashion Café in Jakarta with a Business Consulting partner (and former auditor) and his Indonesian senior manager. This partner, like my BC colleague from New York, was in the small HR group within Business Consulting, but unlike my colleague—an experienced hire from a large company—everything this partner had learned about human resources was self-taught. As we ate among the mannequins of supermodels Claudia, Christie, and Cindy, surrounded by appalling poverty and pollution, the partner proposed to the New York BC partner that they team up to develop a survey for the companies in his region about ethical behavior. Of course, he would be the engagement partner and the work would originate in Jakarta, so he would get the fees, but he needed real HR skills to get it done. That meant trouble for the New York manager. If he went back to his New York boss and told him about this project, his boss would go bananas, saying he was taking time away from work that should be done in the New York office.

Yet not only was the Jakarta partner trying to feather his own nest, he also was proposing what seemed to me to be a completely unethical type of business building. I feared that the survey he wanted to design would have little, if any, intellectual capital behind it and would be worded in such a way that *every* client would discover problems—and then Arthur Andersen could, of course, offer the perfect solution. Here I was, all the way across the world, listening to my colleague talk about screwing a bunch of clients, including the one we were working with, not to mention trying to Fee Fuck his New York colleagues. But neither of us took his bait.

After all this insanity, what we were left with was a deal that brought in the originally agreed dollars. We at Ethics were the "winners" with gross revenues of $138,000 out of the $175,000 total. The billable hours wasted in our scramble for fees far, far surpassed what we brought into the Firm. As for intellectual energy to use helping the client? Well, after spending hours fighting with my colleagues, I'd inevitably end up exhausted. That wasn't exactly the type of razor-sharp focus our clients were supposed to be getting.

The struggle reverberated all the way down the line. The managers and others who worked in my group were one step below me in the food chain, and they, like fish gasping for oxygen, needed work in order to bill the hours that then would ultimately give them a raise or a promotion. For me, success was all about fees, and for them, it was billable hours. Every moment I spent tussling with someone else was time on the clock that couldn't be billed by any of us. But that was how it worked.

For the equity partners at Arthur Andersen, however, there were some unique pressures. The unit committee, which decided who got what every two years, also evaluated partners who reached their late forties on what was called their Career Unit Potential, or CUP. Done probably as a way to control and predict the total number of units, the committee looked at the current number of units a partner had accumulated and projected his final amount upon retirement (which was mandatory at 62, but structured so that you'd get the largest payout if you left at 56). Although the CUP could be altered if a partner suddenly brought in or lost a huge amount of business, it was a strong indication of what you could expect.

From that point forward, you'd have your units raised in a straight-line fashion so you could reach the final CUP by age 56. The implications of that, I believe, were very important. On one hand, once you knew more or less what you were going to be making for the rest of your life, it was reasonable that you'd begin acting in a way to preserve it rather than endanger it. On the other hand, knowing that your CUP would be measured far before it was time to leave the Firm meant that your mid-forties was a time to seriously push the envelope. If you brought in enough units early on, your CUP would be higher. So you ended up with a bunch of conservative-acting "old" men who weren't even 50, pushed from below by a hyperaggressive bunch of partners only a few years younger. At the same time, because Arthur Andersen published and distributed a list of what every single partner in the Firm earned, there was a lot of ego pressure as well. If that jerk in the Detroit office was beating you out, well, you had to prove yourself, didn't you?

While competition was also intense at Arthur Andersen's rivals, the system put the Firm in its own league. At Pricewaterhouse-Coopers, for example, revenues are credited, when appropriate, to more than one person, group, or office. If you bring in business worth $2 million that ultimately is done by another group or office, you still get credit for bringing in the $2 million—as does the consultant or auditor that ultimately does the work. Jim Hatch, who ran the northeast region of Arthur Andersen's Human Capital Services Group from 1996 to 1999, and who has worked at every one of the Big 5 except for KPMG, says Arthur Andersen's approach was the least motivational of all. "It created odd behavior," he said. "One Firm was a crock."

Hatch learned his lesson the hard way: In his second year at Andersen, he brought in $12 million in new business to the Firm, only $2.5 million of which accrued to him (he had allowed the revenues to be split among the principals he hired, never thinking that that meant he'd be penalized for it). Since he'd brought in $3 million the previous year, when he didn't have as many employees, his boss told him he was down for the year and said he wouldn't be getting any new units. Since units were distributed only once every two years, this meant no raise for two more years. "You didn't make $12 million," said his boss, "you made $2.5 million. That's what it says." When Hatch protested that he had no idea it was measured that way, his boss responded, "Well, I guess you learned a lesson, didn't you?" Some lesson: Either Hatch's employees benefited, or he did, but not both.

The absurdity of the system repeated itself endlessly around the world. When I first went to Japan, it was to make a presentation on business ethics at a general seminar for businessmen led by the head of a division of the tax group. The partner also asked that while in Tokyo I meet with an Arthur Andersen Business Consulting partner from the Osaka office who was putting together a proposal on business ethics for a large Japanese telecommunications company. The Osaka/Tokyo team wanted our group's credentials (they had no experience in ethics), research and information on U.S. companies, models, charts, and so on.

I went to meet with the Business Consulting partner to negotiate fee arrangements and fell right down the rabbit hole. My Japanese Arthur Andersen colleague and I sat across from each other on the broad sides of a large conference table. A translator sat next to him, and various U.S. and Japanese managers were arrayed on either side of each of us. You would have thought this was a major peace negotiation, but it was really just a good old Arthur Andersen Fee Fuck. Day One of negotiations lasted seven hours and consisted, basically, of the Japanese partner telling me that we should give his group every bit of research we had, interview ethics officers in U.S. companies for them, put together a presentation for them to the client, and let them use our credentials—all for a whopping $11,000 in fees.

After interminable discussions, I thought we had agreed on shared responsibilities and shared fees—somewhere about $100,000—for our group, though I still felt uneasy about them using our credentials to prove that their group was qualified to do the job. The next day, we met again—to wrap things up, I assumed. But discussions started as if nothing had gone on before. Five hours later, we were nowhere. The arguing and debating continued for weeks, over 10,000 miles, with intermediaries, demands, and threats. It was lunacy. We finally did some work for the partner on the proposal and subsequent engagement. But the members of my group who did the work were appropriately upset—at me, primarily—because most of their billable hours were wiped out by the enormous discount we had to take to meet the pittance Tokyo/ Osaka allocated to us.

This kind of situation was by no means exclusive to Asia. My colleague Debbie Weiner and I spent a day with a Dusseldorf partner who was pitching business ethics services to one of the Dusseldorf office's largest clients. We provided credentials, gave him copies of several presentations, walked him through the steps of sample engagements, and sent him in a cab to JFK as he promised that we would be part of any engagement. Then, of course, Dusseldorf got the job. The partner sent us a big thank-you and an e-mail explaining that although our group's credentials helped convince the client that Arthur Andersen had the ethics capability, the client didn't want Americans working on their project. Sorry, but thanks! Why this was the norm, in a firm that once had been so devoted to doing the right thing, was a mystery to me. Arthur Andersen had both the resources and the opportunities to do truly global work, but chose instead to encourage backstabbing, fee-grabbing, and Balkanization.

* * *

The brutally competitive atmosphere within the Firm made a mockery of its principles and of its culture. Sure, Arthur Andersen had always been a competitive place, where up or out was the rule and those who didn't produce didn't last. But the air was so thick with internal tension that it seemed hard, some days, even to breathe. If you had any leanings toward paranoia, this was not your place. Or maybe it was your place, because, for once, your conspiracy theories would be right on target. People were under tremendous pressure to bring in money, and instead of seeing collaborators or colleagues, they now saw rivals and fee suckers. We posed anything but a united front. When the phone would ring, and it was another consultant or auditor in another area, my first reaction would be "Oh great! They have something they want to bring me in for." Then came the second reaction: "Oh shit! They're hoping I have something I can bring *them* in for." Too often somebody just wanted something for nothing.

The infighting for fees made even day-to-day interactions unbearable. One new "luminary"—a financial specialist whom we'll call Jack—was brought in to the New York office in 1997 to work with two other existing partners. But for the first two months he was there, the other two partners simply wouldn't speak to him, let alone tell him what he was supposed to be doing or how he might best adapt to the Firm. Because he had plenty of his own contacts, he tried to drum up business on his own for a while. But ultimately, Jack, who had some 20 years of experience, became fed up. He walked into one of the partners' offices (conveniently located two doors down from his own) and confronted him.

"What's going on?" he asked. "I've been here for two months and you haven't once stepped into my office and said hello." The partner, a career Android, looked at him blankly and said, "I didn't have anything to do with hiring you. I wasn't involved in this decision." More than anything, it seemed to Jack, his erstwhile colleague saw him as a threat.

Then he went to the office next door and asked the same question of his other partner. "I've been here two months, man," Jack said. "What's up?" This partner tried to smile, but the words that came out were ugly. "It's nothing personal, but I'm motivated by money," he said. "I don't have time to be nice to people. I'm just about making money. That's why I'm here."

"To me, the two responses were both accurate in some ways about the culture," said Jack. "One person, since he hadn't been involved, wasn't going to talk, and the other was all about money. And yet these were the partners in my group, the people I was supposed to be working with the most closely." Jack left after a few years, and now works for a financial services firm where the atmosphere is comparatively cordial. "I had never been in an environment like that," he said.

The end result of all of this pressure and conflict was nasty. As far as I could tell, it was very, very hard to get your money's worth from many of the consulting services offered by Arthur Andersen. As a client, you had a few choices. You could actually get a well-thought-out, carefully prepared project, but you'd quite often find yourself being overcharged for the privilege of the Firm's attention. Alternatively, you could pay what you said you would—and get a lot less than that. The trade-off was clear: good service, for which clients were routinely overcharged, or poor service, which is what clients got if they negotiated a flat fee or a low fee. It seemed to me to be one or the other, and I had plenty of experience with both.

Let's start with overbilling, more appropriately called "Billing Our Brains Out." For the audit itself, it was very hard to overbill. An audit had become a commodity, with fairly standardized services and fees. But what the Firm gave up on the audit side, it had a chance of making up on the risk consulting side, whose revenues were considered part of audit. In fact, the audit group was now called Assurance and Business Advisory.

Prior to joining Arthur Andersen, I had done a lot of work with a subsidiary of a large insurance company, work with which they had been very satisfied. So when I got a call from their public relations person just after I started at Arthur Andersen, saying that the company wanted to set up an ethics office, I told her I could certainly help, though I was now with a new firm. Our job was to help the newly appointed business practices officer get going. Since she was new, the project looked like a blank slate—which meant, I quickly learned, a blank check. The client wanted some basic education on what an ethics and business practices office did, and some guidance in establishing the components that did not already exist, as well as the development of some training materials.

It should have been a $50,000 to $75,000 engagement. It wasn't. We took advantage of our neophyte and steadily built a dependency on our team by such things as giving her weekly "homework" assignments to help her learn about her new position, and devising a monthly step-by-step plan that basically said to her that she wouldn't be able to sustain her responsibilities without us being present. Before she knew what hit her, she had an action plan priced at around $250,000 a month. We had seen a key vulnerability—that the client didn't really have an official budget and that the contact was new in her position—and pounced. After about a month and a half of this, the CEO, whom I knew well, finally put a stop to it. I had worked with this company before, and I knew they trusted me. But I was struggling to make it in this culture, and Billing Our Brains Out was the only way I saw to do so.

Billing Our Brains Out was relatively easy. My group was brought in by a major bank with a division that had gotten into big trouble for retaining funds from abandoned accounts. It is normal for banks to hold on to funds when the owners of the original accounts cannot be located. But after a certain period of time, these accounts are declared abandoned, and the funds must be turned over to the state in a process called escheatment. This division, under pressure to make the numbers, decided in the mid-1990s to simply take that extra money—described to me as the equivalent of the gold dust that had flaked off big gold bricks—and move it into earnings. The company ultimately pled guilty to three felony counts and was fined $60 million.

Andersen wasn't the auditor of this bank, but had already gotten its internal audit and its fraud groups involved in the investigation. As part of the settlement, the federal regulators mandated that the company conduct a training program on escheatment in particular and ethical behavior generally for all personnel in that unit around the world. It would have to be completed and signed off on in three months. The head of Andersen's internal audit group in New York called me. "This is the kind of thing you do, isn't it?" "You bet," I said.

Yes, there was work, and plenty of it to go around. The New York office was thrilled. And now it was time for the main event—the jockeying for fees. Six of us sat in a conference room at Arthur Andersen—a financial services audit partner, two financial services managers, and three ethics people—and duked it out. Despite the fact that this wasn't a client, the audit partner became the engagement partner on the job because he had some experience in escheatment, albeit none in any of the types of programs we were setting up. We drafted a brief proposal, did the dance, and came up with a plan that didn't really satisfy anyone. However, this time we had an edge with the client, who had no choice but to spend.

Ultimately, we put together a good program, using case studies and role-playing to address a range of ethical issues from escheatment to conflicts of interest to managing earnings. The client was pleased, as were the Feds. But the client, remember, was also desperate. So we Billed Our Brains Out, charging more than $1 million for what should have been about a $500,000 job. We billed time on the subway, we billed time rewriting our notes, we billed as much as we possibly could. I rationalized what we were doing by telling myself they were paying a premium for the short time frame and the intensity of the work. After all, if I need a skirt hemmed on short notice, I pay a premium to the tailor. But that was not part of our negotiation: We had simply given them a price and they paid.

For such successful billing, we were publicly praised by Joe Berardino, then head of Metro New York Audit, at the next New York area partner meeting at the Rhiga Royal Hotel. Joe read from a slide listing each of the new consulting groups and incoming revenues. When he came to Ethics, he read off, in his most earnest and praiseworthy tone, the magic number: $1,000,000. He wasn't praising us, of course, for the quality of what we did, but rather for the seven-figure fees. But I didn't care. I felt like a rock star, like a hero. That day was the only day in four years that I felt truly valued by Arthur Andersen. Back in my RRM days, we boasted that our competitive edge was quality. Not anymore. Now I was in it for the money. I guess I was finally beginning to understand this Firm. We, at least, had given the client something worthwhile. But we also had happily ripped them off.

•    •    •

Billing Our Brains Out may have been Arthur Andersen's favorite technique for generating high revenues, but it wasn't the only one. If a client resisted on fees, the most likely scenario was a project completed in as short a period of time as possible, with as many inexperienced, lower-paid people doing the work as possible. In my entire time at Arthur Andersen, I never heard anyone get in trouble for the quality of the work they did. They were reamed out for billing beyond a contract's allowable number of hours, for eating time (spending more time on a project than was economic, given what the client was willing to pay), for not charging enough, for not coming up with another reason to keep working with the client. After all, in a partnership, every dime not spent was a dime in a partner's pocket.

It hadn't always been that way. When Leonard Spacek ran the Firm, he was somehow able to convince his partners, time and again, to sacrifice earnings for investment. In the early 1950s and 1960s, he put a cap on partner compensation and allowed them to be reevaluated only every three to five years, so that "the rest of the money could flow down to the new partners and to the cost of developing the Firm." Partners didn't expect to get rich in those days; they hoped for a good career at a place with a good name. "We didn't make those investments because we wanted to," said one partner in the Firm's official history. "We made them because we thought we had to in order to build the Firm."

Those attitudes didn't outlive Spacek. More typical was a constant focus on earnings and, of course, on units. As Joe Berardino said when I asked him to explain why he wouldn't allow a senior consultant in my group to fly business class to Tokyo so that we could work together on the plane, "Because it's my money."

The centerpiece of Arthur Andersen's billing system was the PFA, or Planned Fee Adjustment. Most firms had such a tool, although it went by different names. The PFA was the official discount you gave to virtually every auditing and consulting job, because the hourly rates were so inflated that the cost of every job if billed at the actual rate would probably be uneconomic for even the clients with the deepest of pockets.

Here's how it worked: Each of us had hourly billing rates, which were set by a faceless committee, based on our experience level and fees brought in (or perhaps randomly—it was never explained). Every year we received a document telling us what our new rates were, and they always went up, regardless of the economy. Moreover, the rates went up for the clients in June, but the nonpartner salary increases didn't take effect until September. So the Firm billed at the new rates without employees getting higher pay for three months. It was sort of a freebie for the Firm, a bonus for the equity partners, and no one ever questioned it, as far as I know.

Once you had a sense of what the client was willing to pay, a manager would create a budget that fit the cost. If you priced an engagement at $200,000 in hours billable at the absurdly high Firm rates, but the client wanted to pay only, say, $150,000, you'd offer the job at $200,000 but sell it at $150,000 by announcing that you were giving the client a 25 percent discount. Then you'd record the 25 percent PFA in the books, so that you ended up with a gross fee of $200,000 but a net fee (the true fee) of $150,000. Managers had leeway to set up their own PFAs, but if they went over a certain percentage, they had to get several partners to sign off.

Actually, the PFA was a loss leader, with the expectation that in the next phase of the project (remember the Roach Motel) the discount would instantly vanish. It also let us play a little game of "good client discount" made famous by used-car salesmen, telling clients that because they were sooo special, we'd give them a break just this once. "My mentor called it a 'hook and run,'" remembered one former Arthur Andersen manager. The idea was to discount the first piece of a business dramatically, but then, in the process, "discover" other problems that had to be dealt with immediately. "The instruction is to do a bang-up job, bust your ass, do this piece and then notice things that need to be done. Then you'd say here's your assessment and oh, by the way, this is a mess, this is wrong, this needs attention, but we've got a plane to catch. And they're, like, NO! You've got to stay! And we'd say, we'd love to stay, remember our full rates are $XXX, and they'd say okay, fine."

It was a classic consulting strategy, yet the PFA was determined in an ad hoc fashion, with no real basis in anything, not even the salaries of the people involved. One person who worked in my group actually asked Joe Berardino to explain the logic behind the PFA during a group meeting. "You set up a project, win a contract, and up front you are supposed to anticipate how much money you are not able to collect? If you can't charge that, why not charge the right amount?" the manager asked. Joe's response was as Android as it gets. "Because," he said, "that's the way it's always been done."

The combination of the Fee Fuck and the PFA meant big trouble for the client that set limits on what it was willing to pay. Just before I left Arthur Andersen in 1999, we won a government contract, in part thanks to my sales efforts. The contracting agency knew I was leaving Arthur Andersen, but also knew that I would continue to work with the Firm for a while on a consulting basis, and we all agreed that I would be overseeing the project, a survey of the executive branch of the U.S. government on several specific ethics issues. The government agency wanted to use a survey our group had developed, known as IntraSight, which assessed a number of organizational and program factors and related them to desirable outcomes for an organization.

Because the project involved a survey, another Arthur Andersen group based in St. Charles that specialized in surveys and data processing was recruited to be part of the team. They knew surveys, but they didn't know anything about ethics. But since I was leaving Arthur Andersen—and the Firm was not willing to let me, as an outside consultant, head the project—the St. Charles group became the key Firm contractor. I did my best to review everything and send detailed comments and revisions to St. Charles. Yet it wasn't in St. Charles's interest to have me involved, since any fees paid to me meant less for them. And the engagement was already going to be a relatively low earner, since the government sets consulting rates that are significantly lower than Arthur Andersen's standard rates. In addition, fees for the project were capped, so Billing Our Brains Out was out of the question.

Faced with what seemed like a loser project for them, the St. Charles folks did the logical thing in this convoluted system, but not the thing that would help the client: They told me I could work no more than fifty-six hours on the project (at a discounted fee I had agreed to when I signed a consulting agreement with them upon my resignation). The project was supposed to take up to eight months to complete, so right away I knew we were in trouble. There were at least three and possibly four all-day meetings in Washington built into the scope of the work, taking up 24 to 32 hours of my time off the bat. With the remaining hours I had to review all survey material, do the interpretation of the data analysis, and write up the results. It couldn't be done, and the group knew it, but I believe that's what they had in mind.

In the end, the St. Charles group did the project the way it wanted to, and my input was ignored. It soon became clear that the client's project leaders were increasingly upset about quality issues and believed, naturally, that I was in charge of fixing them. I spoke with them at length and was well aware that they expected me to "make everything better." After all, I was one of the reasons they had selected Arthur Andersen. I tried to help, but the St. Charles people never responded to my suggestions or comments. And then one day I received a copy of an e-mail message, either by mistake or by some Freudian slip, from the government agency lawyer to the agency project leader saying, "I really think Barbara Toffler could clear up this mess, if she would just be willing to get involved. But she just doesn't seem to care." Not only did I care—by this time I was "eating time" by the bucketfuls! From what I could tell, the St. Charles people didn't incorporate any of my suggestions.

•  •  •

Another key line of business for accounting firms was cleaning up the messes their own competitors made. Accounting fraud does tend to come in waves, and is discovered most often after a market collapse, since no one is interested in investigating much when stock prices are high and everyone's making big money. Yet regardless of economic cycle, accounting problems do occur from time to time, and after a firm like Arthur Andersen exhaled with the "there but by the Grace of God go I" line, it would parachute in to save the day. Since someone had to do the forensic accounting needed to understand what had gone wrong, and since the accounting and consulting firms had all the resources to do so, it meant instant big bucks for the firm that landed the cleanup gig. One case in point was the 1997 discovery of cooked books at Cendant Corp., a company created by the merger of high-flying conglomerates HFS and CUC. Arthur Andersen wasn't the auditor in this case—Ernst & Young was—but once the damage was done, there was a major opportunity out there.

Arthur Andersen used its Fraud group to pore through Cendant's books and find out what had gone wrong at the company. The multimillion-dollar project, featuring hundreds of worker bee staffers going through every receipt and document at the company, was later trumpeted on the Firm's Web site as a shining example of the kind of specialized work that it could do. Nowhere did it mention the fact that another company's screwup was the business opportunity of the year.

Running the Cendant project was the new head of the Fraud group, a former forensic accountant with the FBI. He, like all of us, was under massive pressure to bring in big bucks, and when Cendant landed in his lap, he was in consultant heaven. Actually, Joe Berardino had brought in the work and had tried to get them to hire my group too, but the client needed the Fraud group—and Ethics was discretionary. The Fraud partner did, however, ask me to do an ethics presentation for a group of Cendant employees in the control division, setting my budget at $5,000 tops.

I wasn't about to do a boilerplate presentation, given the significance of the Cendant difficulties, so I spent time preparing a customized session, including writing two cases after consultation with the then-CFO of Cendant. The session went over well, but I did commit the sin of spending more time on the presentation than I had been told. I had eaten time, but it was not a huge amount, and Fraud had some $7 million in fees coming in. So I asked the Fraud partner if he would pay me an additional $1,500, since I had spent fifteen hours, not twelve and a half. I was chump change in the Arthur Andersen scheme of things.

It was like asking a starving man for his last crust of bread. "Not a penny more," he said. "You knew what they wanted to pay, and you were stupid to spend any more time than you were getting paid for. The client wouldn't know the difference anyway." Technically, he was absolutely right. I was, indeed, stupid: I had assumed again that it was better to do a good job than to present something I'd be embarrassed about. As a result, I had to take the dreaded Unplanned Fee Adjustment. This was not the prenegotiated discount, but what happened when you couldn't manage your time. It was grounds for dismissal if it happened enough.

If you could cut a corner, you did. Mary Gottschalk, the derivatives specialist, came to Arthur Andersen in 1995 and left after two years, mainly because, she said, the Firm had no respect for expertise. The last straw for her occurred when an enormous public software company came looking for help managing several billion dollars in cash and deciding whether it should be in equities, bonds, hedged, or something else. Gottschalk knew that an Arthur Andersen colleague in San Francisco was an expert in this area, so she wrote him into the proposal. Her boss was furious. "You have to take him out," he insisted, saying that he'd give her someone in New York and she could train him. Gottschalk was appalled: This person was exactly what the client needed, yet because he belonged to another office, he couldn't be part of the solution for this hugely influential company. She refused to sign the proposal and quit shortly afterward. "It was about how to maximize the money and they would do whatever it took to [do that], including putting people on [projects] who were unqualified," she said.

Qualified or not, all of Arthur Andersen's employees were expected, by the late 1990s, to be masters of creativity when it came to figuring out ways to sell more services—audit or consulting—to clients. There were regular meetings of what were called SOAR teams—Sales Opportunities and Resources—as well as Crown Jewel teams and Elephant Target teams. Like most consulting firms, Arthur Andersen wanted to exploit every possible void. Everyone who had (or might have) anything at all to do with the client would attend, from the auditors, to the internal auditors, to the tax specialists, to the consultants hoping to wedge their way in. Some would call this client service—but in my experience it seemed to be more about raping the client than serving it.

With audit clients, the engagement partner on the account usually led the meetings. Over the course of an hour or two, the status of the account would be reviewed, and then everyone would pitch in with ideas on how to boost that book. It was all about cross-selling—offering the soup, the nuts, and everything in between. The meetings were boring, actually, but they also had the effect of increasing the pressure. You were on the team, so you'd better deliver. One senior manager in Chicago remembered an audit meeting in 2001 for a huge client. The global managing partner for the client stood up and said, "We do $11 million with [name] now. By next year, I want this to be a $14 million account." Somewhere, somehow, we were all going to have to come up with another $3 million in fees in one year—and make the client feel good about paying it.

● ● ●

Apart from the infamous maroon ethics binder, which was so unwieldy you couldn't even begin to process it, I could find no indication that ethics was ever talked about in any broad way at Arthur Andersen. When I brought up the subject of internal ethics, I was looked at as if I had teleported in from another world. We are inherently ethical people, the attitude seemed to be, so why would we need any training? It was true that the Firm recruited people who were screened for good judgment and good values. But then they were left alone. If questions of accounting arose, there was the Committee on Professional Standards to consult. But what if someone violated a rule or decided to ignore the Committee's recommendations?

As a private partnership, Arthur Andersen didn't have any of the same restrictions on gifts, dinners, and so forth that most of its clients did. In fact, our group spent plenty of time putting together those types of policies for other companies. But when it came to its own policies, the Firm took full advantage of its ability to invite clients to the U.S. Open (tennis and golf), host fabulous dinners, and buy tables for events at favorite charities and political causes of its clients. Buying influence was simply considered part of the drill, and all of the major accounting firms did it. I had issues with this—how was a firm charged with certifying numbers allowed to spend millions enticing CFOs to stick with them? But when I found out that some colleagues actually billed the client for the expense of entertaining them, I decided to look into it.

The call came to me in the fall of 1998 from a longtime partner in the New York office, who'd been contacted by a manager on a major, longtime audit client. The manager was concerned because his boss, both a prominent partner in the office and the Firm and the advisory partner on this audit (the partner providing some extra oversight on the largest, most important clients), had taken his daughter and the daughter of the client's CFO, as well as the CFO, to a New York Yankees game in a limousine, which waited there for the entire game and then took them home to the suburbs.

What had bothered the manager so much wasn't the expense of the day—it was a bit eyebrow-raising to entertain the daughters, but not so unusual—but the fact that the partner had told him to charge the excursion back to the client, listing everything as audit-related expenses such as transportation or a client-related trip. "You can lose it in the rounding," I was told he had said. The manager, distressed, called another partner, who in turn called me as someone with a background in ethics and related the story. This was an accounting firm: Wasn't this a form of cooking the books? I didn't feel it was my place to confront the partner—I wasn't even supposed to know about this—and the partner who had called me did not want to confront a fellow Android. I decided to take it up another level.

I called Bob Kutsenda, chairman of the Risk Management Executive Committee. I had met him when I attended two Risk Management Executive Committee meetings, and I assumed this situation fell into his bailiwick. I said I had heard from a partner in the New York office, who had expressed concerns about a very high-level partner. Kutsenda called me back and conferenced in Gary Goolsby, another committee member. I told the story, without identifying the "high-level" partner, but I think they knew whom I was talking about.

Both men made a lot of empathetic noises and told me they would definitely look into the matter. I never heard from them again. I have no idea whether anything was ever said to the offending partner, but I did not feel comfortable taking it further. Certainly, many of the schemes I've described here may sound familiar to people in other service firms. Arthur Andersen was hardly the only firm or company to succumb to the constant pressure to deliver during the 1990s and early part of this decade. But the end result was the continual reinforcement of the idea that it was okay to play with numbers. That's what accountants did, by definition, but that laxity of approach certainly would come back to haunt the Firm later. Billing Our Brains Out or compromising quality was what we all had to do to get ahead—or to keep up. So that's what we did.

# Lord of the Flies

6

> *Who runs Arthur Andersen? Hell runs Arthur Andersen.*
>
> —JIM HATCH, former Andersen partner

IN MY FIRST YEAR OF GRADUATE SCHOOL, I had an experience that taught me a powerful lesson about leadership. It was the first meeting of a course on group dynamics for graduate psychology students and psychiatry residents. Our professor was already sitting at the front of the room as we ambled in. At the appointed time, we settled down and waited for him to begin. Nothing happened. We just sat there for more than half an hour, fidgeting, waiting. We stared at the professor expectantly, but he didn't say a word. He just calmly looked around the room, a blank mirror reflecting our quizzical expressions. Intimidated, we didn't say anything either. It was incredibly uncomfortable. About 40 minutes into it, he said, "You have just demonstrated group dependency. You're all waiting for me, as the leader, to do something. There was no reason that one of you could not have spoken or acted."

But we hadn't. It was fascinating. Here we were, graduate students, social workers and psychiatry residents, collectively thinking, "Someone please tell us what to do!" We were all over 25 years old. Everybody had had a good education, and yet we all sat there, paralyzed, as if we didn't have a right or the ability to make a move.

With an inactive leader and no one else designated to take a leadership role, we all thought, "I can't take responsibility." This, I believe, is what happened at Arthur Andersen. As things began to spin out of control, the leadership that existed was distracted and angry, providing neither strategy, direction, nor cohesion. And while not every one of the 85,000 employees fell into a state of abject paralysis, they did emulate, I believe, the classroom dependency I experienced so many years before. Even if you knew that the culture was changing for the worse, because the people in the most powerful positions didn't know or didn't care, you were left in the position of waiting, quietly, for someone else to act.

Organizations need strong leaders, with good, solid values, to function effectively. Leaders provide the goals, the vision and the strategy, and the values and principles that guide people in their pursuit of those goals. Certainly there have been experiments with leaderless societies. Many of my friends joined communes in the 1960s to live unbounded by any formal authority. But in any leaderless group, individuals will eventually take on specific roles to help the group survive, though ultimately that may also work against the best interests of the group as a whole. Leaders do emerge to fill the void. But rather than being elected or formally appointed, these leaders are often the individuals who are best able to deal with the external threats to the group—and who therefore increase the dependency of the group members, who see them as saviors. This leaderless dependency, I believe, caused Arthur Andersen to morph into a place reminiscent, in some ways, of the novel *Lord of the Flies*.

William Golding's 1954 novel tells the story of a group of British schoolboys who survive a plane crash onto a remote island in which all the adults perish. Left with no adult leaders, the boys attempt to set up their own form of governance. But the group feels threatened by hunger and unknown island beasts, so it allows the aggressive Jack to emerge as the leader. Some members of the group become Jack's loyal followers, and they become the "hunters." The hunters' violent and destructive behavior works well against the outside threats, but it is devastating when used against those in the group who want to live by the rules of traditional British society.

Out of the leadership void at Arthur Andersen's American unit, leaders such as Steve Samek and Joe Berardino emerged with the ability to manage the threat of the possible loss of Andersen Consulting revenue and the increasing consulting competition from what, by 1998, was the Big 5 (Price Waterhouse and Coopers & Lybrand merged that year). But the very aggressive tactics used to fight their "beasts" also helped to dismantle the culture. Unlike *Lord of the Flies*, it was not the Navy but the Department of Justice that stepped in.

Arthur Andersen has always been a partnership, and in a partnership leadership is more complicated than in other forms of business because it is diffused. Faceless committees make group decisions, and no one truly holds the ultimate decision-making authority because the "leader" serves at the will of the partners. In a crisis, action is particularly difficult. Yet for much of its history Arthur Andersen was headed by a series of strong leaders, from Arthur Andersen to Leonard Spacek to, for a time, Harvey Kapnick. They ran the Firm and wielded both inside power and outside political capital. They commanded respect.

As of 1997, however, the folks at Andersen seemed to be falling into the black hole of group dependency. Duane Kullberg had resigned in 1989, frustrated by the tensions between Arthur Andersen and Andersen Consulting. Larry Weinbach had jumped ship, leading to the infamous power struggle between Wadia and Shaheen—which neither managed to win. By the time Andersen Consulting filed for arbitration, there was effectively no one with any strong power base at the helm of the worldwide Firm. After both Wadia and Shaheen failed to win the confidence of the partnership, W. Robert Grafton, a board member who seemed to me to have ascended for his lack of baggage rather than his compelling personality, was chosen as the interim CEO of Andersen Worldwide. He would hold that position while the arbitration played itself out. Immediately after the arbitration decision was announced in August 2000, with its disastrous conclusions for Arthur

Andersen, Wadia stepped down as head of the accounting side, and Lou Salvatore, our New York office managing partner, became the interim CEO for much of 2000. (He told others he had absolutely no interest in the job on a permanent basis.)

Not until early 2001, after a campaign lasting several months, was Joe Berardino, by then managing partner of the North American audit practice, elevated to run what was now simply called Andersen—and by then it may well have been too late for this storied old Firm. For much of the 1990s—arguably the most critical period in Arthur Andersen's history—the Firm was rudderless, its core values of integrity, stewardship, and public responsibility replaced by greed. Money was seen as the great healer, and so the leaders who emerged were those whose clear focus was on raising the revenues. Berardino was certainly of that ilk, and he had helped to structure a deal with SEC chairman Arthur Levitt that protected much of the Firm's ability to provide both accounting and consulting services. From Andersen's perspective, the new hero, like *Lord of the Flies'* Jack, was the person who defended the Firm against external threats.

Long before that, however, the leadership system that had been so carefully constructed began to decay. One of the first rituals to go was the annual all-hands global partners meeting. With no sense of whether the consulting group would remain part of Andersen Worldwide, the default decision was that there simply were no global partnership meetings for the entire Firm in 1998, 1999, or 2000. Only in October 2001, after Andersen Consulting, now called Accenture, had split off and Joe Berardino had taken over, was a meeting finally held in New Orleans for the remaining partners. And that meeting was marred by the events of September 11, which prevented many people from attending.

Another important consequence of the lapse in leadership was the dissolution of Andersen's vaunted Public Review Board, the board of outside independent experts that had carried out their own quality reviews every year since 1974. When the Public Review Board was first created by Harvey Kapnick, he said,

> A public accounting firm has a significant responsibility to the private sector of our economy, not only to clients but also to

investors, creditors and the public. . . . We believe the establishment of this board is a constructive and beneficial step that
should enhance the efforts of our firm to carry out its function
in the business and financial community.

The board was never formally dismantled, says Donald Jacobs,
retired dean of Northwestern University's Kellogg School of Management and a member of the Board. Rather, it was another casu-
alty of the Andersen-AC split. "It was an entity of Andersen Worldwide," Jacobs said. "Once the arbitration started, [the two units]
were really completely separate. There was no entity for us to be-
long to."

*　*　*

To be fair, strategic thinking when so much is in flux would have
been difficult for any leader. After the filing of the arbitration in December 1997, no one knew what the structure of the Firm would be
going forward. The one thing the managing partners of Arthur Andersen thought they could control, however, was the short term.
That meant the active and energetic pursuit of anything that would
help the Firm get a piece of the ever-escalating stock market, which,
by the beginning of 1998, was several years into a raging bull market.

At Arthur Andersen, greed took on a different tenor than it did
in the publicly traded companies it served. The Firm was unable to
gain directly from a company's meeting its earnings projections or
an executive cashing in stock options, and partners were extremely
limited in which stocks they could own. But it could certainly get
close to the action. A client that made its numbers and whose stock
soared would have lots more discretionary income to spend on a variety of consulting projects. That meant more for the Firm and
more units for the partners who kept their Crown Jewels happy. The
Firm had, since the days of its founder Arthur Andersen, specialized
in taking on clients that were small but had the potential for massive growth. Now it had to do its best to spot the next upstart en
route to becoming a New Economy winner.

At the same time, AA was in a brutal market-share war with its
rivals to maintain its clients and win over new ones. One way to do

this was by offering some kind of value-added to the audit. Seeking to prove that audit wasn't a commodity after all, most of the Big 5 introduced new and improved versions of their basic offerings, much as Tide did with its new stain remover or Tropicana with no-pulp orange juice. For Arthur Andersen, the new and exciting product was called the Business Audit. Several years in development, it was rolled out to great fanfare in 1997 as the most in-depth, analytical audit approach out there. Read one Arthur Andersen marketing piece:

> Imagine an audit that focused on the critical business environment, transactions and risks that affect your company. Imagine an audit team with the technological tools and insight to help you successfully manage those risks and deliver recommendations that truly benefit your business. These images might just change the way you view an audit.
>
> By engaging Arthur Andersen as your independent auditors, you need not imagine. We have already transformed the traditional audit.
>
> Auditing used to mean examining the balance sheet. But you deal with more than your financial statements. You deal with a multifaceted business, with tough issues and the people who face them.

The Business Audit was seen as an Audit Plus. Unlike the traditional audit, it would look at areas that hadn't previously been part of a standard annual review, such as the strategic business environment. If it required more work, the Business Audit would probably also cost more. The Business Audit was the biggest new product introduction during my time at the Firm, and its launch went far beyond the metaphorical smashing of a bottle of champagne across Andersen's prow. The Firm prepared a multicolor sound and light video and a deluxe PowerPoint presentation on the Business Audit, and dispatched Jim Hooton, a longtime Houston audit partner, to introduce it around the world. Hooton was slick, smooth, and smart, with a drawl and a fast temper. He came off as a cross between Billy Graham and Sylvester Stallone. The presentations were all about synergy, with multicolored cylinders and arrows meant to prove it. Even we consultants were expected to understand the Business Audit, because we would presumably be working with the auditors as they discovered issues that needed a consultant's touch. The Business Audit was supposed to define the future culture of the Firm.

But the Business Audit didn't really catch on. So, a year later, in April 1998, AA held a global meeting for the partners of the Assurance and Business Advisory Group in Orlando, Florida. While the Firm did its best to focus on the critical importance of the Business Audit, what I remember most was the extreme level of tension between the Americans and non-Americans. On the first night, everyone gathered for a buffet dinner on the pool patio, a casual, all-American meal. Unfortunately, several of our global colleagues, like the Japanese partners with whom I was talking, expected a full sit-down dinner. After traveling 10,000 miles, they wanted something more than a breaded shrimp and two mini-quiches. Following the rather skimpy repast, we were treated to a fireworks display. As the multicolored lights exploded into the sky, the strains of "Stars and Stripes Forever" and "The Washington Post March" blared over the speakers. It was all very Fourth of July, except that this was Arthur Andersen, one seamless *global* firm. Many of the non-Americans were highly offended. "This is supposed to be an international meeting," one of the Japanese partners hissed. "Why are they playing only American music?" Both the Japanese and the French groups got up and left in search of a real dinner.

Things deteriorated further the next day. For the morning session we were divided into broad industry groups, so that each breakout group had representatives from several countries. Audit partners were supposed to report on how they had implemented the Business Audit. It quickly became clear to me that the Business Audit seemed to be viewed by many as a U.S. initiative, and that most of the non-U.S. partners wanted nothing to do with it. One presentation, by an Italian audit partner in the financial services group, was typical. He walked us through the steps his team took during an audit of one of his top clients. He then defiantly said that what he was showing us was not the Business Audit but an example of the kind of audit his office always did. His basic message was that the Italians had been doing good audits for a long time, and that they didn't need anyone telling them how to do their business. A lot of heads nodded in angry agreement. As an American, I felt uncomfortable; as a consultant, I felt a part of someone else's war. By noon, the air was thick with tension. They probably should have added Tums to the lunch menu, given the agitation so many members of this one global Firm seemed to be feeling.

The increasing international tensions were about more than the Business Audit. According to a former high-ranking European partner, there was a serious split between the U.S. audit practice and the rest of the global Firm over Andersen's direction going forward. Many of the European practices wanted to move aggressively into corporate finance and other areas that had little to do with audit—and didn't require those skills—while the U.S. auditors wanted to ensure that audit, defined broadly to include all the consulting services I and others were doing, remained the core. "The troubling feeling I was getting was that [U.S.] audit partners themselves were not content with their position in the Firm," said the former partner, "and were anxious to prove that they did have a very valuable contribution to make." The result was a meeting that was anything but jovial.

That afternoon, we were asked to break up into country groups to discuss the ways in which we could all work together to help get the Business Audit going. Since there were relatively few consulting partners present (most of the audit-related consulting groups were, at that time, in only U.S. offices), auditors and consultants were grouped together. Each breakout room had a screen that played a video of Joe Berardino listing the items to be covered. But this, too, started a diplomatic row. Berardino was the head of North American Audit, not the global head. Why was he addressing the group at all? And why in English? Tensions erupted. The French appeared to take the greatest offense at this one. Furious, they began crumpling up napkins and paper cups and throwing them at the screen. "Why couldn't they at least have a European leader on the screen?" someone scoffed. No one seemed particularly jazzed about the Business Audit itself.

But the rollout had far bigger problems than intercultural disputes. The real issue was that many clients didn't like the new audit one bit. If the Firm was planning to delve further into their operations, several clients said, that must mean that Andersen must not have been doing as much as it could have or should have all along. One senior manager in the Chicago office described to me his Business Audit presentation to a client who'd been with the Firm for close to 50 years. After finishing, he said, the CFO turned on him and charged that if Andersen had been auditing them for all this time and needed more information because they didn't know the company well enough, then maybe they ought to drop them as their auditor. The auditor mumbled something about "serving you even better," but the client wasn't having it. The equally disturbing alternative for many clients was the idea that Business Audit might be simply a ploy to raise prices and "discover" something that would necessitate a need for consulting services of some kind.

The Business Audit had problems internally, too. Not only did it address issues that had not previously been part of the formal audit, it offered, as its pièce de résistance, a sophisticated, highly complex technology through which all the new information would be processed. All new audits and consulting assignments had to be filtered through the Business Risk Model, which purported to identify every single kind of risk a client could face (there were 76 of them, which were summarized in several boxes on a laminated card we all carried around with us). Every one of those 76 risks—and each risk subcategory beneath it—was ostensibly measured, and the data were to be fed into the fancy new computer program designed to support the model. Every auditor and consultant, along with the entire computer support staff, needed training in this new Rube Goldberg approach. The auditors were already under tremendous pressure to maximize revenue. Now each one of them had to go through many hours of new training modules while juggling all their commitments. The Business Audit also put more emphasis on macro issues and less on the micro part of checking every number, relying more on sampling than in the past. And what you were supposed to say to the client if you actually found a big problem was less than obvious. From talking with many audit partners and managers, and from my own observation, it seemed that the Business Audit was, to quote Shakespeare, "full of sound and fury, and signifying nothing."

A memo to all partners in September 1998 underlined the importance of the new system to the Firm—and the frustration with its slow adoption. Written by Michael Bennett, the global managing partner for the audit group, Berardino, and Greg Jonas, managing director of financial assurance, it was both about selling new services and about reducing Arthur Andersen's own litigation risk. The targets for implementing the Business Audit were not being met, it said, despite the strategic importance of the system. With 40 percent of clients there had been no progress in implementing any portion of the Business Audit. From here on out, partners would be measured on their progress, and those who didn't meet goals would be considered to have a "deficiency" when review time came around.

That meant you wouldn't get a raise if you didn't do your part on the Business Audit. Yet at the same time, if you successfully used the new tool, which purported to be better at ferreting out fraud or mistakes earlier, you might actually put your compensation at risk. That is because the Firm had made it clear that any restatement of earnings or litigation for a "quality flaw" would torpedo a partner's chance to earn new units. In a perfect Catch-22, the partners and their staffs were caught between two conflicting standards. On one hand, you should try your best to implement the Business Audit. Yet if you found a problem that changed the audit through your new approach, you were discouraged from calling for anything that could lead to a restatement. The logical choice would be to try to resolve things behind the scenes.

The schizophrenia continued. Although the first of Andersen's myriad of earnings scandals were only beginning to appear, there seemed to be a growing realization that the pressures of the bull market might lead to some serious problems for the Firm. The same memo mentioned that the Business Audit, because it was more comprehensive, should decrease the risk of litigation by helping the Firm identify clients it should resign from. It would be a win-win solution for both the client and the auditor. Yet at the same time, the Firm desperately needed the new business the Business Audit might bring in. "BA is key to implementing other planks in [Assurance and Business Advisory's] strategic pyramid, particularly our need to grow risk consulting services and integrate other service categories, i.e., cross-sell other AA services," the memo read. By the end of 1999, according to Arthur Andersen's U.S. annual report, the Business Audit had been "introduced" to "nearly all" of the Firm's U.S. clients. Yet just as this purportedly more sophisticated tool was being rolled out, Andersen rushed headlong toward New Economy clients—whose very essence, of course, was risk.

*   *   *

Arthur Andersen jumped into the arms of the New Economy with the reckless abandon of an infatuated teenager. Sure, every consulting firm, accounting firm, investment bank, venture capitalist, and public investor was piling on too. But for Arthur Andersen, the motivation was a complex mixture of greed, envy, and insecurity. Watching its bitter rivals at Andersen Consulting, which had refashioned itself as the "market, architect, and builder of the New Economy," make money hand over fist, the reputation the Firm had—still—as being "just accountants" burned deep into its collective soul. Like the librarian who takes off her glasses, shakes her hair loose, and transforms herself into a vamp, this once-practical, plodding, and reliable icon of American professional service firms was about to give itself a radical makeover.

We had a lot of work to do. At a New York fiscal year kickoff meeting in late 1998, we walked into the room to find, beside each of our places, a little toy dinosaur. It was time, announced Lou Salvatore, to start afresh. No longer would we be thought of as the dinosaur of the industry! I was half expecting a sleek lynx or a speedy cheetah to suddenly appear in the room, but no such luck. We were stuck with the dinosaur.

Lou talked a lot about the Firm's decision to raise the salaries of first-year employees, and justified it (they had been vastly underpaid) by saying that we had to start to think of the investment banks as our peer group. Retention was becoming a bigge problem than ever, as the New Economy beckoned with stock options and high salaries, and onetime guaranteed Androids left for the more lucrative pastures of their clients. Still, the comparison to investment bankers felt like quite a stretch. Investment bankers made big money making deals happen. Auditors were supposed to be checking the numbers to make sure everything was kosher. What, exactly, were we aspiring to?

Next, we watched a series of videos of focus groups of clients asked to say what came to mind when they thought of Arthur Andersen. "Steady, sure," "a little bit old," "a little bit tired" were among the descriptions. Then they asked the groups what kind of a car they thought of when picturing both Arthur Andersen and Andersen Consulting. Adding to the inferiority complex, the clients described AC as a Ferrari or a Mercedes while labeling Arthur—to embarrassed snickers around the room—as an Oldsmobile or a Buick. People became agitated. "Nobody wanted to be called a Buick by clients," said Natalie, my colleague. Finally, Lou instructed us to take our dinosaurs and throw them away, trashing our stodgy old image in the process.

The dinosaurs had been relegated to the dustbin of history. Now all we had to do was to let down our hair and whip off our glasses. But it wasn't that easy: Even the changing of the dress code required an agonizing number of discussions and rules. One day in 2000, the e-mail went out finally permitting employees to wear business casual. But this didn't mean you could bring your dog to the office or use a scooter to get to the bathroom. "The e-mail was hysterical," said one manager in the Chicago office. "No mules, no skorts, no stretch pants, no leather, no gauze. In the summer, we weren't supposed to wear crew neck undershirts. We had to wear V-necks. They sent people home!"

Around 1999, the Assurance and Business Advisory Group had reorganized its consulting group yet again, this time under the rubric of risk. Risk had become the Firm's buzzword of choice, and a neat way in which to package all of our pricey and glamorous services. After all, not every company needed consulting services—but who could say they didn't want to reduce risk in such a fast-paced, ever-more-confusing business environment? Our group and all of the others in audit-related consulting, such as fraud, derivatives, and so on were organized under what was called Business Risk Consulting and Assurance Services, or BRCA. We still remained separate from Business Consulting, the technology and human resources folks who were not part of the audit umbrella. Since an audit was, by definition, about safeguards, the new unit was the perfect complement. Now there would be a head of BRCA in every major office, usually an audit partner. Little changed with the new name, but we had a new global leader in Mike Bennett, a charming, youthful Houstonian who had won kudos for building the firm's first Computer Risk Management consulting group. CRM helped clients manage their information risks over things such as firewalls and the anticipated problems with Y2K.

After Bennett got the new position as head of global audit, I e-mailed him a few times, sharing my concerns about the infighting and the general atmosphere within the consulting group, and expressing my hope that he would involve many of us in resolving tensions and setting a new course. I was happily surprised when he suddenly popped his head into my office on his way from a meeting down the hall with Berardino. All smiles, he announced: "Your troubles are over! Tomorrow is the first day of the rest of your life!" I wasn't sure what he meant, but I felt that he had heard me, and I liked his enthusiasm.

In April 1999, Steve Samek, Berardino, and Bennett called a three-day meeting in Orlando for the hundreds of worldwide BRCA partners and senior managers. The purpose of the event was to stir up enthusiasm for the new group. On a more pragmatic level, it was basically a great big sales meeting, designed to juice everybody up to sell, sell, sell. It was also meant to sell the New Economy to us. The emerging leaders of the new culture wanted to turn us all into voracious hunters.

Although I was hopeful that this really was a new beginning for our group, I was seriously thinking about leaving the Firm. Perhaps because of my frustration, many things about this meeting seemed either ridiculous or hypocritical. To build enthusiasm, Andersen took us to Universal Studios, where we were invited to the "Twister" attraction, modeled after the film starting Helen Hunt. Dutifully, the mostly male group shuffled onto the "set," a mock-up of a Kansas farmyard in the moments before a big storm. Then as we stood scrunched together behind a fence, simulated winds began to blow, lights flashed, and miniature furniture, cars, and cows flew into our line of sight as a funnel cloud swept across the landscape. We survived, with nothing more than slightly disheveled hairdos. I suppose some deep thinkers might have suggested that this was meant to show us how we dinosaurs were being buffeted by the winds of dramatic New Economy changes. But in retrospect it looks more like an unintended metaphor of the whirlwind of corruption that would sweep us up and smash us into a million pieces like some mobile home in Texas. Whatever the point, it just seemed silly.

Equally absurd had been the kickoff presentation, earlier that day, of Ben Zander, a minor-league orchestra conductor who was building a career as a motivational speaker. As we sat in the spacious hotel ballroom, Zander scampered around the room like a leprechaun, trying to inspire a mass of people from around the world whose feelings for one another ranged from, at best, disinterest to, at worst, abject hatred. He made us stand up and stretch, jump around, and shout out happy phrases. I looked over at our leadership—Berardino, Samek, and Bennett—sitting on the side of the room, smiling benignly like a bunch of cardinals. They all appeared to have gone through some serious media and image training since the last time I'd seen them. Samek and Bennett, two Androids who had heretofore specialized in bland, were positively slick! (When I called Bennett a few days after the meeting to set up a conference call, I told him I wanted to get on his agenda soon, before he became a talk show host.) Needless to say, they didn't feel the need to participate in these embarrassing exercises.

Zander's shtick was basically that the New Economy demanded a new way of thinking. For example, he informed us, when something good or interesting or different occurs, you should shout out, "This is fabulous!" And when something bad happens, you turn it into an exciting lesson and crow to the world, "This is fascinating!" Zander's relatively obvious point was that we should work together like an orchestra, each with our own instrument, ultimately creating a beautiful sound. The reality of the Firm, however, was that we were indeed each playing our own instrument, but unlike in an orchestra, there was no harmony in collaboration. We simultaneously made our dissonant sounds in hopes of drowning each other out, and they were as painful to play as they were to hear.

As Zander bounced around the ballroom, I stood and looked at my colleagues (I decided to emulate the leadership and keep my feet firmly planted on the ground). There they were—French, Japanese, American, German, Italian, Australian, Brazilian—staring straight ahead, grim-faced, each one in his own little world. For once we were unified, if only in our feelings of ridiculousness. Later, when I was called up to the stage along with some other practice leaders to talk about our respective businesses, the debunker in me escaped again. "We're a new service line," I said, "so we've had our ups and downs. This year's been a little tougher. But what I learned from watching Ben is that the next time Joe Berardino says we're not making our numbers, I'm going to say, 'But Joe, it's fabulous!'" Everyone laughed, partly because of my cheekiness but also because I mangled the phrase. What I was supposed to say, and would have known had I paid more attention to leprechaun Zander, was "fascinating." Maybe I wasn't cut out for the New Economy.

Yet when I think back on that meeting, the most stunning recollection of all is the glitzy presentation we all sat through on the Arthur Andersen "world-class client." As we watched, triumphant music blasted from the sound system and the enormous screen came to life in an explosion of red, green, and blue. An upended E appeared next to the word ENRON. Enron was Arthur Andersen's dream client, the model for tomorrow. It was innovative, it was dynamic, it was one of the most successful stocks in the market, and best of all, it had a seemingly unquenchable thirst for both audit and consulting services from the Firm. Members of the Enron team stood on the stage and talked about what each of them was doing to help this dynamic company. Then came the numbers on how much Enron was paying us, bathed in an hypnotic glow. They were in the multimillions—on both the audit and the consulting sides. One Enron, we realized, was more valuable than literally thousands of our other clients.

The message was as clear as day: This is what we are shooting for with all of our major clients—an intergalactic, multidisciplinary effort from as many different service lines as possible. Enron is the future, and everyone must work to bring in an Enron. By the time the fiscal 1999 annual report was published, Enron, along with WorldCom, another company already cooking its books, was listed among the Firm's four most important clients.

By the beginning of 2000, this accounting firm whose employees were barred from owning stock had set up a $500 million venture capital fund, Arthur Andersen Ventures, to invest in Internet start-ups and to take equity instead of fees. At the same time, it discarded the doors' logo for the orange orb, declared that its vision was "to be *the* partner for success in the New Economy," and published a book, *Cracking the Value Code: How Successful Businesses Are Creating Wealth in the New Economy*, with Steve Samek as one of the authors. Featured prominently were examples of such companies as Internet incubator idealab! and audit client Qwest Communications, which in 2002 would have to restate at least $1.2 billion in earnings.

Andersen also announced a strategy focusing on what it called the Emerging 10, or fast-growing entrepreneurial companies. The clients that found themselves hopelessly stuck in the past got the boot. "Clients that were either not growing or unprofitable were culled, saw fee increases, or were switched to an alternative service delivery model," the 1999 report said. The idea to migrate unprofitable clients away from the Firm's best resources seemed to me to indicate that its interest in a thorough audit was directly proportional to the fees the client brought in. Sure, every company had to have an audit, but those that weren't growing would have to be serviced by some other firm. And the New Economy only intensified the pressure for more consulting. In fiscal 1999, more than 30 percent of the Firm's total U.S. fees came from services that didn't exist or were just starting in 1995. Given that Business Risk Consulting had posted 50 percent growth that year, it wasn't hard to see where the Firm wanted its energy focused.

All of this meant that the risks were mounting everywhere. Take the enthusiasm over the group that conducted a client's *internal* audit if the client requested it. It wasn't unheard of for the Andersen staffers doing the external audit and those doing the internal audit to sit in the same room together at the client. One former manager saw it happen at a large client in Minnesota: "They worked very closely [together]. They would share documents. It seemed like a conflict to me." And to me, too. In case of trouble, it would be like having the cops and robbers on the same team. Yet when my colleague Natalie asked the head of the group how one firm could do both, he said simply, "It's allowed." I was struck by how both the Firm and its most loyal audit clients, who embraced outsourcing their internal audit function to Andersen, rationalized the concept. The idea seemed to be that in the rapidly changing, highly complex world that all companies were facing, *risk* was the enemy. What better way to manage your risk than to make sure that your internal and external auditors saw life from the same perspective?

Although it wasn't discussed much publicly, the Firm was not blind to either its own internal risks or those of the New Economy. Standard procedure upon acquiring a new client had for years been the completion of a risk-assessment questionnaire for new clients or projects, called SMART, or the System for Managing Acceptance and Retention. With the launch of BRCA, a new version of SMART was produced for our group. The questionnaire was very similar to the audit SMART. Such factors as "potential negative publicity," the presence of "legal protection clauses," and "independence violations" had to be assessed as part of the process. Now there were also specific questions about related regulatory agencies, other audit firms that might be doing the external audit, and e-commerce vulnerabilities.

At the end of any SMART, you had to give points to each section and come up with a total assessment of the potential risk the client or project posed for the Firm. "Management integrity and behavior" and "potential negative publicity" were each worth 150 points, while financial risk of the client was worth just 75 points. If the risk profile was considered "maximum," several more executives had to sign off on the form, sometimes going all the way up to the global managing partner. But at the bottom of the form there was also a section about the engagement economics, including estimated net fees. Clearly, the risk was being assessed in part based on the reward expected. The new system also included a question about the "competencies" necessary to fulfill the engagement. There followed a list of all the consulting services by name—a handy-dandy guide to consulting services that could be urged on the client.

There was another problem, a common concern with any questionnaire: The system was subjective and easy to manipulate, just as the previous system had been. Most people knew, or could guess, which questions would lead to which answers. If you felt you were drowning in paperwork already—or if you were feeling in need of business and you didn't want to take a lot of time getting sign-offs—it was easy enough to answer questions to produce a normal or a high, but not maximum, risk outcome. To truly answer some of the questions thoroughly would require due diligence, which took time from fee-generating activities. Plus, SMART assessments were usually completed by a senior consultant or staff person two or three years into his career. These younguns weren't exactly known for their experience and sophisticated risk-assessment capabilities.

So while the leadership was clearly aware of client risk, the process for assessing it did not emphasize the consequences. For high- or maximum-risk audit clients, the audit team met prior to the audit, or "busy," season to discuss the particular risks. At my request, I sat in on two such meetings in the fall of 1998. As I recall, each meeting was attended by the audit team partner, senior manager, and one or two other team managers, as well as the industry group head, and was chaired by Joe Berardino in his continuing role as Metro New York Head of Audit. The group talked through an outline that included questions like: Where were pressures on the client in the past? What new opportunities faced the client, and what pressures might they bring? What was the integrity of the company—past and present? Then they discussed an action plan. The key issues I recall were the rapid, heavy acquisitions both clients were doing, and, in one case, the health and energy of an audit partner who had been ill. My sense of these meetings was not that the Firm was considering resigning from the client or challenging the client, but that the auditors on these engagements needed to be careful. The Firm understood its risks. But it didn't take adequate action to confront those risks.

Under the leadership of Berardino and Steve Samek, New Economy clients that were both high risk and high income producers seemed to become a badge of honor for the Firm's U.S. practice. The highest-risk clients seemed to be those that did massive acquisitions in fairly short time periods (thereby acquiring enormous debt), those whose stock was volatile, or those who were using deregulation to transform themselves into high-flying energy dynamos. Those were the WorldComs, the Enrons, the Global Crossings that Arthur Andersen lusted after and then bragged about. They seemed to legitimize the Firm within the New Economy culture.

•   •   •

The formal leadership was absent, distracted, or fighting its own battles. The vision was money. The traditional culture had suffered a mortal wound. But no one knew it yet. In 1997, the first of the epidemic of accounting scandals that would ultimately engulf Arthur Andersen began to unfold. Waste Management, a rollup of regional garbage collectors, environmental companies, and random other things founded by Dean Buntrock and a partner, had grown into one of the greatest success stories and hottest stocks of the 1970s and 1980s. If Enron and WorldCom were the dream clients of the New Economy, Waste Management was the ideal of the old one.

The ties between Waste Management and Arthur Andersen went all the way back to the company's beginnings. The Firm was its auditor even before it went public in 1971, and it felt a special connection to this up-from-nothing Chicago success story. For most of its existence, Waste Management was a thing to behold, a corporate machine that saw gold where others saw garbage and made thousands of acquisitions. Waste Management made trash sexy and its executives, investors, and accountants rich. It also was used to playing hardball in an industry long known in some parts of the country for unsavory business practices. Over time, most of the national garbage market was divided between two behemoths—Waste and Browning-Ferris Industries—both of whom regularly faced antitrust suits, paid their fines, and went on accumulating. Not that the investors minded much: The stock rose from a split-adjusted $1.84 to the mid-$40s by the early 1990s. Buntrock was feted on the cover of *Fortune* and was the fourth-highest-paid CEO in *Business Week*'s Executive Pay list in 1991, raking in over $12 million for the year. "No company in this business, anywhere in the world, can match Waste Management's range of experience and store of technology, its financial prowess and management skills," wrote author Timothy Jacobson in his adoring book *Waste Management: An American Corporate Success Story.* "Many companies everywhere envy its balance sheet."

In 1996, when I was still in Chicago, there was an elegant party to celebrate the 25-year anniversary of Waste Management's going public and the Firm's long relationship with the company. It was, in some ways, a family reunion, since every CFO and chief accounting officer in Waste Management's history had come from Arthur Andersen. Not that this was so unusual: A common trajectory for auditors with extensive experience at one client was simply to take a job there, where they might be paid significantly more money to sit on the other side of the table than they did when they were at the Firm. The SEC would later speak out against those transitions, but at the time this was a fairly standard practice. Those of us who weren't on the Waste audit team didn't know anything about the cooked books at the time; the company wouldn't begin to restate earnings until 1998. But even then I found the idea of an auditor and its client celebrating at a gala party together unsavory. They were acting like they were on the same team—not as if one was supposed to be the other's gatekeeper.

And then the music stopped. After more than a decade of being a growth company, Waste Management's forays into international markets and other sectors flopped. The company lost its momentum and became mired in industries such as recycling and environmental cleanup that, it turned out, didn't have the cost efficiencies of American trash. But no one knew this, because Waste Management allegedly disguised its growing financial woes by such tricks as extending the lives of its garbage trucks and other assets on its balance sheet to make income look better. "From his earliest days in the business," Jacobson wrote presciently in 1993, "Chairman Dean Buntrock had a concept that quickly became a bedrock business principle at Waste Management: Every truck is a profit center."

The Securities and Exchange Commission settled charges against four Andersen executives and the Firm in 2001 (the Firm paid $7 million without admitting guilt). It alleged that Andersen's auditors, including partners Robert Allgyer, Walter Cercavschi, and Edward Maier—who in addition to being a concurring partner on the Waste account headed up the risk management practice for the Chicago office—spotted the incorrect accounting and brought it up with more senior management. Cowed by the client's executives and afraid of losing the $7 million in audit fees and $11.8 million in nonaudit fees they had collected between 1991 and 1997, the SEC charged that the auditors simply caved when the company refused to implement the changes they wanted. The partners did propose "action steps" to fix the problems, but Waste rejected them. So they allegedly simply certified the audit and decided to hope that the company would see things their way the next year instead.

After a few years of this, according to the SEC, the partners brought their concerns to Robert Kutsenda, an Android who made partner in 1975 and rose to the position of Central Region Audit Practice Director. His job included consulting on "significant auditing, accounting, financial statement presentation and reporting problems encountered during an audit." In 1995, Waste Management had booked a $160 million gain that it planned to use to cancel out the expenses that had been accounted for illegally in prior years. When Kutsenda was asked whether Andersen should then qualify its audit report, he allegedly said no. He argued that the numbers were "immaterial," an accounting term that meant the changes wouldn't have an impact on earnings, even though this represented 10 percent of pretax income. Just a few years later, the whole scheme would fall apart as the company merged with a competitor. The stock collapsed, and, in February 1998, Waste Management restated $1.7 billion in earnings—at the time, the largest restatement in corporate history.

The pressures were intense. Waste Management was considered a Crown Jewel client, but it had in 1991 limited the total amount it would pay for an audit while placing no restrictions on nonaudit services. Robert Allgyer, the engagement partner, had been selected for his "personal style that . . . fit well with the Waste Management officers," and he also held a senior position at the Firm cross-selling other services to Waste and to other Chicago-area companies. According to a former SEC official, the partners eventually brought their concerns all the way up to Steve Samek, then the head of Commercial Audit Services, who okayed approving the audit and continuing to press for change from the inside. (Samek would later become the Firm's managing partner for the United States.) The CEO of Arthur Andersen—Dick Measelle—was also briefed, the official said, although neither man's name appeared in the final settlement. Even without the Business Audit, it seemed, Arthur Andersen's systems worked. It was the culture of integrity that appeared to have failed.

The Firm knew full well that it was under investigation for several years before finally settling with the SEC in 2001. So what did it do to instill confidence, to change behaviors, or to let its staff know that what had happened at Waste Management was a serious black mark that could destroy trust, the only thing an audit firm has going for it? To my knowledge, virtually nothing. The case was not discussed openly. The Firm's ethical responsibilities were not questioned or discussed, despite the fact that members of the senior leadership had allegedly signed off on the decisions. And, in fact, Waste Management kept the Firm as its auditor and boosted its revenues, paying an amazing $48 million in audit fees alone and $31 million in nonaudit fees in 2000. Only after the collapse of Enron did Waste end the relationship. The only reference I ever heard to the scandal was a bit of black humor uttered by a young audit partner in New York. "Be careful how you count the trucks," he'd say with a knowing smile. An opportunity came and went, but the leadership was focused elsewhere, on new Crown Jewels and Elephant Targets, on its rivals at Andersen Consulting, and on discarding the dinosaur image.

And of the executives involved? Well, by the time 2001 came around, all but one, Robert Allgyer, who resigned in 2000, were still at the Firm, still partners, still earning their units. They did not admit to guilt under the terms of the settlement, but in 2001 Allyger, Cercavschi, and Maier were barred from serving as accountants for three years. In the meantime, Cercavschi soldiered on as a partner in the audit division until 2000, when he was moved to the business process outsourcing practice. He also kept his job as the lead recruiter for University of Illinois–Champaign students at the Firm. Maier, who headed up Chicago's risk-management office, later would be named as having approved some questionable transactions at now-bankrupt Boston Chicken, according to a still-pending lawsuit. The SEC later ruled that franchise start-up costs had been improperly accounted for at Boston Chicken.

Robert Kutsenda, the highest-ranking person named in the settlement, would be suspended in 2001 from practicing accounting for a year. During the investigation, Kutsenda was put in charge of the Firm's prestigious Risk Management Executive Committee, the committee that looked at Firm risk as a whole and the committee that ultimately decided to rewrite the document retention policy. After all, if anyone should know about risk, it was Kutsenda. But to put him in a position of making risk-related policy while he was under SEC investigation could turn the most idealistic observer into a bitter cynic.

The Firm and Waste Management settled shareholder lawsuits in 1998, paying out a portion of the $228 million total. But the settlement of civil charges and the $7 million fine—the largest ever paid in an SEC enforcement action—would not be announced until June of 2001. Included in the settlement was a clause stating that the Firm could not ever again violate any securities laws. It was this clause that may have ultimately sealed the Firm's fate later, when its involvement in Enron was exposed. Proclaimed Richard H. Walker, the SEC's director of enforcement:

> Arthur Andersen and its partners failed to stand up to company management and thereby betrayed their ultimate

allegiance to Waste Management's shareholders and the investing public. Given the positions held by these partners and the duration and gravity of the misconduct, the firm itself must be held responsible for the false and misleading audit reports issued in its name.

It already was too late. Even as Waste Management simmered away, Arthur Andersen's pot was beginning to boil over with accounting-related scandals. Next, there was Sunbeam, the high-flying appliance maker run into the ground by the controversial, brash, and arrogant CEO, Al Dunlap. Dunlap had made a career out of parachuting into troubled companies, slashing them to bits, and then selling off assets or the troubled companies themselves to thunderous shareholder applause. But his way of making the numbers, according to many reports, was to browbeat and intimidate his employees into doing whatever it took. Dunlap took over at Sunbeam in July 1996 and promised great results. Wall Street enthusiastically bought the story, boosting the stock to a high of $52 a share in March 1998 from $12.50 before Dunlap signed on.

But what was going on inside the company was anything but a turnaround. The SEC would later charge that Dunlap, his key lieutenants, and Arthur Andersen auditor Philip Harlow were engaged in a "massive financial fraud." According to the SEC, Sunbeam's CFO, Russell Kersh, allegedly made use of a virtual laundry list of fraudulent types of accounting and nonrecurring charges. In 1996, Sunbeam purposely inflated its loss, creating a "cookie jar" reserve that would later be used to pad earnings and create the illusion that Sunbeam was in the midst of one of Dunlap's patented turnarounds. Dunlap apparently hoped to sell the company at an inflated price, reap the benefits, and move triumphantly to his next "slash-and-burn" project. Next, Sunbeam perfected the art of "channel-stuffing," or giving major incentives to customers to buy merchandise that they wouldn't be able to sell for some time, if ever. Grills, for example, were "purchased" by customers—and recorded on Sunbeam's books—at substantial discounts in the winter, when it was obvious that they wouldn't be used for months, if ever. Sunbeam then promised to hold the goods in its own warehouses until the customers were ready to take them. Already stuffed to the gills with grills, the whole system was bound to collapse.

This "bill-and-hold" strategy was an accepted accounting process under GAAP only if several specific criteria were met, such as the fact that the practice must be the customer's idea, not the vendor's. That wasn't the case, yet Sunbeam's outside auditor, Andersen, issued unqualified audit opinions for both 1996 and 1997. According to John A. Byrne's comprehensive book *Chainsaw: The Notorious Career of Al Dunlap in the Era of Profit-at-Any-Price*, in a meeting of the board in early 1998, Andersen partner Harlow told the audit committee that he didn't see a problem with the grill storage. In the spring of 1998, the house of cards began to come tumbling down: Amid reports of major earnings problems, the board of directors met and fired Dunlap on June 13. It would later be discovered that almost one-third of Sunbeam's 1997 earnings were a result of accounting fraud. Arthur Andersen was forced to admit that it no longer stood behind the company's earnings, and Sunbeam ultimately restated its earnings downward by over $100 million. The firm filed for bankruptcy in February 2001.

Again, the issues from Andersen's side centered on materiality and judgment, not a lack of knowledge or awareness of the problem. Although accountants often claim that they are not responsible for ferreting out deliberate fraud by a client, Harlow apparently understood at least some of what was going on. According to *Chainsaw*, during the 1997 audit, Harlow and Larry Bornstein, his Arthur Andersen colleague, questioned the accounting treatment of some transactions, such as some sales on consignment, but the controller, Robert Gluck, defended them as immaterial, and Harlow then changed his mind. He would stick to that belief all the way through a dramatic board meeting at which Dunlap asked him whether he stood by his numbers.

Unnerved by Dunlap's own performance at that meeting, the board asked him to step down. Within a few weeks, the SEC had opened an investigation into Sunbeam, and Arthur Andersen then suddenly withdrew its unqualified audit. A new team of Arthur Andersen auditors was brought in by Andersen to complete the review and do a restatement, along with Deloitte & Touche, which, in typical

Big 5 form, had appeared to clean up a rival's mess. Yet Andersen's lawyers later alleged that both the initial audit and the restatement were accurate, as odd as that sounds, because the standards and thresholds were different for a regular audit and one that had been restated. "I'd never seen that defense before," said Carl Stine, an attorney at Wolf Popper LLP, one of the law firms that filed the class action suit against Andersen and Sunbeam. The argument was never tested, however, since Andersen settled the suits for $110 million without admitting wrongdoing in April 2001.

In May 2001, three months after top Andersen executives teleconferenced to discuss problems at Enron and one month before the Waste Management suit was settled, the SEC sued Dunlap, four other Sunbeam executives, and Andersen accountant Harlow for civil fraud. Harlow was, as of early 2002, still employed as the managing partner of Andersen's Fort Lauderdale office. In a statement, Andersen said, "The SEC allegations reflect professional disagreements about the application of sophisticated accounting standards. They are not indicative of fraud."

The Sunbeam and Waste Management failures were occurring almost simultaneously as the Business Audit was in the midst of its rollout. It's no wonder that the Firm was becoming increasingly concerned about fraud—yet neither case was a result of auditors being left in the dark. The cases were seen as one-offs, things that happened to every firm once in a while as the result of overzealous litigators. "I don't remember anything changing significantly," said Bob Lorenz, a former partner, as these stories became public knowledge.

But there was still so much more under the surface. "It's almost like someone at Andersen broke a mirror," said Jonathan Hamilton, editor of the newsletter *Public Accounting Report.* Broke a mirror—or forgot to look into it, perhaps. As the Chicago, Fort Lauderdale, and Houston offices were struggling to manage their star clients, the Phoenix office found itself embroiled in the biggest nonprofit bankruptcy in history.

This time, it was the Baptist Foundation of Arizona, a charitable organization for Southern Baptists that collapsed in a Ponzi scheme allegedly masterminded by its top executives. In November 1999, the foundation went under, bilking 11,000 mostly elderly religious investors out of $590 million in savings. The collapse was hardly a surprise to Arthur Andersen—or at least, it shouldn't have been: The warning signs were numerous, yet the Firm allegedly never dug below the surface. According to the evidence provided at trial in May 2002, the senior manager on the account, Ann McGrath, the engagement partner, Jay Ozer—who had in the late 1980s audited one of Charles Keating's failed savings and loans, resulting in Andersen's paying a $24 million settlement—and the Phoenix managing partner, Jack Henry, allegedly all decided to take management's word that there was no funny business going on.

The trouble began in 1996, when several in-house accountants and one attorney at the Baptist Foundation resigned, citing concerns with the company's financial management. One, L. Richard Polley, wrote to Bill Crotts, the CEO: "I regret to inform you that the Lord has led me to resign my position as Trust Accounting Manager for the Baptist Foundation of Arizona. As you know, I have been concerned for some time about our business practices. . . . I do not believe that our Lord and Savior, Jesus Christ, would have us conduct His business in a manner that withholds important information from our investors." Polley said the Foundation's relationship with two businesses that owed it millions of dollars was not independent, and that in fact those businesses (ALO Inc., and New Church Ventures) were controlled by people affiliated with the nonprofit.

One of the Baptist Foundation accountants who resigned in 1996 was Karen Paetz, who had handled the bookkeeping for ALO and NCV and came to believe that Crotts and other executives were "selling" distressed real estate to the two businesses, which Crotts had helped to set up, at grossly inflated prices. The Foundation was being paid with worthless IOUs from ALO and New Church Ventures, she believed, but the financial statements looked as though these were legitimate, arm's-length sales. In February 1997, when Paetz knew Andersen was about to begin its next Foundation audit, she arranged a lunch with Andersen's McGrath. She said that she warned McGrath that the two businesses were in fact controlled by executives connected to the Foundation, and that she had serious questions about its management.

Around the same time, the CFOs at two longtime Andersen nonprofit clients who ran Baptist charities told their Andersen audit partner in the Dallas office that they had heard about possible financial shenanigans at BFA, and said that its debt was too high. According to information presented at the trial, the partner called his boss, who then called one of Andersen's top lawyers in Chicago, Don Dreyfus. Dreyfus, in turn, called Richard Corgel, the practice director responsible for the Phoenix office, and told him about an "anonymous caller" and what he reported. Corgel's notes, which were presented at the trial by Baptist Foundation of Arizona Liquidation Trust trial attorney John P. "Sean" Coffey, a partner at Bernstein Litowitz Berger & Grossmann LLP, read: "credible inquiry—anon. source. . . . Is BFA a Ponzi scheme?" Other than Ozer telling Crotts about the anonymous call seven months later, no action was allegedly taken. The Baptist Foundation went on to take in more than $200 million in additional money from unsuspecting investors.

In April 1998, the alternative Phoenix paper the *Phoenix New Times* ran an investigative series in which it charged that the foundation was a sham and that it had returned just $1.3 million to its own Baptist community while giving $140 million to companies associated with current and former Baptist Foundation directors. Shortly thereafter, an outside financial adviser named Deeann Jo Griebel was asked by a prospective client to look into the advisability of an investment in the Foundation. Using publicly available information, she came to the conclusion that most of the debt owed to the Baptist group was owed by one entity, ALO, whose president was a former director of the Baptist Foundation—and that this company had no money. That meant, she concluded, that the Foundation was unlikely to ever collect its receivables.

After meeting with Baptist officials and getting unsatisfactory answers to her questions, Griebel tracked down a public filing—easily obtained by anyone—that showed that ALO's net worth was a negative $105 million. She decided to speak up. "In public accounting, we were taught that the code of ethics was that if you came across something done by another CPA that you felt was flawed enough to jeopardize the public, that you needed to give that CPA a heads-up," she testified in court. Griebel called Andersen's Phoenix office twice and the Chicago headquarters once, leaving her name and the message "This is Dee Griebel, my CPA number is 3930E. I've looked at the Baptist Foundation audit. They're broke. [Andersen needs] to withdraw their audit opinion immediately. Call me," according to her testimony in the case. No one ever did.

While all of this was going on, Arthur Andersen issued unqualified audits of the Foundation, which in turn used those audits to bring in more and more churchgoing investors. Andersen executives were allegedly aware of each of these events. They brought up concerns with management, but never, according to the court documents, conducted an independent investigation that could have exposed the pyramid scheme. Andersen later claimed that it was not the responsibility of an accounting firm to identify management fraud, but star witness Dr. Dan Guy, an expert on auditing standards and detection of fraud, disagreed strongly. When asked during the trial if Andersen had lived up to its responsibilities as of December 1998, Dr. Guy said: "They did not because information came to their attention which required investigation . . . and an auditor is obligated, absolutely obligated, to go back, investigate, find out if the financial statements are reliable based on the new information."

Caught in a barrage of lawsuits and its criminal indictment for the Enron case, Andersen abandoned its plans to fight and settled the suit on March 1, 2002—the last business day before trial—for $217 million. After it was indicted two weeks later in the Enron scandal, Andersen then said that its insurance carrier wouldn't pay the claim. The court quickly reset the trial for April 29, 2002, the week before the Enron trial was to begin. After six days at trial, Andersen agreed to settle again for the same $217 million. Ozer and McGrath gave up their accounting licenses, and Andersen did not admit or deny any wrongdoing. "They never stopped stonewalling," said Coffey. "I thought the case against Andersen was as gross an example of misconduct by an audit firm as I've ever heard of in my career. I took the case thinking it was a rogue audit team, but I came to believe that there was a deeper culture of corruption at Andersen when it came to covering up what they were doing wrong." The criminal fraud cases against the Baptist Foundation executives are still in progress.

Many more scandals would soon unfold—and the one name common to most of them was Andersen. There was McKesson-HBOC, the drug distribution megamerger in which it was later alleged by the SEC that HBO & Co., an Andersen client, had falsified its earnings in 1998 and the beginning of 1999 by such techniques as backdating revenues. The company had to restate $300 million in earnings. There was Boston Chicken, which loaned the money to franchisees to start new restaurants and then booked the start-up costs as revenue, a controversial accounting decision that was okayed by Maier and Steve Samek in the early 1990s. Later, when the SEC required the franchises to change their accounting on these matters, it became clear that Boston Chicken's franchise losses were greater than the company's earnings. Two years later, in 1999, the company went bankrupt. A lawsuit against Andersen by Boston Chicken's bankruptcy trustee is pending.

Later, there would be the bankruptcy and criminal investigation of Global Crossing, the sizzling telecommunications company that collapsed under a mountain of debt (and whose CFO, Joseph Perrone, was the company's former auditor when he was at Arthur Andersen). And in July 2002, Andersen client Qwest Communications International announced that it had, through "error," improperly accounted for some 220 transactions worth $1.16 billion between 1999 and 2001. As of the end of 2002, Qwest was under investigation by the U.S. Department of Justice and the SEC. In 2001, Qwest paid Andersen $8.3 million in nonaudit fees and $2.2 million in audit fees, and Global Crossing paid $12 million in nonaudit fees and $2.3 million in audit fees in 2000, the last year it reported such fees.

The final shock, however, may have been the alleged massive accounting fraud at WorldCom, a prized audit client that paid Andersen some $12.4 million in nonaudit fees in 2001. On July 21, 2002, WorldCom declared bankruptcy with $107 billion in assets, surpassing Enron as the largest bankruptcy ever recorded in the United States. Again, there was fraud—the company, allegedly through its CFO, Scott Sullivan, improperly accounted for as much as $9 billion in expenses—but no one at the outside auditor claimed to have had a clue. It took an internal auditor to uncover the cooked books, on a shift so large and so rudimentary that accounting experts expressed disbelief that Andersen could fail to catch it. The senior audit partner, Melvin Dick, a well-regarded Android of 27 years, said simply that Andersen had conducted its audit according to generally accepted accounting principles. No charges have been filed against Mr. Dick.

I was startled when I heard that Mel Dick was the WorldCom audit partner on the hot seat. I had met him only once, in a hotel restaurant in that trip to Denver with Steve, my fraud colleague. As Mel and some associates entered the restaurant, Steve pointed him out. "That's Mel Dick, the audit partner on US West. He is one of the most respected and important people in this Firm. He's someone you should know."

Certainly, in a Firm with this many clients, some amount of litigation is viewed as inevitable, and it is true that accountants are not always expected to be able to detect fraud on the part of management. But they are, as the Firm itself noted in its memos on the Business Audit, expected to try. And litigation risk had been an issue long before the late 1990s for all accounting firms. Not even counting Enron, Andersen paid more than $500 million to settle claims against it between 1997 and 2002, an amount far surpassing that of any of its competitors, according to *Public Accounting Report*. As of October 2002, three of the five largest bankruptcies ever recorded were Andersen clients with accounting problems.

But to me, to have so many high-profile blowups occurring almost simultaneously and not have it register that something was terribly wrong, clearly explains why the Firm collapsed. Perhaps Rep. Bernie Sanders, Independent of Vermont, put it best when questioning Mr. Dick at the House of Representatives Financial Services Committee hearing:

> It appears very clearly that Arthur Andersen failed in their audit of WorldCom, you failed in the audit of Enron, you failed in the audit of Sunbeam, you failed in the audit of Waste

Management, you failed in the audit of McKesson, you failed in the audit of Baptist Foundation of Arizona. What was Arthur Andersen doing? I mean . . . it is incomprehensible to me that a major accounting firm could have such a dismal record in trying to determine what the financial health of a company is. It's almost beyond comprehension.

# Arthur the Terrible

*You find out these things are like cockroaches:*
*If you see one you're reasonably sure there are others.*
— GREGORY JONAS, Arthur Andersen's managing director
for financial statement assurance, October 1998

ON AUGUST 13, 1998, Robert G. Kutsenda, Gary B. Goolsby, and Gregory J. Jonas—three senior Andersen partners running the Firm's Risk Management Executive Committee—called a special meeting of the group to look at the Firm's internal risks, based on a flurry of troubling issues that seemed to be popping up all at once.

There were plenty to address. In 1998, no one at Andersen knew that rampant fraud at some of its most important clients would morph into a mushroom cloud that would engulf the Firm. But the senior leadership must have known that the risks to the Firm—and to the profession—were growing by the day. There were more complex audits to do, the new Business Audit system to learn, and the threat that the cash cow of Andersen Consulting could disappear. There were massive shareholder lawsuits after the public blowups of Waste Management and Sunbeam, along with ongoing SEC investigations. The pressure for Andersen's biggest clients—the public companies—to make their quarterly earnings estimates or face the brutal discipline of an angry market was everywhere.

The leadership crisis inside Andersen had been written about un-favorably in major business publications. The Firm was trying to put through the most radical overhaul of its audit practices in a generation. New jobs in start-up companies were stealing the best and brightest from the profession, and turnover was on the rise. And suddenly, Arthur Levitt Jr.'s Securities and Exchange Commission had begun to make noises about challenging the largely self-regulatory system for accountants. Earlier that summer, Levitt's new chief accountant, Lynn Turner, had visited Andersen execu-tives and members of the Big 5 firms as part of a meet-and-greet be-fore he took over in the new position. He indicated that the SEC was paying very close attention to the spate of earnings scandals.

In response to the various pressures, the three Risk Manage-ment executives called a meeting in Chicago for August 24. The goal was to formulate an action plan that would reduce Firm risks in 1998 audits, since, they said in a memo, recent media reports about fraud and "cooking the books" were raising concerns about Andersen and the entire auditing profession. The meeting would go over the possible causes of fraud and consider what the Firm might do about it, both internally and with the SEC.

Although the meeting was mostly for senior partners, practice directors, and members of the legal department, I was invited at the suggestion of Toby Bishop, a partner in the Chicago fraud practice and a Brit known best around the office for his cold-weather attire of velvet-collared tweed coat, bowler hat, muffler, and umbrella. Toby primarily did research and development in the area of fraud prevention and detection, and had been talking to the committee about developing a fraud-prevention program for audit clients and enhancing the current risk-assessment system for new clients with some items that better identify the potential for fraud.

The Ethics group had, on our own, been developing some tools to look at ethical concerns in potential and present audit clients. These were designed to broadly assess a company's ethical vulner-abilities and to determine whether companies had in place the pro-cedures required by the Federal Sentencing Guidelines for Orga-nizations. We had drafted a set of proposed additional questions to the risk-assessment system. Toby and I had discussed our parallel projects—more often competitively than collaboratively—so I was surprised, but pleased, when I got the invitation to attend just a few days before the meeting. Greg Jonas also set up a conference call a few days later to discuss how the Ethics group's work could be included in the ongoing risk-management project.

Reading the premeeting preparation materials and agenda, I was impressed to see a brief analysis of the current business context and the possible actions: The fanfare at the Business Audit meetings had been all about client risk, never mentioning Firm risk. But these materials seemed to signify a real attempt by partners to take a serious look at troubling issues. The outline defined the various types of risk (reputation, litigation, regulatory) that financial reporting failures caused or could cause for the Firm. Presciently, it noted as part of the business context for the fourth quarter of 1998 that the Firm needed to be prepared for "big impacts of aggressive accounting [that] will be felt when [the] economy tanks."

Looked at four years later, it was a perfect road map of everything that could (and would) go wrong at the Firm, from the reputational risk related to congressional hearings and SEC investigations to the costs of litigation to the increased time and money pressures on engagement teams, and, of course, the potential problems from aggressive accounting. The memo expressed concerns about the client, about the Firm, about analysts, the SEC, Congress, and Arthur Andersen employees' careers. The only omission—and it was a glaring one—was the Firm's responsibility to the investor.

I arrived at the O'Hare Westin, enthusiastic and newly optimistic. Until now, our group's efforts in regard to risk assessment and management had been completely self-generated and relatively unnoticed. But this meeting seemed to play directly to our skills. We all hoped there might be an opportunity to help address some of the problems we saw as rampant. The invitation had been sent to about fourteen partners, including Kutsenda, Goolsby, Jonas, and Don Dreyfus—one of the Firm's top lawyers and the man who would later supervise Nancy Temple, the lawyer whose Enron-related notes convinced the jury to convict Andersen of obstruction of justice. The Firm's top leadership, including Joe Berardino, Steve Samek, Jim Wadia, and Mike Bennett, received copies of the materials.

We met in a small hotel conference room and sat around rectangular fold-out tables arranged in a square, with a blackboard in the front of the room and the ubiquitous coffee and bagels. The quarters were close and stuffy, which may have contributed to what felt like a lack of oxygen in the room. Despite the content of the meeting, the tone was calm and businesslike, with no particular sense of urgency. Bob Kutsenda led the meeting, standing in front of the blackboard and laying out the various fraud risks. He was a mild, serious, and sallow-complected man, whose presentation style was a perfect match for his appearance. He had a perpetual look of worry on his face and never smiled (although I didn't know it then, at the time he was under SEC investigation with regard to Waste Management). Never, however, did he convey a sense of impending doom.

After a lengthy discussion of problems and possible root causes, the meeting turned to focus almost solely on the risk of client fraud—and, of course, the impact on the Firm. Toby presented his ideas for a client fraud-prevention program, and I was invited to say a few words about the work that our group was doing. Everyone responded politely but noncommittally, and at the end of the day another full-day meeting was set for September 1, one week later, to work on action steps. It seemed to me that everyone was much more energetic when discussing possible root causes in the external environment than they were when it came to internal pressures like revenue demands and partner units.

That same week, the external temperature went up another notch. On August 26, Lynn Turner met with some members of the Auditing Standards Board, a senior committee of the AICPA, including some Andersen partners, and mentioned several concerns. One of them, according to a memo circulated afterward to the risk-management committee, wondered where the auditors had been during all of the recently announced frauds. The Andersen partner who wrote the memo noted that Turner seemed interested in a cooperative relationship with accountants, but that he also expected to see some real action taken to address the spate of fraud cases. Also at the meeting, according to the memo, a member of the Public Oversight Board, a self-regulating group for the industry, emphasized that the problems popping up were more about audit execution than standards. A few weeks later, the SEC announced new rules that defined "improper professional conduct" by accountants. With these, the SEC had much more power to censure, suspend, or bar accountants from auditing.

On August 28, Natalie Green Giles and I spent about an hour and a half on a call with Greg Jonas to discuss our work in the context of the meeting. Jonas asked that I make a brief presentation at the September 1 meeting, looking at the range of ethical concerns an audit firm might address with a client. Prereading materials for the meeting were again distributed, including minutes of an August 5 Risk Management Executive Committee meeting raising some internal concerns. One was the Document Retention, Elimination, and Destruction policy. "Overall, the firm is retaining too much information," the memo read, noting that a task force had been formed to make recommendations. Clearly, the Firm viewed "too much information" as a risk. The minutes also referred to an internal focus group that had found "a gap" between how auditors were compensated and rewarded and the need to evaluate risk. The Firm appeared to understand that what it was asking its auditors to do and what it was paying them to do were not the same things—that partners were being incentivized not on their risk-assessment skills, but rather on the business that they brought in, risky or not.

The document most important for the upcoming meeting was a draft of a plan to lessen the Firm's risk from financial reporting problems. It was an impressive piece of work. It listed action items by root cause, organized around three potential motivators, the type of action, and, finally, the timing of such an action. The causes included the fact that the market pummels companies that disappoint on earnings, and that the CFO's and controller's role had become more about helping to make the numbers than keeping track of them. Then it moved to auditor risks, noting that audit partners were often assessed on how satisfied their client was, and that partners sometimes felt pressure to keep the client happy at all costs as a result. The members of the committee who had composed this document seemed to understand exactly what was happening within the Firm.

We met at the O'Hare Hilton, and again the group was relaxed and professional. We went through all of the problems as well as proposed internal and external action steps in a fairly orderly and intellectual manner. No one said anything particularly startling, nor was there any evident sense of panic about what we were discussing, although there did seem to be a sense of resignation that some of these risks were simply inherent in such a pressured environment. The idea was to come up with possible short- and long-term solutions to keep the Firm from getting in trouble. Although the risks were spelled out graphically, they still seemed abstract and far away. The chance of a congressional investigation into accounting, for example, was judged unlikely without more major scandals.

After a brief review of the previous meeting, Greg invited me to give our group's presentation. My goal was to review the action plans proposed and to elaborate in some areas. I urged broader preventive action, since much of the fraud initiative focused on things that had already gone wrong, and also suggested additional risks such as increasing harassment suits in Latin America and the increasing number of companies that were piling on new acquisitions, often with insufficient due diligence.

The presentation seemed to be well received, and it yielded a formal assignment for our group. During the meeting, Kutsenda distributed the draft of a "Cooking the Books—Audit Alert" memo that was to be sent out sometime in the next month or two to all U.S. audit personnel, from partners to staff. The committee members discussed the fact that it was often difficult to get people to pay attention to Lotus Notes messages. Kutsenda then asked me if our group might be able to help design a memo that people would pay attention to and that would communicate the gravity of the Firm's concerns. We eagerly signed on.

The Risk Management Executive Committee seemed to be moving forward. Three days after the meeting, an initial action plan was distributed to all the attendees. There were two parts to the memo—an "agreed upon" action plan and a list of possible additional actions. It had been decided that the Firm would require an extended consultation with senior-level partners on all audits above a certain level of risk by October 31, 1998, addressing issues such as fraud, when to issue a going-concern opinion, aggressive interpretation of accounting rules, meetings with the Audit Committee, and client retention. This extra consultation would be required both at the end of audit planning and before sign-off. For maximum-risk clients, the engagement managers, partner, and concurring partner also had to meet with the audit division head and the audit practice director. For certain high-risk audits, they had to go even farther up the chain. We were also sent a list of short- and long-term internal and external actions, with instructions to rank the priority of the various possibilities.

I ranked the action steps and sent the memo back to Greg Jonas, trying to emphasize the point that the planned actions made sense, but only in the context of understanding the culture of the Firm and its relationship to the client. For example, I agreed strongly with the idea of adding a question asking whether senior management was pressuring a client to make its numbers to all fraud and risk-assessment tools used in an audit. I stressed, however, that getting an honest answer to this question required a lot more work than a simple survey. Another suggestion was to implement and better communicate the idea that restatements would be harmful to one's career. I saw this as motivating partners and managers to do anything to avoid a restatement rather than encouraging them to force a client to do one if problems were found. I noted that such harsh measures probably wouldn't be helpful. Unless part of a comprehensive program, they might actually inhibit change, I wrote.

Next Natalie designed and revised the "Cooking the Books" memo to make sure it was perceived as critically important and not just another piece of junk in the inbox. The point of the memo was to make everyone aware of the growing risk of accounting fraud and what to look for as an auditor or consultant. Yet making sure this actually happened was no insignificant task, because one of Arthur Andersen's biggest communications problems was the sheer barrage of Lotus Notes memos, instructions, voice mails, and other materials that we had to look forward to every morning. The amount of information we received was truly unfathomable, with no way to distinguish between a new audit rule and an invitation to a company picnic. In fact, a consultant I hired to work with us for 56 hours a month eventually decided to quit—not because of the work, but because, as she said, "you are paying me primarily to read e-mails. Right now it is taking me probably forty hours a month just to get through all of the stuff that comes through. I can't believe you want to be paying me for that."

The voice mails weren't much better, particularly those that came from Steve Samek. Everyone dreaded getting them, because he was truly one of the most long-winded, blustery, inefficient message-leavers I have ever encountered. Because he ran the U.S. practice, his messages would jump the queue, so you couldn't get to your own voice mails without listening to him first, all the way through. It was like that famous Dudley Moore skit in which he plays the piano, appears to finish, and then starts all over again— fifteen or twenty times. Many of us did eventually discover that you could press "#" and skip to the end of the message—saving us long stretches of time that might be better used helping clients.

Our group suggested a unique visual presentation, with a color and background that would make this Cooking the Books memo stand out from the slush pile, and a bold heading showing that this was a top priority for the Firm. We also made a strong recommen- dation that the memo address the problems related to *implementing* the new policies, such as concerns about possible cost overruns, the difficulty of raising sensitive issues with clients, and, internally, for managers with their partners. We suggested a Lotus Notes response mechanism, so that the leadership would know who received the memo. Finally, we recommended having a more concrete support system for people to use if in fact they spotted potential fraud, which, naturally, would be a very stressful and possibly terrifying experience. The draft memo had just the standard "If you have any questions, please contact your Audit Division Head" and so on. "What if someone contacts one of these individuals and that person does not have a reasonable answer to the question?" we wrote.

Ultimately, in October 1998, the memo went out, under the names of Berardino, Samek, and Goolsby, with a catchy bold font but no color, and no greater attention to the realistic barriers, or to the thing that worried me the most—what to do if a young staff member or manager actually found a problem. If there was a problem with the culture itself, we wouldn't be able to change things with these memos. Waste Management, to take one example, had made use of consultations of higher-ups—none of whom forced the Firm to take a stand.

Overall, my experience at the Risk Management Executive Committee had been positive, and it seemed that there was finally some awareness of the fact that the Firm was sailing in treacherous waters. "We knew years ago that fraud by management was the killer, the thing that was most cancerous in an audit, and that the audit profession was not doing enough to detect fraud," said Jonas in a recent interview. "We thought we were on the leading edge of what auditors should be doing." Yet apart from the Cooking the Books memo and an earlier note on how to deal with going-concern issues, I am not aware of any significant internal steps that were taken on the action plan in the following year, particularly those that had been classified as more long term or cultural in nature. Perhaps they were sent and I lost them in the crush of memos. But if such was the case, it is likely that few others noticed them either.

Looking back, I think this was a critical juncture for the Firm, a point at which great leadership could truly have made a difference. Yet I also acknowledge the other pressures on the partners. Becoming a tougher audit firm might have meant losing some major clients, and that would have had a direct financial impact on their livelihood. So the leaders did what, unfortunately, many leaders do when times are tough: They punted the ball. They released a few warning memos and essentially crossed their fingers and hoped everything would work out. It didn't—not for the Firm, not for its thousands of worldwide employees, not for its clients, and not for the investors, who trusted that the numbers they read were accurate. Yes, it would have taken a special leader to stand up to all of these groups and his own partners and acknowledge that something was spinning out of control. Such leaders are indeed rare. At Arthur Andersen, they didn't exist.

Of the Cooking the Books memo's authors, Samek had allegedly been briefed (and had signed off) on the issues at Waste Management, Goolsby would lose his position during the Enron scandal, and Berardino would resign after living through the criminal indictment of his Firm. These men were not ignorant: They were fully cognizant that the Firm was at risk of being embroiled in more and more earnings scandals. They tried, nominally, to warn the Firm with these memos. Yet they did not or could not change the culture to provide the incentives for people to spot—and raise—problems. They didn't ask the Firm to take a hard look at its own behavior, but rather placed the blame externally, on regulators and on bad clients. At the same time they asked their staff to be vigilant, top executives were tightening the screws on budgets, boosting revenue targets, and, possibly, approving potentially questionable numbers with top clients.

To me, the Cooking the Books memo represents what could have been for Andersen. It should have been a start, not an end, to solving a major problem. There could have been a detailed internal plan that addressed these critical issues and put the Firm back in a powerful leadership position within the industry. There could have been public recognition and reward for those who had the guts to stand up when things were wrong. But there wasn't. There was only a memo.

● ● ●

And then came yet another major distraction. Although no one seemed too worried at the meetings, there suddenly was a real possibility of regulatory action against the Big 5, thanks to a shift in the point of view of SEC chairman Levitt, a patrician yet relatively liberal investor whose father had been New York's comptroller. Levitt, along with Sandy Weill, Arthur Carter, and Roger Berlind, founded the investment firm eventually known as Smith Barney, and had been at the helm of the SEC since 1993. He had made a name for himself as a reformer by changing the makeup of the boards of the NASDAQ and other exchanges to be more representative of the public investors, and by making a push for better accounting rules relating to derivatives.

But the Big 5 hadn't viewed him as someone likely to take on the profession itself. Even before Levitt had come to town, the industry had enjoyed a string of years in which few new rules or regulations were issued, and the ones that had been attempted, such as treating stock options as an expense on the income statement, had been roundly defeated. The economy was booming, the market had made people rich, and as we all know all too well today, the appetite for regulation is greatest in a bust, when people have lost big and are furious about it, not in a period where everyone thinks they've got a comfortable seat on the gravy train.

The industry had it all wrong. According to one former senior SEC official, Levitt began to grow concerned over the attitude of the firms back in 1994, when the Financial Accounting Standards Board, the industry's rule-setting group, proposed counting stock options as an expense on a company's income statement. The bitter fight that ensued destroyed people's careers and unified many of the country's most influential companies and politicians behind the principle that stock options were crucial to the success of our economy—and that nothing could or should be done that would make them more difficult to use. Levitt, who originally supported the expensing of options, ultimately caved in and told the Board to back down because he felt the political costs would be too great. He did, however, pay close attention to how involved the accounting firms had become in defending big business. "From the Commission's perspective," said the official, "they were taking the sides of the clients," rather than the side of the investor.

Levitt began to feel that the firms had lost their supposed neutrality when it came to business issues. Whatever their clients wanted was what they wanted. Natural for a lobbying firm, perhaps, but for an accounting firm? Conscious of the special role that accountants played in our society, he wondered if everyone else had forgotten about it. At the same time, the SEC looked at the growing portion of revenues coming from consulting at the major firms and grew ever more concerned about a conflict of interest, just as Congress had during the 1970s, when it began to question the growing consulting practices of audit firms. In a 1996 speech, Levitt said, "I caution the industry, if I may borrow a biblical phrase, not to 'gain the whole world, and lose [its] own soul.'" No longer, he remarked, were there people like Leonard Spacek in the industry who saw the need for true reform and spoke out. Instead, the industry acted like a bunch of children with one favorite word: No.

Levitt was also upset by the reaction of the big accounting firms to the creation, by the SEC and the AICPA, the accounting industry group, of the Independent Standards Board in 1997. The board was supposed to look at issues relating to ethics and independence within the accounting industry and make new rules to address them. The two firms to oppose the creation of the Independent Standards Board were KPMG—which, according to Lynn Turner, had several senior executives who believed that the SEC had no true right to regulate the industry—and Arthur Andersen. They lost, but then a vicious fight erupted between the SEC and the industry when it came to figuring out who would serve on the board. Andersen, like the others, wanted as many people from the profession as possible, as opposed to public figures with no connections to industry.

Ultimately, a compromise gave the Independent Standards Board four public and four private members (the CEOs of KPMG, Ernst & Young, and PricewaterhouseCoopers, and Barry Melancon, head of the influential and change-phobic AICPA). Gridlock ensued. "It was doomed from the beginning," says Russell Horwitz, a former senior adviser to Levitt. Levitt ultimately refused to attend the Board's inaugural meeting. The Board began to address the perceived conflict between auditing and consulting, but in January 2000 threw up its hands, saying it was a major issue that demanded the SEC's perspective and ability to look at the pressures going on within the industry. With the approval of the accounting profession, including Andersen, and the SEC, the Board would disband in 2001.

Yet Levitt hesitated, at first, to move against the industry. He had already been through some bruising political battles, and he knew he faced a well-funded, ferocious, politically connected adversary in the Big 5, all of which were substantial and regular contributors to the campaigns of such influential lawmakers as Rep.

Billy Tauzin, who in 2001 became the chairman of the House Energy and Commerce Committee, and the failed 2000 Senate campaign of John Ashcroft, who later became Attorney General. But in 1998, a trifecta of spectacular frauds hit the news. Following Waste Management and Sunbeam came Cendant, an Ernst & Young–audited client and the result of a merger of two firms—one of which, CUC International, turned out to have cooked its books to the tune of more than $500 million over three years. Levitt and his team saw an opening. In the late summer of 1998, they held a retreat in which they resolved to push for changes to boards, particularly audit committees, and their relationships with auditors and management.

That September, Levitt gave a speech titled "The Numbers Game" at New York University, in which he put auditors, securities analysts, companies, and boards of directors on notice that a major shift was underway:

> If a company fails to provide meaningful disclosure to investors about where it has been, where it is and where it is going, a damaging pattern ensues. The bond between shareholders and the company is shaken; investors grow anxious: Prices fluctuate for no discernible reasons; and the trust that is the bedrock of our capital markets is severely tested.

Levitt discussed several of the most popular forms of earnings management, from "big bath" restructuring charges (one of the techniques that would soon be used by WorldCom to mask its problems), to the premature recognition of revenue (Sunbeam), to the abuse of the concept of materiality (Waste Management). He called for changes in the accounting rules, more enforcement on the part of the government, better and more qualified audit committees, and better work from outside auditors, and he announced the formation of a blue-ribbon panel to study the issues and come up with recommendations within the next few months. The culture of focusing on short-term earnings at the expense of everything else had to change, he said. Levitt also asked the Public Oversight Board, a unit of the AICPA, to put together a panel to dismantle and analyze the audit process itself, later called the Panel on Audit Effectiveness. Levitt continued:

> I need not remind auditors they are the public's watchdog in the financial reporting process. We rely on auditors to put something like the Good Housekeeping Seal of Approval on the information investors receive. The integrity of that information must take priority over a desire for cost efficiencies or competitive advantage in the audit process. . . . Today, American markets enjoy the confidence of the world. How many half-truths, and how much accounting sleight-of-hand, will it take to tarnish that faith?

To the comfortable world of the Big 5 and all of its clients across Corporate America, the speech was a warning shot. Several CEOs of major companies, such as Sandy Weill of Citigroup and Lou Gerstner of IBM, contacted Levitt to tell him he'd gone too far, even though, according to Turner, they had been invited to attend more than a month earlier and some of their companies' executives participated in the information-gathering meetings the SEC had prior to the speech. A few weeks later, I received a phone call from a partner in the Firm's Boston office who had been approached by former New York governor Mario Cuomo. Cuomo needed help with a speech he was preparing on ethics related to the Levitt speech. Natalie and I prepared a lengthy, detailed memo for Governor Cuomo, with a copy to the Boston partner. We never heard a word from anyone after that, nor do we know if Cuomo included our information in his address. But at the time I thought that the Firm might be able to capitalize on this interest and become an educator to leaders, investors, and the general public.

At Andersen, no one knew Levitt's speech was coming, but they clearly understood that a sea change was happening. Already, the Risk Management Executive Committee meetings had seemed focused on coming up with a strategy that would keep the Firm out of the regulatory spotlight. Now, should the Firm actively oppose what the SEC was proposing, or instead get out in front of the issue and support the parts of Levitt's plan that didn't have much impact on the auditors?

After the speech, the SEC moved to launch its Blue Ribbon Committee on Improving the Effectiveness of Corporate Audit Committees, featuring such big names as John Whitehead, former chairman of Goldman Sachs; Jim Schiro, head of Pricewaterhouse-Coopers; and Philip Laskawy of Ernst & Young (there were no Andersen representatives). For several months afterward, many issues that were important to Andersen and its rivals—changes in the accounting for materiality, new rules for audit committees, and so on—took center stage. They required participation and analysis, but none of them were life-or-death issues. With the obvious exception of the ongoing investigation into the problems at Waste Management and Sunbeam, the heat was off, and Andersen could go back to its favorite activities—cross-selling services and fighting with Andersen Consulting.

In the spring of 1999, the Blue Ribbon Committee presented its recommendations, including the requirement that all public companies with a market capitalization greater than $200 million have audit committees of independent directors, three of whom had to possess financial skills, and one person with accounting training. The outside auditors would from then on be accountable to the board of directors—not management—and the committee would have to assess, with the outside auditors, the quality of the accounting as well as the numbers themselves. In December 1999, the requirements were approved by the major stock exchanges and phased in over the course of the next year.

Publicly, Andersen did back many of the Blue Ribbon Committee's conclusions, such as the increased responsibilities and skills of a company's audit committee. "[Andersen was] very supportive of what we did on audit committees," said Turner. In 1999, Berardino and Jonas coauthored a piece in *Financial Executive* magazine called "Power to the Audit Committee People." "Audit committees alone have the combination of insider knowledge, an expressed responsibility to represent shareholder interests, and, perhaps most important, the power of oversight," they wrote. Obviously, this was a reform that would put more responsibility on a company's board to investigate problems—and not necessarily on its outside auditor—but the Firm did take a leadership role in this area. It also backed stricter rules on materiality, says Turner, and was more supportive on that concept than the other firms were.

Yet when the SEC turned with a near-religious zeal to the issue of auditor independence and the idea that the fast-growing consulting groups might be hurting that independence, Andersen lashed out like a wounded animal. "There was only one thing they were intransigent on," said Turner, "and that was auditor independence. Their basic message was always consistent: No changes that would restrict the services auditors provide."

It was quite a far cry from the approach of Leonard Spacek, Arthur Andersen's leader in the 1950s. Spacek took on his own industry with the ferocity of a pit bull, warning that the myriad of interpretations and the lack of a true ruling body would lead to trouble. "I would like to tell you that our profession is standing steadfast to our principles and responsibilities," he said in a speech. "This I cannot do. . . . I find that the most serious problems of our profession are caused by our indulgence. . . . We just wait for the catastrophe, because we do not have a sufficiently strong or self-appraising accounting profession to right this public wrong before, not after, serious injury results." Spacek died in 2000 at the age of ninety-two, just before the catastrophe he had warned of finally occurred.

But the SEC's ammunition was building. One key event was the announcement in January 1999 that a group of employees at one PricewaterhouseCoopers office were found to have owned stocks in companies that the firm audited—a clear violation of the independence standards every firm was supposed to live by. At first, it was called an oversight resulting from the 1998 merger between Price Waterhouse and Coopers & Lybrand, but a 1999 investigation discovered that the violations were rampant throughout the organization, going all the way up to Jim Schiro, head of the firm. "There was widespread total noncompliance," said Greg Corso, a former senior counsel at the SEC. PricewaterhouseCoopers settled and accepted a censure before the widespread nature of the violations came to light. Suddenly there was a gun, and smoke seemed to be curling out of it.

Another break for the SEC was the fact that the Big 5 suddenly had very different business objectives. In February 2000, Ernst &

Young, sensing trouble to come and facing huge pension payments for its aging partner base, sold its consulting unit to Cap Gemini for $11 billion. Now its head, Philip Laskawy, signaled a willingness to support the SEC if it moved to limit the consulting work auditors could do. It seemed to be a classic case of realpolitik: If Ernst & Young didn't consult anymore, why should anyone else? Then there was PricewaterhouseCoopers, which, knowing that the SEC had it corralled in the independence matter, was in no position to resist. It was time for battle.

In late 1999 and early 2000, the SEC began to hold a series of meetings with the heads of the Big 5 to discuss placing major restrictions on the types of consulting and nonaudit services they could offer. The main goals from the Commission's perspective were to completely ban auditors from providing information technology consulting and internal audit services to their audit clients. These were two of the most profitable consulting services offered by the industry. In the throes of the bull market and the New Economy, the other three firms were in no mood to make a deal. KPMG had already been planning to spin off an interest in its consulting firm in an IPO, but had initially hoped to maintain control of the board and the profits. Deloitte's consulting arm was growing like gangbusters. And Andersen, with a leadership team of Grafton, Samek, and Berardino, was 100 percent opposed. Grafton, in particular, opposed any type of compromise, Turner remembered. From the Firm's perspective, it had to fight. War had been the default setting at Andersen for a long time anyway, between the infighting and the ongoing battle with Andersen Consulting. The Firm had worked so hard to re-create a profitable consulting unit. To risk losing that one, too, seemed unfathomable.

It was going to be an epic struggle. But Levitt was concerned in early 2000 that the SEC, which was already working through the corporate governance changes and the fight to implement Regulation FD (full disclosure)—which limited the amount of private guidance a company could give analysts—might be accused of overregulating. Then there was the political muscle of the Big 5, who were supported by some of the most powerful people in Congress, such as Tauzin, Rep. Michael Oxley, chairman of the House Financial

Services Committee, and Senator Charles Schumer. "We had a series of debates about whether to go forward with new rules on auditor independence," said Horwitz. One day, Levitt looked at a copy of a business history book by Joel Seligman called *Transformation on Wall Street* and swallowed hard. He saw a very disturbing parallel between his tenure and the SEC of the 1970s, when so many business frauds caused investors to lose their faith in the honesty of corporations—and, as a result, in the stock market. Levitt saw how many of the same issues had emerged yet again—and decided that it was time for resolution.

Things got very hot very quickly. The Panel on Audit Effectiveness, also referred to as the O'Malley Panel, came up with more than 200 recommendations when it released its report in 2000. Its conclusion was that "most, if not all" of the auditing standards needed to be rewritten and that "forensic auditing," the in-depth analysis used when a fraud is suspected, be made part of every audit. It also recommended that the Public Oversight Board, a group formed in 1977 to oversee the accounting profession, be given more power.

The industry's response said it all. In December 1999, the SEC had asked the Public Oversight Board to perform a special investigation into whether the major accounting firms were complying with SEC and professional rules governing auditor independence. In late April 2000, a committee of the AICPA, dominated by senior partners in the Big 5, including Andersen, voted to suspend all funding for the Public Oversight Board's investigation. This would have been the first time ever that the board itself was going to inspect the firms as opposed to the firms inspecting one another in "peer reviews." The peer reviews were more of a backslapping exercise than anything else, since no Big 5 firm ever issued anything other than a clean bill of health to its peers. It was clear who held the purse strings.

Ultimately, the suspension of the Public Oversight Board's funding and Deloitte & Touche's "clean" peer review of Andersen, just weeks before Enron imploded, put the Board out of business in March 2002. It was another reason why, later that year, Congress, through the Sarbanes-Oxley Act, established a new Public Accounting Oversight Board independent of the profession, with outside funding and powers to write auditing standards, inspect the accounting firms, and take disciplinary actions when necessary. Unfortunately—and predictably—the early efforts of the board to choose a leader ended in a haze of political infighting and, ultimately, the resignation of SEC Chairman Harvey Pitt in November 2002.

The SEC met with all of the firms before announcing, in May 2000, that it was going to issue proposed rules and put them out for public comment a month later. The plan was to ban accountants from offering their audit clients internal audit and IT consulting services, and to require that company fees paid to auditors for nonaudit services be disclosed to the investing public. To Andersen, KPMG, and Deloitte, the SEC was a bully kicking sand in their face. Before putting out the rules, Levitt, then-SEC general counsel Harvey Goldschmid, and Turner flew to New York for a meeting to tell the firms that the rules were coming the following week. Levitt urged the three to keep the lines of communication open and to work behind the scenes rather than debate the issue on the front pages of national newspapers. The three were joined by the AICPA's combative leader, Barry Melancon, although he hadn't been invited to the meeting. "We might as well have been in an icehouse," Turner remembered. Grafton looked straight at Levitt and said, "Arthur, if you go ahead with this, it will be war."

The SEC had hoped to keep the discussions behind closed doors, but the accountants had other plans. They decided it was time to call in the dogs—the members of Congress that they had long supported for moments like this one—and the lobbyists they had worked with in the past, such as Clark & Weinstock, with former congressmen like Vic Fazio and Vin Weber on its payroll. Suddenly, Congress began to paint the SEC as a gang of oppressors. A bipartisan collection of big names, from Senator Schumer to Representative Tauzin to Representative Tom Bliley, attacked the SEC for moves that could dismantle the suddenly shaky stock market, which had plunged precipitously in April 2000, and for offering such a short comment period on the rules (75 days). In a lengthy letter to Levitt dated April 17, 2000, from the House Commerce Committee, the signatories (Tauzin, Oxley, and Bliley) threatened hearings on the SEC proposal if they didn't get satisfactory answers to a list of 15 multipart, complex questions such as this one, No. 2:

> What empirical evidence, studies or economic analysis does the SEC possess that demonstrates accounting firms providing tax advice to audit clients are less independent than those firms that do not provide such advice? Are there any specific administrative findings that have concluded the provision of tax advice resulted in a specific audit failure by the same firm?

Hearings were, indeed, held by Senator Rod Grams, featuring Senator Phil Gramm and others castigating the SEC for what they called a lack of evidence supporting the rules. Political blood spilled, but neither side would budge. On July 26, the three firms announced:

> The Commission is rushing to judgment by means of a process that is fundamentally flawed and without any factual justification. Moreover, we are very concerned that the proposal will undermine audit quality and have a number of other unintended consequences that will injure investors. We believe that the new measures recently implemented to enhance the role of audit committees in ensuring auditor independence should be allowed to work before a rule of this magnitude and complexity is considered.

Still, the SEC pressed ahead. Politically, a compromise would be better, but Levitt was having a terrible time even getting any members of the group to show up at a meeting. Then, in August, the puzzle pieces shifted again when Andersen's arbitration decision was announced—and, to the shock of everyone, the accounting side lost big. In a heartbeat, Andersen, shorn of Andersen Consulting, went from being the world's largest professional services firm to the fifth-largest—and one with relatively bare coffers at that. In the confusion that ensued (Wadia resigned by noon on the day of the announcement and Salvatore replaced him as interim CEO of Andersen), the Firm continued to stonewall. In testimony before Congress on September 20, Joe Berardino defiantly declared:

> The future of the profession is bright and will remain bright—as long as the Commission does not force us into an outdated role trapped in the old economy. Unfortunately, the proposed rule threatens to do exactly that. A broad scope of practice is critical to enable us to keep up with the new business environment, attract, motivate and keep top talent, and thereby provide high quality audits in the future.

Yet behind the scenes, the Firm's position was shifting. I can only surmise that given the accounting scandals it already knew about, and its suddenly vulnerable financial position, some members of the leadership, or Berardino, at least, felt it would behoove the Firm to have a decent relationship with the SEC. If a compromise couldn't be reached, the firms might have sued the Commission, and another lawsuit probably was not something Andersen was eager to take on that point. Until late 1999 or early 2000, the point person for Arthur Andersen with the SEC had been Grafton. He didn't take a leadership role within the Big 5, but rather stayed within the bloc of KPMG, Deloitte & Touche, and Andersen.

Suddenly, Berardino began to emerge as a force within the Firm. Grafton was on the way out. Samek, once a contender for the top slot, was now discredited owing to his involvement with Waste Management, and Salvatore, though seen as a major player, said he had no intention of taking the top slot on a permanent basis. Berardino, head of North American Audit and Business Advisory services, filled the void. I had had a tempestuous relationship with him, but I recognized that he was an excellent politician. He was smooth—not in look as much as in style—and he did convey the appearance of someone who wanted to make things happen.

One day in October, the Firm blinked. Berardino called Levitt, wondering whether there was any room for compromise on the proposed ban on internal audit and information technology consulting. Hoping to get negotiations rolling again, the SEC came up with a counterproposal—one that ultimately worked, but one that, given the events of today, seems awfully tame. Rather than an outright ban on the services, a firm would have to meet a list of restrictive criteria for each client in order to be allowed to perform the two services, such as making the company, not the auditor, manage and accept full responsibility for the project and make all the key decisions. Turner said the SEC believed that few companies would accept these conditions and, as a result, would opt to not use their auditors for these services. Internal audit consulting also wouldn't be banned, but rather restricted to 40 percent of the total for any audit client and subjected to the same criteria.

There was no movement from the Gang of Three—Andersen, Deloitte, and KPMG—but now PricewaterhouseCoopers and Ernst & Young, the two compromisers, got wind of the possibility of a deal and met with Levitt in a fury. "They were for a business deal. They were never for investors," said a former SEC official. "When it looked like we might be cutting a deal with the other three, they said we were cutting them off at the knees and backstabbing them." (A month earlier, PricewaterhouseCoopers had entered into talks to sell its consulting division to Hewlett-Packard for $18 billion, so it, like Ernst & Young, wanted the other Firms out of the business.) After this meeting, Levitt wavered, torn by the anger and bitterness from the two firms, but regrouped the next day and moved on.

Time was growing short. The presidential election was too close to call, and the SEC worried that a Republican victory would undo everything it had worked for. The firms, for their part, saw the election as an escape hatch. They managed to get Congress to ask for a delay in the rule making until after the election—when it was widely believed Levitt would retire. So the SEC decided to go for broke, announcing that the day before the election they would put through the final rules—either the compromise or the original, more restrictive plan. Then the presidential election paralyzed the entire country. The following Friday morning, Jim Copeland, head of Deloitte, asked for a final meeting at Levitt's office. Grafton attended by telephone, but Berardino, in Paris, wasn't available. The SEC offered the criteria rather than an outright ban, but stuck to one critical point: that the final rule would have a definition of independence based on whether or not a "reasonably informed" investor would consider an auditor's action to have the "appearance" of independence. "In our mind," said Turner, "it all got down to whether or not investors *believed* the auditor to be independent. That was the crux for us."

The three firms asked for an hour alone to hash it out, but failed. KPMG refused to support the appearance clause, saying that the definition of independence should be up to the auditor. "In the back of our mind," said Turner, "we had Waste Management, Sunbeam, et cetera. We had the evidence that showed you would have to be brain dead to let the fox guard the chicken coop." The SEC was going to try to go ahead with or without the firms' cooperation.

After the meeting ended that Friday, Levitt directed the staff to prepare two different rules for the commissioners to vote on—one that put in the SEC's original desires and one that included the compromise. And then the stars suddenly began to align. First, Berardino called from Paris, dismayed to hear that no deal had been reached, and, the following Monday morning, asked for some time to bring in both Deloitte and Andersen, at least. A few hours later he called back, saying the two firms would support the rule.

Within the same few hours, the news broke that PricewaterhouseCoopers' deal to sell its consulting arm to Hewlett-Packard had collapsed. Suddenly, PricewaterhouseCoopers' head, Schiro, the man who just two weeks earlier had been furious with Levitt, called him and said it might be in the best interest of the industry to make a deal. The SEC folks pressed the advantage: Turner added to the final rulemaking a requirement that companies disclose the amount of information technology consulting fees they had paid to their auditors and whether or not audit committees had had a formal discussion about auditor independence. After a tense conference call the next day, Ernst & Young's boss, Phil Laskawy, gave in too. With four of the Big 5 on board, the SEC declared victory— of sorts. Yes, it had put through strong regulations, but what it achieved, unfortunately, did little to halt the epidemic of fraud that was already spreading.

The motivations for Berardino's move are even today not entirely clear. Was it a realization that audit independence was truly at risk, a stark political move by Berardino to gain control of the Firm, or both? Was it a clear-eyed assessment of the facts, one that made him realize things wouldn't get any better? I don't know the answer, but I do know that Berardino managed to ride that compromise to success on both sides of the fence. On one hand, he earned the respect of Levitt, who later said that he was the most reasonable of the five executives to deal with, and on the other, he was suddenly seen as a leader within his industry.

Yet inside the Firm and in public, Berardino portrayed the deal as a victory for the industry. "We would have sued" if the SEC had put the rules through as originally planned, he claimed in an interview with *The Chicago Tribune.* "We didn't want to, but we would have." His perception inside the U.S. Firm, at least, as the man who had stood up to the SEC—not the one who made the final compromise—helped get him nominated to become Andersen Worldwide's chief executive. Five months after the arbitration decision, Berardino received 90 percent of the partner vote and took charge of a firm that, it turned out, was already in free fall. While Turner acknowledges Berardino's willingness to negotiate, he says that nothing would have happened without the failure of the PricewaterhouseCoopers deal with Hewlett-Packard. "It wasn't just Berardino," he recalled. "At the end of the day, Grafton, Samek, and Berardino were all businesspeople as opposed to public accountants. Meaning that their focus was more on running the business than on the concerns investors might have."

Trying to assess the winners and losers in retrospect is a tough thing to do. Certainly, Berardino was a short-term winner, although had he spent less time fighting and more time looking at the company he was about to run, he might not have been the long-term loser he is today. Nor did any political capital he gained with the SEC make an iota of difference once the U.S. Department of Justice began to consider an indictment. Levitt and his team were able to put through many important changes, but it was already too late for the reforms to take hold. Their worries were well-founded, but they didn't ultimately help the hundreds of thousands of people who lost their life savings. In the end, the tangle between the two Arthurs—Levitt and Andersen—was another distraction for the Firm, a convenient way to demonize the forces pushing for change from the outside and ignore the signs that the real change was needed from within.

# The Cobbler's Children

## 8

*The cobbler's children have no shoes.*

—OLD ADAGE

"S O YOU'RE WITH ARTHUR ANDERSEN NOW. I hear they don't do anything with ethics."

John Buckley smiled as he said those words to me and the telecommunications executive I was trying to pitch, but his voice had a hard edge. As I stood among rows of spangled dresses, feathered headdresses, and rows of purple and gold plastic beads at Mardi Gras World, the place where the most fabulous costumes and floats are stored, I wished I could slip on one of the outfits, down a Chivas or two, and melt away into the steamy New Orleans night. But I was at the gala dinner for the 1998 annual conference of the Ethics Officers Association, and Buckley had me in his crosshairs. Now at Raytheon, Buckley had been at Digital Equipment Company, a client of mine during my Harvard Business School days. He was saying to all within earshot what I knew to be true, and it made me cringe.

It is often said that the cobbler's children go shoeless. It's an old line, but, in this case, a very true one. Arthur Andersen, with KPMG the first of the then–Big 6 to sell ethics consulting services, was indeed barefoot when it came to its own conduct by the standards required by the Justice Department's Federal Sentencing

Guidelines for Organizations, and by my own standards as an "expert" in business ethics. And I, too, was getting blisters.

My job, as head of the Ethics and Responsible Business Practices group, was to sell other companies services that would help them act more responsibly. Yet I was constantly undermined in my attempts to do so by one simple fact: While we at Arthur Andersen thought it was important that *you,* the ethically challenged corporate client (who, more often than not, had its books audited by the Firm), get its house in order, we didn't feel the same compulsion to do any navel-gazing of our own. How do you sell as "essential" programs and services that your own firm refuses to embrace? How do you respond to the question "If this stuff is so necessary—and you're the best—how come your firm's not doing any of it?" When I pointed this out, I was seen as at best a nuisance and at worst a complainer who "simply didn't get the way things worked around here." Outside the Firm, I felt like an insincere spinmeister.

Arthur Andersen's lack of interest notwithstanding, ethics had become a hot topic almost everywhere else in the business world. By 1997, 95 percent of U.S. corporations had embraced the Justice Department's Guidelines by installing some kind of ethics program, an ethics officer, and a "mechanism for the prevention, detection, and reporting of criminal activity" and other wrongdoing. Also, several large not-for-profit organizations, such as the United Way, were implementing such programs, having themselves been exposed for their own poor ethical practices. The ethics business had grown dramatically since I first entered the field in 1978. There was more interest in the topic than I had ever seen before, but I was having more trouble tapping into that interest than ever before, too.

One result of all this activity was the establishment of the Ethics Officers Association (EOA), a "trade group" for executives with this title. Founded in 1992 at the Bentley College Center for Business Ethics by Mike Hoffman, the Center's director, and Craig Dreilinger, a consultant, with a membership of a dozen, by 1997 the group had become an independent organization of 283 members. (As of 2002, membership had grown to more than 800 companies.) These corporate ethics officers, drawn from legal departments, internal audit departments, or managerial ranks, banded together to define and develop their function—and to identify new needs and find new resources. The annual Ethics Officers meeting was a potential treasure trove to every business ethics consultant, a place where you could connect with just about every company in the world with an interest in ethics.

Mike Hoffman and I go way back, having met at the First Bentley Business Ethics Conference, which he organized in 1978. Over the years we have sat on panels together, participated in discussion groups, and shared ideas as professional colleagues. Ed Petry was someone I had known professionally since the mid-1980s. So it seemed no big deal for me, as head of the Ethics Group, to call Ed and request an invitation to the annual meeting. "Ed, I'd really like to come to the New Orleans meeting," I said. "Can you put my name on this list?" There was a long pause. A very long pause. "But Arthur Andersen doesn't have an ethics program or an ethics officer," Ed said, slowly and deliberately. I could feel my face getting hot. "That's not strictly true," I stammered, launching into the spin I had developed over the past months.

And it was not *technically* true. Arthur Andersen did pay a lot of attention to what it called "Independence and Ethics." Independence has been, for many years, one of the key SEC requirements for public accounting firms. What independence means for an accounting firm is the elimination, as much as possible, of real or potential conflicts of interest that might compromise the integrity of an audit. Independence relates to stock ownership or board membership of audited companies, loan and brokerage relationships, and other such activities. For example, no member of a public accounting or audit firm, be it partner or employee, could hold even one share of stock in any audit client. The reason for this is clear—to avoid any perception by the public that the way a firm conducts an audit is affected by its relationship with the client. At Arthur Andersen, this form of independence was an ingrained part of the culture.

But it wasn't that way for everyone. Accounting firms and independence got major media attention in 1999, when the newly merged firm of PricewaterhouseCoopers was found to have violated SEC independence standards by owning stock in lots of companies audited by the combined company. PwC was required to set up a $2.5 million fund to increase awareness of independence in the profession—a paltry slap on the wrist compared to Arthur Andersen's later punishment. It seems to me highly unlikely that that type of independence violation could have happened at Arthur Andersen, because of the way "independence" was defined and embedded in the firm's culture. However, other eyebrow-raising aspects of independence issues, like entertaining clients, golfing with them (often at AA's expense), and providing summer employment for clients' children, were not as ingrained. In fact, these activities, which were undertaken especially to build interdependence with the client, were always encouraged. In addition, when consulting activities grew and brought new possible conflicts of interest that could compromise auditor independence, the Firm did not—via e-mail, memo, voice mail, or additions to the Independence and Ethics binder—address the new reality.

While I was at Andersen, the point person at the Independence and Ethics Office was Sue Quinlan. Her office distributed the form we all had to sign annually listing banks we used, our mortgage holders, the investment firms we dealt with, mutual funds (though these were exempt from the ethics and independence requirements), new stock purchased, and so forth. Sue's office reviewed the documents and contacted anyone in violation of independence standards. So while Arthur Andersen didn't do anything about ethics specifically, and hadn't done anything at all to respond to the Justice Department's Federal Sentencing guidelines requirements, I was still within the bounds of truth when I responded to Ed Petry.

• • •

I arrived in New Orleans for the October conference convinced that I should probably keep a low profile, despite the fact that I was eager to see many old friends, former clients, and even a few potential new clients. Buckley quickly foiled my plan, stopping me cold with his comments. My potential client was, of course, all ears. Once again, I launched into my "not strictly true" patter, this time adding a now-standard part of my sales pitch: "And did you know that in 1987 Arthur Andersen spent $5 million developing and distributing an ethics program for undergraduate business majors?" I didn't mention the fact that the program had fizzled out in 1994 because of the Firm's partners' unwillingness to continue to fund it.

Buckley wasn't buying any of it. Perhaps Arthur Andersen's known arrogance and my own led him to delight in a small game of humiliation. Holding on to my arm (I guess so I wouldn't escape), he called over one of the PwC ethics managers and introduced us. "Why don't you tell Barbara what you all are doing over at PwC," Buckley chortled. "Maybe she could learn something." I smiled graciously and stood there awkwardly while I was instructed, utterly humiliated. It was a low moment personally, and I realized that not only did Arthur Andersen have nothing going on in the ethics field, but that everyone knew it—and thought worse of the Firm, and me, as a result.

Naive, stupid, co-opted, or simply stubborn, I kept plugging away. There was also the annual Business Ethics Conference sponsored by the Conference Board. I had been one of the speakers at the Board's first conference in 1988, leading two discussion sessions in which actors performed scenes from plays dealing with ethical issues in business. It was a great success, and yielded numerous opportunities for my firm. In the ensuing years I had chaired panel discussions and served as a speaker. As a source of potential new business clients, the Conference Board's Business Ethics Conference was right up there.

Earlier that year, in February 1998, I had called Jeff Kaplan, a New York attorney who was serving as coordinator for the ethics conference, and requested a spot somewhere on the May program. Jeff was blunt. Only speakers from companies with recognized ethics programs could appear on the conference roster, and yes, some independent "experts" would also speak, but I wasn't an independent expert anymore.

"There is a way you can speak next year at the 1999 conference," said Jeff. "Arthur Andersen can sponsor the Conference Board's Ethics Conference—$20,000 will take care of it—and then you can be on the program." (I'm not sure about the ethics of an ethics conference selling speaking slots, but given the land of slippery slopes I was living in, I didn't lose much sleep over it.) Spending $20,000 for what could be a client gold mine seemed like a no-brainer for me, but it would take a bite out of our group's budget. So I set up a meeting with Joe Berardino, who as head of audit for North America, could approve an expenditure in the name of the Firm. Sponsoring the conference would be prestigious for the Firm, I said, and I felt it was critical for Arthur Andersen to be seen as a leader in business ethics. I also told him how embarrassing it was for us to be considered deficient in this area. We were, after all, a place that thought straight and talked straight, right?

Joe's answer was short, to the point, and as smoothly dismissive as ever. "The Firm's not interested in supporting an ethics conference. If you want to do it, take it out of your budget." In the overall Arthur Andersen budget, an expenditure of $20,000 would have been negligible (or, to use a pet accounting phrase, "not material"). But there was no further discussion. He just turned me down flat. For me, $20,000 was a big deal, and I knew that my decision to spend money on something the Firm did not stand behind was likely to come back to haunt me. But I decided to do it anyway, partly because I really thought I could drum up business and partly to soothe my own bruised ego. These were, after all, my people, most of whom, I thought, respected me and my past work. Maybe the Firm—and I, by association—would look like players again if we sponsored the conference. I called Jeff Kaplan back and said we were in.

Our group appeared at the 1999 conference in full force. I was relieved—and inwardly troubled—to see the name Arthur Andersen splashed all over the conference literature. It felt hypocritical, but I was desperate for the exposure. At least the 150 or so companies there, more than half of which were in the Fortune 500, knew we were in the game. Yet we were pretty limited in what we could actually say, since presentation of client projects by consultants was strictly taboo. We did manage to get one of our clients onto a panel to talk about a project we'd done with them, but otherwise, we were simply the money folks. I learned that lesson all too well during the final session when the moderator, a longtime competitor of mine, responded to my raised hand with a sardonic quip that made me wince: "Sure, Barbara, take the floor. You paid for it."

•   •   •

Frustrated by my internal struggles and embarrassed by the fact that my former clients and associates in the business ethics community saw Arthur Andersen as a joke, I became increasingly unhappy, and so did my group. The seemingly constant humiliation, the endless conflicts with my "colleagues" within the Firm, and the consequent uphill battle to sell services began to take a toll on the relationships within the Ethics Group. Here was a team of highly educated, talented, and underpaid individuals, working at something they believed in and cared about, and getting nowhere fast. Our once cohesive group of eight began to fracture, with infighting about how to market our services, resentments over who was assigned to what project, and cliques that were beginning to resemble neighborhood gangs. All of their frustration and resentment began to focus on one target—me.

As the head of the group, I was supposed to be the rainmaker, bringing in big projects for the team to tackle. But I wasn't bringing in enough, and much of what I was bringing in didn't count to the Metro New York office. "They should be giving us work," wailed one manager. They should be giving *us* work? I suppose that would have been nice, but that wasn't the way it worked at Arthur Andersen. I was working so frantically at trying to sell, sell, sell that I lost my ability to be a good manager—and the group let me know it by deputizing Natalie Green Giles to tell me so. I knew it was true, but I was too exhausted to do anything about it. Instead, I lay awake many interminable nights, my mind spinning frantically to find some new business angles. Team members and others at the Firm made fun of my long voice-mail messages that invariably said "Received at 4:12 A.M." Yet I was too fried to motivate my team or myself. I was disrespected on the outside, thwarted on the inside, and now the only people I trusted were furious with me too. The pressure was almost intolerable.

But every time I felt like giving up, a little shred of hope would keep me hanging on a little bit longer. Sue Quinlan, of the Arthur Andersen Independence and Ethics Office, and I had spoken a couple times, and she had expressed genuine interest in what our group was doing. So in early 1998, she called me with an appealing suggestion. On her rounds of the major U.S.-based offices, Sue was coming to New York to deliver a talk on the importance of independence to the Metro New York managers. She had been allocated three hours, but said she had only enough material to last an hour. Would I like to take her remaining two hours to talk about ethical concerns within the Firm? I lunged at her offer. Not only was this an opportunity to provide some guidance, it was also a chance to learn something about what Arthur Andersen managers—the employees who bore the greatest day-to-day responsibility for overseeing audits and other projects—thought about their own ethical responsibilities.

On the appointed day in the spring of 1998, about 120 managers in their late twenties to early thirties sat tightly packed in a conference room at the Parker Meridien Hotel. Sue made her presentation, a pretty straightforward dos-and-don'ts session about independence in a public accounting firm. Then I was on. I began my program by putting a stakeholder "wheel" up on the blackboard. At the center of the wheel was "You, Arthur Andersen manager," and at the end of each "spoke" I listed a different stakeholder: client, public investor, partner, firm, SEC, community, government, fellow employees, family.

"As an Arthur Andersen manager," I said, "you have an obligation to every stakeholder shown here." There was a general nodding of heads.

"Okay," I continued, "which one is most important?" I waited patiently for someone to pipe up. But no one did. No hands, no response. I asked the question again. Eyes shifted around the room in discomfort. A few people openly turned around in their seats to see if anyone was observing the session. Again I waited. Then I spoke. "It can't be that hard to answer: To whom are you most responsible?" Finally one young manager timidly raised his hand. Very quietly, he said, "The partner." Hmmmm, I thought. "Anyone else?" Another hand went up: "The partner." And another: "The partner." "Anyone disagree?" Silence.

"What about the public investor? What about the client?" I asked. "They're important," someone responded, "but not as important as the partner. My career depends on the partner." "So what does that mean?" I asked. "It means I do what my partner tells me to do," he said. "And what," I continued, "if your partner asks you to do something you think is wrong?" No one dared to breathe. "Would you do it?"

Finally, a timid voice spoke up: "I guess I might ask a question. But if he insisted I do it, yes, I would. Partners don't want to hear bad news." Realizing something really strange was going on here, I followed up: "But would you tell anyone else?" Again, very softly: "No. It could hurt my career." No one contradicted him. They just shifted in their seats and waited in misery for the session to be over.

I was stunned. Not that I hadn't run into the "Just following orders" and "Shoot the messenger" syndromes before. They, unfortunately, are standard operating procedure in far too many companies. One of my earlier clients, a major insurance company, had ended up with a $2 billion "bill" to reimburse bilked customers, because the sales agents were afraid to speak out thanks in part to the generous commissions all were earning. Arthur Andersen had for so long stood apart as a place where "the right thing" was honored and respected. But these young men and women, so carefully selected, so rigorously trained, exhibited little independence of thought, sense of individual accountability, or—and this was the most chilling part—any sense of responsibility to the public investor, the true primary stakeholder of any public accounting firm. Somehow, somewhere, the mission expressed best by Leonard Spacek of a firm with "a professional responsibility to the public" had derailed. This was not a place that held itself above. It was a place that operated in the below. And not only did the employees not understand that their role—as guardians of the public trust—was a special one, they didn't even understand what they had lost.

I went back to my office with Debbie Weiner and Susan Jayson, members of my group who observed the session, and we tried to make sense of it. "My God," I said. "Can you believe it? Their main stakeholder is their partner?" I wouldn't have been so shocked if they had said the client; after all, the almost religious importance of the client had been drummed into my ears more times than I cared to remember. But if they were loyal only to the partner—who, in turn, depended on the client for his own career—the potential for wrongdoing was a lot greater than I had imagined.

Another intriguing nugget that came out of this session had to do with the disappointing results of the Business Audit. Throughout the spring of 1998, it had become increasingly evident that despite the splashy dog-and-pony shows, the lengthy e-mails and voice mails, and the general leadership drum-beating, the new Business Audit was going no place fast. Given that this new tool ostensibly was supposed to prevent or mitigate client and Firm risk, and had implications for the ethical performance of both clients and the Firm, I decided it was fair game for discussion at that same Independence and Ethics session.

Generating discussion in this area proved to be even harder than the stakeholder subject. It was like pulling teeth. Clearly, the participating managers did not perceive this environment as a safe venue for confidential chat. What little discussion there was suggested that managers somehow felt that the Business Audit could put them at risk. Maybe, we thought, the Business Audit wasn't working because an effective business audit meant uncovering problems—problems that the partner had never discovered or acted on. If my only stakeholder was my partner, I, too, would feel deeply conflicted about bringing them up. We decided we needed to do some serious investigation.

And we had the perfect laboratory. Because the AICPA required that every member of a public accounting firm have 20 hours of continuing professional education a year, Arthur Andersen encouraged anybody to present what were called Technical Sessions that anyone could attend, for which they would receive continuing-education credit. Technical Sessions could cover any topic that related to work, and the selection process was less than rigorous. All you had to do to host one of these things was to let the marketing department know the title and date of what you wanted to deliver, and a room would be assigned and a memo distributed. Our group had done a couple of such sessions before, on the Federal Sentencing Guidelines for Organizations, and on Responsible Business Practices consulting. So we decided we'd do a Technical Session on the barriers to use of the Business Audit. On June 24, 1998, Susan and I delivered a session in the New York office to about 30 partners, managers, and seniors, called "Business Practices: Is Your Client at Risk?"

In preparation for the session, Debbie and Susan conducted a small internal study, interviewing approximately a dozen managers at different levels about their concerns with the Business Audit. The findings were straightforward: (1) clients objected, believing that the Business Audit was just a new way for Arthur Andersen to sell more consulting services or, at least, to charge more for the audit, (2) managers might be expected to evaluate situations that they didn't understand, (3) managers were terrified that with the Business Audit they might actually find real problems and risks for the client that would force them to bring "bad news" to the partner, and (4) as an added kicker, despite the Firm's heralded commitment to training and support, many managers had not been trained in how to use the new tool because it would keep them from spending time at the client. We weren't surprised: It only confirmed what we thought—that there was something rotten in the culture of Arthur Andersen.

The goal of the session was to let the participants discuss in this more public forum their problems with the Business Audit, to suggest resources for addressing those difficulties, and to emphasize the changing environment that increasingly put both clients and the Firm at risk. I used a framework I had developed years before that identified four sources of risk for an organization. The basic idea is that while it is instinctive to think that most wrongdoing is the result of "bad apples," the reality is that a large percentage of unethical or illegal problems in organizations are the result of some combination of other factors—all of which a responsible manager can address. Our message was this: As an auditor using the new Business Audit, you will learn more about your clients' vulnerabilities than you ever have before. And, as your clients' "Trusted Business Advisor," you need to be able to point them toward these sources of risk. Of course, we hoped they might think about their own culture using the same framework.

To allow participants to practice using the model, we presented several brief scenarios dealing with timely situations, each beginning "What are the possible risks if . . . ?" Follow-up questions sought to identify what the auditor should be looking for and how those concerns should be brought to management and to the partner. One of the scenarios we used mirrored Enron, although we didn't know it at the time:

> In response to deregulation of portions of the energy industry, your client has recently restructured its operations. Its goal is to substantially increase its revenues from non-regulated businesses. The management team is viewed as "entrepreneurial" and has set ambitious but realistic financial targets. The assistant controller expresses concern about deregulation and the lower rates the competition is introducing into the marketplace.

Given my years of experience using these kinds of materials with managers and executives, I expected a vibrant, maybe heated, discussion. But I had neglected to consider the dampening effect of having partners in the room. (I had been naively hoping that the session might prove educational for the partners when they heard the concerns of the manager.) Once again, getting anyone to respond was painful. It felt like a junior high school math class. When I tried to draw people out, they looked everywhere but at me or at each other, or went to the back of the room for coffee. Every so often, a manager would venture a response. But every time one opened his mouth, one of the partners would inevitably interrupt and condescendingly explain what was wrong with the manager's thinking or why what the manager thought was a problem wasn't.

Near the close of the session, I asked the managers if they felt uneasy in raising client problems to their partners. One murmured that sometimes he did.

I was amazed to see a partner—who had frequently shared concerns with me that the beloved Arthur Andersen of the past had become a brutal place to work, a place with constant pressure to sell, where no one would dare challenge a partner—rebuke the manager. "That's ridiculous," the partner said in a voice dripping with condescension. "Of course we welcome your comments." Knowing how this partner had so often complained of being patronized by more senior partners, I was stunned by the reaction. It reminded me of how abused children often grow up to be involved in abusive situations themselves: While they know it's wrong, it is also what they know best. At Arthur Andersen, apparently, no matter what you thought privately, a partner still always outranked a manager, and to challenge that hierarchy with uncomfortable questions just wasn't done. Anyone who dared got the equivalent of a public spanking.

The rest of the session was useless. At the end, no one applauded or told us we had helped explain the resistance to the Business Audit. I felt as if they saw me as a rabble-rousing troublemaker: To some partners I was just stirring things up, while to some managers I was making things harder for them.

They had a point. No one had ever given us the go-ahead to study the culture or business practices of the Firm. We had clearly shown inappropriate chutzpah in asking such "subversive" questions of young employees. As I'd been told many times before, that was not my job. My job was to be a rainmaker bringing in consulting business, not to interfere in internal matters or waste my very valuable hours (my billing rate at this point was nearly $500 an hour). But I couldn't help it. I was feeling frustrated, demoralized, and stained by association with a firm that seemed to thumb its nose at basic responsible management. I was exhausted from fighting my colleagues for fees, angry at having my group's methodologies and materials ripped off by my "partners" and delivered with little concern for quality by inexperienced juniors, and humiliated at being seen by respected professional associates as a sellout, someone who went for the big bucks and compromised her own beliefs. Thoughts of leaving again crossed my mind. But at the same time I, too, still heard the call of the almighty buck. I was making more money than I ever had in my life. How could I give it up?

●   ●   ●

Then, on August 20, 1998, opportunity knocked again. When I arrived in the office that morning, I had an e-mail from a manager in the London office whose interest in our group had triggered the development of a small ethics unit in the United Kingdom. He had attached an article from a U.S.–based newsletter, *Ethikos,* about Coopers & Lybrand's $1.5 million internal ethics program. Part of it read:

> Twenty years ago, employees . . . were accountants who subscribed to a professional code established by the American Institute of Certified Public Accountants (AICPA). But now the firm is involved in other lines of business, like management consulting. Indeed, consulting is an area that has "grown exponentially, faster than auditing" [said Vincent M. O'Reilly, Chairman of Coopers' Ethics and Business Conduct Committee]. "As our other lines of business grew, we hired people with diverse backgrounds who had no idea of the professional code." Moreover, accounting guidelines don't cover all issues likely to arise these days . . .

Dammit, I thought. That should have been us! In truth, the thought was that should have been *me.* It sounds arrogant, I know, but I considered myself one of the leaders of the "contemporary" business ethics movement, and one of the first to bring business ethics out of academia and into the real world. I thought I was going to be a trailblazer and instead stood on the sidelines as other firms seemed to be doing it the right way. At this point I could pack up and leave—or fight to force Arthur Andersen to act responsibly and to do whatever I could to restore my own diminishing reputation.

I immediately drafted an e-mail memo, attached the article, and by midday sent it off to Mike Bennett, Joe Berardino, and a group of partners in positions of power and involved with the new risk consulting activities. Just about all of them were partners with whom I had discussed my concerns that we had no internal ethics program. I ended the memo with these words:

> Finally, the points raised in the article below about audit firms moving into broader consulting activities, and the need to consider business practices in these newer areas, are certainly applicable to us. We tell our clients that they are at increased ethical risk when they move into new markets, undergo regulatory change, acquire new businesses, etc. [As well,] our group [ERBP]—as I'm sure has occurred with other consulting service lines—has, on occasion, been questioned by potential clients about conflicts of interest and other related issues. I hope we can begin a discussion on the possibilities of developing an Arthur Andersen internal ethics program.

I might as well have tossed it in the wastebasket or flushed it down the toilet. I never got any response.

Then, in the beginning of 1999, Sue Quinlan called again. The Office of Independence and Ethics had decided to make a CD-ROM to serve as a self-administered course on independence and ethical standards. Would we, she asked, like to do a piece of it? I am not a big fan of computer-based training for anything as nuanced as ethics—my opposition to it had gotten me in hot water when I first started at the Firm—but given the Firm's previous disregard for internal ethics activities, I felt any effort should be enthusiastically supported. I guess I'd fallen pretty far. I told her we were in.

The purpose of the CD-ROM, which would be distributed to partners, managers, and seniors, was to present the Firm's Independence Standards as a trip around the world, then test the "traveler" on his or her retention of the information. The topics were straightforward: independence relating to investments, loans, and broker-dealer accounts, family relationships, insider/confidential information, fee arrangements, and board memberships. And, oh yeah, ethics. We were allotted a whopping 10 minutes of the

60-minute video to get Arthur Andersen's employees straight on ethical behavior.

Jeff Salters, one of our managers, took the lead on the project. He and I spent some time on the phone with Sue, trying to eke out some information on what the Firm would consider appropriate material for the ethics portion of this Firm-wide statement. It soon became clear that there really wasn't much the Firm had to say. As far as we could determine, being ethical meant obeying the independence standards. I was struck, once again, by the fact that probably every publicly held company audited by Arthur Andersen had a more extensive set of policies related to ethical behavior than did the Firm—the one who puts its imprimatur on a company's numbers! And certainly every corporate computer-based ethics program I'd run into covered a substantial range of issues that included values, mission statements, responsibilities to stakeholders, conflicts of interest, gifts and entertainment, competition, privacy, and political contributions. Few of these showed up in any Andersen documents—and virtually none were deemed necessary for the CD-ROM.

Still, we tried. We decided to go with a more structured version of our Independence and Ethics and Business Audit Technical Sessions, and Jeff developed brief caselets with multiple-choice responses. But then we hit a roadblock. The lack of a safe way to report a problem with an audit, a client, or colleague had been *the* gut-grabbing issue at both of the earlier sessions. We realized that we needed to provide an answer, so we called Sue Quinlan and asked her what someone in that situation should do.

"I guess you tell your partner," she said. Terrific. We knew how likely that was to happen. And what should a partner who had concerns about wrongdoing do? She didn't know. We hunted through the ethics binder. Buried somewhere within it, Jeff finally found a single sentence that advised an employee with a concern to report it to a "senior person in authority." Having no idea what that was supposed to mean, I called John Geron, the New York Audit Practice Director and a member of the Risk Management Executive Committee, to find out.

John was a tall, distinguished-looking man in his fifties. His flowing white hair and deep, resonant voice were more characteristic of a onetime matinee idol than a CPA. He also seemed to be truly concerned about the matters raised at the two Risk Management Executive Committee meetings I had attended, and genuinely interested in what I had to bring to the table.

"John," I said, "I need your help with this CD-ROM we're working on. To whom does a manager report an audit problem if he doesn't want to tell his partner? And to whom, exactly, does a partner report wrongdoing?"

John laughed his deep rumbling laugh. "Good question," he said.

"All I can find," I continued, "is a directive to tell 'a senior person in authority.' Who would that be?"

I thought he might step up to the plate and say, "Me." Instead, he said, "You got me. Let me see what I can find out. I'll call you back."

I figured it was a good thing I wasn't an audit manager sitting there with a client's cooked books or odd-looking off–balance-sheet transactions trying to figure out what to do. Ten minutes later, John called back, laughing. "Couldn't find out anything more than 'a senior person in authority.' I guess that's not much help."

I thought I had lost the ability to be shocked at this point, but it still threw me for a loop. These were questions that no one had even considered, it seemed, for many years. So what did I do? I caved. I was too drained to try to fight yet another battle, so I put the CD-ROM through, directing people with problems to report them "to a senior person in authority," whoever the hell that was.

*   *   *

It was just before this unhappy experience that I had that fateful run-in with Robert, the consultant who told me to double my fees because that's the way things were done around here, and who had delivered the $600,000 sticker price to the stunned general counsel. Back home after that horrible phone call with him, I was too wound up to eat or sleep. After waking up my husband a few times to tell him the story over and over, and rearranging all of my files—again—I went out to the kitchen and made a cup of tea, mind and stomach churning. I felt like a used-car salesman, but I was supposed to be an ethics consultant. The irony didn't escape me.

I got up the next morning and did something that should have gotten me fired from every professional services firm in the world. I marched to my desk and called the general counsel of that European bank, a pleasant, soft-spoken man who seemed to truly care about his company and wanted to do everything he could to ensure that the merger had the least disruptive effect possible on the bank's employees. I told him the truth: We were ripping him off.

"Arthur Andersen has the talent and skills to deliver exactly what you need," I said. "But you don't need all those people, and you shouldn't be spending all that money. We're overcharging you, probably by 100 percent. And that's wrong. I thought you ought to know." I exhaled sharply, both terrified and relieved. I shouldn't have done it, but I felt a lot better all of a sudden.

There was a long pause. And then, in the calm and thoughtful tone he used throughout our discussions, the general counsel thanked me and hung up the phone. We didn't win the project. And as far as I know, no one ever found out about my phone call. But the experience was, for me, the beginning of the end.

In the meantime, I did follow up with Geron on the issue of Firm risk. I felt he really understood how critical this problem was, even if he didn't have answers. We had several discussions about the range of risks to the Firm that were becoming increasingly evident, and the reluctance of leaders of the Firm to address them. One day, John gave me an opening. He invited me to make a presentation to the new Global Risk Management Committee on the topic "Managing Internal Ethical Risks" at its meeting on April 26, 1999. Ten of the 16 members of this committee had been on the Risk Management Executive Committee that had earlier discussed the new risks in this environment. The executives I knew the best, besides John, were Bob Kutsenda and Gary Goolsby, because, aside from the Risk Management meetings, I had held a few conference calls with them to find out how to "report" the partner who was entertaining clients and charging it back to the client's company. Although, like so many issues I raised, I never got any answer or result from my discussion on this with the two men, I had gotten to know them a bit better.

Our group was charged up. Maybe, this time, someone would listen. John scheduled my presentation in a prominent place on the agenda of the first day of a two-day meeting—right after Bob Kutsenda discussed the overall risk-management strategy of the Firm. He also arranged a planning session of the two of us with Bob for a few days before the GRM meeting. It wasn't a long meeting— Bob never took his coat off, and his luggage stood by the door in anticipation of his departure for LaGuardia, but he stayed long enough for John and me to lay out the proposed presentation and for him, in his role as committee chairman, to okay it.

As I strode into the conference room in our offices, I felt more excited than nervous. I'm not sure why; it was the biggest and best opportunity I'd ever had to show a group of the most important people in the company that something was seriously wrong, and I suppose they could have reacted angrily to what I was about to say. But at this point, it didn't really matter. I had one foot out the door anyhow—why not tell them what they needed to hear?

My 90-minute presentation, prepared by our group, pulled no punches. I led off by discussing the Firm's current external risks. I talked about the fact that the SEC was looking carefully at the accountants in the wake of high-profile accounting scandals, and that the press and the public were beginning to ask serious questions. As one example, I mentioned the October 1998 *Business Week* article "Where Are the Accountants?" as well as the increasing complexities of issues and accounting technologies. The world was getting more complicated by the day, and it was hard for anyone to keep abreast of all the changes in this fast-moving new economy.

Then I drilled down. I talked about the internal risks that we had noted over the past year, the reluctance to bring "bad news" to partners and the implications of that; the fact that Arthur Andersen employees didn't see the investor as someone to whom they were accountable; the few and conflicting messages about where to go for help. "Arthur Andersen has become the proverbial cobbler of shoeless children fame," I said. "We are recommending best practices to our clients we do not ourselves follow."

The next slide read:

> Based on limited assessment and observations to date, [we believe] Arthur Andersen faces an unacceptable level of risk. What we don't know CAN hurt us. Ignorance of wrongdoing is no defense.

Arthur Andersen's needs were as follows, I said:

- an official, institutionalized reporting mechanism

- a live, interactive assistance medium to clarify policies and procedures

- a consistent process for investigation and follow-up

- to strengthen the culture to increase employees' comfort in coming forward with information and questions

Finally, I offered some possible solutions, including a proposal to do an in-depth assessment of the vulnerabilities of the Firm through confidential interviews with partners and employees at all levels.

When I finished my presentation, I stopped, took a deep breath, and scanned the room before asking for questions. People actually seemed interested, I thought, daring to hope that I'd finally gotten through. Like the partners at the Risk Management meetings I attended, the members of the Global Risk Management Committee acknowledged almost all of what I said as true. There was a general nodding of heads, comments about having seen the *Business Week* article, and a general agreement that these were perilous times. But no one jumped up and shouted, "Eureka! Let's do it!" John Geron asked several times, "So what do we want to do? Do we want to engage Barbara's group to conduct an assessment? Or maybe pilot an assessment?" This group of pleasant, polite senior partners of the Firm emitted a bunch of hems and haws that added up to a collective "I don't know."

What I saw was a group of high-level partners who understood exactly what this Firm was dealing with, but had either no authority or no sense of responsibility that something had to be done, and that they could be the ones to do it. It's one of the truisms about a partnership: Where does the buck stop, and with whom? This group had to report in some fashion to the seniormost executives in the Firm—Samek, Berardino, et cetera. (their names were on every bit of communication relating to this committee)—on what they were going to do. But from what I could tell, this radical plan to assess the Firm's vulnerabilities and risks made them profoundly uncomfortable.

John finally came to the rescue. "I have a suggestion. Let's ask Ethics to prepare a White Paper for the Committee to launch a firm-wide consideration of our recommendations. Barbara, do you think your group can have that in a week?" The darkness lifted once again. "Absolutely," I said. During that week, John and I met a couple of times to talk about how we would do the implementation, which, at his suggestion, we included in the White Paper. We agreed that the U.S. practice was probably the most critical as well as the toughest because of the intensely litigious environment here. So we began to develop a plan to conduct the assessment in a few key large (New York, Houston, L.A.) and small (Boston, Minneapolis, Phoenix) offices. Finally, something real was happening.

On June 8, 1999, we delivered the White Paper to the Global Risk Management Committee.

The paper was straightforward and aggressive. We reviewed some of the same external issues I'd mentioned at the meeting, and went on:

> The SEC has sent a clear message that it expects more from the Big Five auditing firms. . . . SEC Chairman Levitt emphasized the auditor's role as the "public's watchdog" in the financial reporting process and questioned whether the "staff in the trenches" of the accounting and auditing profession have the training and supervision they need to ensure that audits are being done correctly. It is also important to consider the extent to which ineffective upward and downward

communications may have contributed to a failure to detect accounting irregularities.

To warn about the increased accountability of organizations for the actions of their employees, we cited the then-recent (1998) Supreme Court rulings on sexual harassment, noting that in the past, employers defeated sexual harassment lawsuits because the burden of proof was on the plaintiffs to prove that the employer knew or should have known about the harassment.

> But the Supreme Court has made it clear that ignorance of wrongdoing is no longer a viable defense. . . . In the future, other court rulings will likely use the sexual harassment rulings as precedent in charging organizations with greater and more defined responsibility to prevent myriad types of wrongdoing, such as independence violations.

Finally, we underscored the inadequate training on the Business Audit, managers' perceptions that partners are sometimes reluctant to bring issues to a client for fear of damaging the relationship, and the now-famous "senior person in authority" resource. We also detailed a two-phase assessment project.

We submitted the paper. Then we waited, and waited, and waited—for nothing. I never heard another word. No questions, no feedback, not even a hint that maybe the Firm was thinking about doing something with or without our group. I suddenly felt like Cassandra, the mythological bearer of bad news, the person no one wanted to listen to. John offered apologies and excuses: More important things needed attention, it appeared.

The letdown was devastating for my group, and it was, I thought, the last straw for me. I had now spent almost four years in an organization that embodied almost everything I believed represented the worst in American business. It was time to get the hell out.

Sometime in April, I had met with Joe Tarantino, head of the New York Business Risk Consulting and Assurance Services Group, to initiate a general discussion about my leaving the Firm. However, I had put off further talks when the Global Risk meeting came up. At the end of June, I again met with Joe to begin to plan my departure. We decided together—by this time, with my service line not contributing much, the Firm wasn't the least bit opposed to my leaving—that I would leave the Firm at the end of September, exactly four years after I got there. We also agreed that I would continue to work with Arthur Andersen as an independent consultant on a few projects, and drafted a formal contract to that effect. The contract enabled me to consult externally to two Arthur Andersen clients that had signed on specifically because they wanted to work with me, and allowed me to employ Arthur Andersen personnel as needed in my consulting work. I stayed in touch with John Geron, who tried to be encouraging. "Maybe," he said, "you can conduct the assessment for the Firm when you're an outside consultant. We can engage you to do it." I think he really believed that could happen. And—do you think I ever learn?—for a while I did too.

It's four years later—and John's call never came. Now it never will.

＊　＊　＊

Ironically, my worst professional moment came a few months after I left Arthur Andersen, when I called the CEO of a former client to have lunch. I had worked with him at my own firm and had had a wonderful experience. I had also worked with him at Arthur Andersen by playing on our history, and he had essentially fired our group for pushing too many services he felt weren't needed. This was a man I respected, a leader who himself had faced a tough time in his own company and handled it forthrightly with integrity and elegance. One of my personal pick-me-uppers when things were tough was the thought of the respect and praise he had given me for the work I'd done with his company. "You never let us off the hook," he told me. It was a compliment I'd carried in my heart for years.

Now, as I sat with him in a private dining room in the financial district looking over New York Harbor, he called me to account.

"Why did you think we should be doing something Arthur Andersen doesn't think is important enough to do itself? You were selling us stuff you didn't think we needed."

Then he summed it all up with one sentence. "Barbara, this is not the you I used to know," he said. I had to agree with him. This was not the me *I* used to know.

# The Fall of the House of Andersen

9

*What happened at Enron is a tragedy on many levels.*
—ANDERSEN CEO JOSEPH BERARDINO,
testifying before Congress, December 12, 2001

T HE FALL OF ANDERSEN began slowly and almost impercepti-
bly. In early October 2001, the Firm, under the leadership of
new CEO Joe Berardino, held its first worldwide partners meeting
in several years at the Ernest N. Morial Convention Center in New
Orleans. The focus was on rebuilding, after the long battle between
Arthur Andersen and Andersen Consulting. Arthur Andersen, by
all accounts, had lost—and badly so. "We'd gone through what for
many partners was a big disappointment," said Bob Lorenz, a former partner. "The meeting was about resolving that loss, saying
'That's behind us and we're going to move forward.'" Combined
with the disintegration of the New Economy and the horrifying
tragedy of September 11, the mood was all grim business.

But even as the partners gazed into a long mirror set up on the
stage, where a deep voice intoned "The Future Is You," Andersen's
future had become blurry. A once-stodgy utility company in Houston that had transformed itself into the poster child of the New
Economy and Andersen's model client was already sowing the

seeds of its and the Firm's destruction. For Joe Berardino, the first hint of trouble came moments after he stood on stage, savoring his first worldwide meeting as top dog. After making a presentation on teamwork, Berardino stepped down from the podium and was approached by a partner who told him that he had some worrisome news. It appeared, he said, that there were some irregularities with Enron's third-quarter report. Berardino was a bit concerned, but "did not take any special note of it," he later said.

It may have been the first time Andersen's CEO learned of real problems at the Firm's star customer, but for other Androids, this was hardly a news flash. Indeed, for those close to Enron, it harkened back to a critical two-day meeting the previous February. It was the annual risk assessment of Enron, where a group of Andersen partners met in Houston and via conference call to make sure the client hadn't run afoul of Andersen's guidelines and procedures. Present were 14 of the top U.S. partners, including Michael Bennett of Business Risk Consulting and Assurance Services fame; Gary Goolsby, the new head of the Risk Management Executive Committee; Robert Kutsenda; and Steve Samek, who had seen his influence decline after Berardino's election but still remained on the most powerful committees. Houston practice director Michael Odom, Houston office head Bill Swanson, and, of course, David Duncan, Enron's engagement partner, were also there.

David Duncan was a lifelong Android and churchgoing family man who had joined the company right out of Texas A&M, soldiering along relatively anonymously for most of his early career. He made partner in 1995, and in 1997 got the Enron account. At the time, the company was in the midst of its transformation from regional power company to global dynamo, so the job was a prestigious one. Though Duncan still was considered a young buck, his status within the Firm surged along with the success of Enron and with the seemingly insatiable appetite the company had for Andersen's wares. Enron paid Andersen $52 million in 2000 in both auditing and consulting services, and the numbers just kept going up. In 2001, Berardino named Duncan to his new Strategic Advisory Committee. He had become a major player.

There was plenty of risk to discuss at the meeting, beginning with an off-balance-sheet transaction called LJM. Named for Enron CFO Andrew Fastow's wife and two kids, it was a Special Purpose Entity that, the partners understood, was essentially controlled by Fastow. For several years, Enron's basic strategy had been to buy an asset such as a power plant or a water source and then create markets around it. To create these markets required taking on a lot of debt—debt which, if held on Enron's balance sheet, could have crippled the company's expansion plans and its high-flying stock. So Enron, along with many other companies, created Special Purpose Entities, business units affiliated with Enron but supposedly separate enough that debt could be parked there instead of with the parent company. While Special Purpose Entities are not illegal, there are tight restrictions on how and when to use them.

At Enron, however, many of the Special Purpose Entities were hardly what they seemed. Not only did they not meet the accounting requirements to assure independence from the parent company, but even as the Andersen partners were meeting, CFO Fastow was allegedly already using them to secretly funnel millions of company dollars to himself and a few carefully selected associates. While the Andersen partners didn't know this fact at the time, there were plenty of other things that didn't seem to sit quite right at the meeting. According to a memo summarizing the meeting, partners discussed the conflicts of interest Fastow faced as both CFO and the LJM fund manager, along with his earnings, the board's views, and the disclosures of the transactions in the financial footnotes. They dubbed Enron's earnings "intelligent gambling" and its transaction structuring "aggressive."

Again, Andersen proved itself adept at recognizing risk. What the Firm didn't know how to do was to stay away from it. "Ultimately, the conclusion was reached to retain Enron as a client, citing that it appeared we had the appropriate people and processes in place to serve Enron and manage our engagement risks," the memo read, adding that it was "not unforeseeable" that fees could reach $100 million a year—a huge amount from any one client. Just as it had in my experience, risk assessment and fee generation went hand in hand. Whatever concerns the partners might have had stayed hidden behind the Firm's famous doors: Just one week later, Duncan met with the audit and compliance committees of Enron's board and told them that the related-party transactions had been "reviewed for adequacy." Andersen would be issuing an unqualified audit opinion for the year 2000.

There were other warning signs. Carl Bass, a member of Andersen's Professional Standards Group—the group that is supposed to oversee accounting decisions—had been removed from working on the Enron account in early 2001 after he objected to some accounting practices. After noting problems as early as 1999, Bass was stifled when Enron, infuriated by his criticism, demanded that he have no dealings with the company and Duncan acquiesced. Bass later testified that memos showing that he had signed off on certain transactions had been changed without his knowledge and that he had demanded that they be revised.

The alarm bells came from below as well, as mid-level Andersen auditors Jennifer Stevenson and Patricia Grutzmacher discovered that another Enron Special Purpose Entity, called Merlin, was not actually independent and that Enron was reimbursing investors in the partnership for losses. Duncan and other senior partners overruled their concerns. As had happened before, some people spotted problems, but an ambitious partner at a star client had easily overridden the system that was supposed to protect Andersen from trouble. It was the same pattern I'd experienced over and over: Keep the client happy, no matter what the consequences. Andersen's work for Enron was overly aggressive, compromised by pressure from the client, and featured an engagement partner who was easily able to ignore and disregard the standards experts and coworkers in his own Firm.

For a few months, Andersen's cross-your-fingers-and-pray strategy seemed to have been the right one. But suddenly, in the summer of 2001, the Firm's demons began to emerge, one by one. In August, Enron CEO Jeffrey Skilling, a slick and cocky one-time McKinsey consultant who had taken over from Chairman Kenneth Lay just months earlier, suddenly resigned, saying he wanted to spend more time with his family. Inside the company, Skilling's departure was bizarre, since anyone who knew him knew that he had openly lusted for the job for many years. Shortly thereafter, Enron employee and former Arthur Andersen auditor Sherron Watkins wrote a comprehensive memo to Lay, detailing a list of accounting problems she saw and expressing the fear that the company could "implode in a wave of accounting scandals."

Although Watkins was no whistleblower—she expressed hope that the transactions could be unwound "quietly"—she also made a call to a friend and former colleague in Andersen's Houston office, James Hecker, to express her concerns and ask for advice. The "ostensibly social call," according to a memo Hecker penned the next day, started with small talk about the state of the Houston job market. Then the tone changed dramatically. Watkins went on to lay out several specific concerns about the accounting at Enron relating to LJM and many other questionable transactions involving Fastow. Hecker, who didn't work on the Enron account, was so alarmed that he immediately contacted Duncan, two practice directors, and another Andersen partner working on Enron. The first page of his e-mail read, "Here's the smoking guns you can't extinguish." After a meeting the next day, the partners, evidently shaken by the news, agreed to consult internal lawyers.

By the time someone decided to rain on Berardino's New Orleans parade with the bad news, Enron was in its death throes. On October 16, Enron announced its third-quarter results—a shocking loss of $638 million and the reduction of shareholder's equity by $1.2 billion in connection with the early termination of "certain structured finance arrangements." Andersen had—finally—forced its client to take the write-down, but by then it was much too late. The actions had taken on a life of their own. The stock plummeted, falling almost 40 percent in the following week, the media pounced, and six days later the Securities and Exchange Commission began investigating. Suddenly, Enron was in free fall. It would file for Chapter 11 bankruptcy reorganization just six weeks later, on December 2, 2001. Until it was surpassed a few months later by an equally devastating collapse, that of WorldCom, another Andersen client, it was by far the largest bankruptcy in American corporate history.

For Berardino and his leadership team, the Enron debacle should have been cause for serious alarm. Just months earlier, in

June 2001, the Firm had settled a lawsuit with the Securities and Exchange Commission over its alleged misdoings in the Waste Management case. A condition of the settlement was that Arthur Andersen consent to a "permanent injunction" from violating
securities laws. In other words, the Firm had been put on warning.
If there was a next offense, there was big trouble ahead, and Berardino, who had been deeply involved in the settlement negotiations, knew it as well as anyone. Yet it appears that he severely misjudged both the anger of the U.S. government and the seriousness
of the situation, preferring to view Enron as an isolated case rather
than the last in a series of embarrassments for the Firm.

Duncan, on the other hand, seemed to understand what he
and his Firm were in for. Enron's sudden fall was the nightmare
every Andersen partner had awakened from, soaked in sweat, a
thousand times. His reputation, his identity as a comer, his partnership units, all were at stake. And then, on October 12, what
looked like two magic words appeared in the subject line of an
e-mail from Chicago in-house lawyer Nancy Temple that had been
sent to Michael Odom and forwarded to Duncan. "More help," it
said. The three terse lines that followed made Duncan feel, he later
testified, justified in getting rid of much of Andersen's documentation relating to Enron. "It might be useful to consider reminding
the engagement team of our documentation and retention policy,"
it said. "It will be helpful to make sure that we have complied with
the policy. Let me know if you have any questions."

And so began the last act of Andersen's nearly 89-year existence. On October 23, Duncan called a meeting, the results of
which led several Andersen employees to embark on a frenzy of
document shredding never seen before at the Firm. I hadn't been
to the Houston office, but if the clutter of work papers was anything
like what I'd seen at the offices where I worked, there was plenty to
do. The massive mechanical beasts whirred all day and late into the
night, fed by an endless stack of papers somehow relating to Enron.
Three days later, as many as 26 trunks and 24 boxes of Enron material had been pulverized into meaningless scraps of paper. In
Portland and in London as well, young employees fed the ma-
chines constantly.

Suddenly, all was quiet again. On November 8, the SEC sub-poenaed information from Andersen relating to Enron. The next day, Temple left Duncan a voice mail telling him about the sub-poena. Duncan understood the message as an order to stop the shredding, On that same day, Enron dropped another bombshell, announcing that its earnings for the years 1997–2000 had been sig-nificantly exaggerated and would be restated—to the tune of an ad-ditional $591 million.

Clueless as he may have been to the orgy of destruction, Be-rardino knew by now that his Firm's reputation was in mortal dan-ger. Andersen was quickly becoming implicated in the scandal as the media and others wondered how the Firm could have let these transactions get through. Yet true to form, the first reaction was denial. Berardino wrote an editorial, published in *The Wall Street Journal* on December 4, suggesting that the failures came from the system rather than the auditor. "Enron's collapse, like the dot-com meltdown, is a reminder that our financial-reporting model— with its emphasis on historical information and a single earnings-per-share number—is out of date and unresponsive to today's new business models, complex financial structures, and associated busi-ness risks," he wrote. It reminded me of the presentation I'd made at the Risk Management Executive Committee meeting in 1998, when I talked about how fraud prevention needed to be more about anticipating than reacting. But it was rather too late for that discussion.

The next week, Berardino testified before Congress and was congratulated by many representatives for being so forthcoming. "Andersen will not hide from its responsibilities," he said, dis-cussing an "error" of $172 million that he felt the Firm's accoun-tants had made. He then went on to talk about needed reforms and what he called a "crisis of confidence" in the industry.

When I read the op-ed, the feelings of humiliation, frustration, and guilt associated with my experiences at Andersen rushed back to me. I threw down the paper in disgust. Later, when I saw Be-rardino attempt to call Enron's failure a "business problem" in his interview on *Meet the Press* the next month, I bellowed at the televi-sion screen, startling my husband, who rushed in to see what had happened. My instant reaction was that the culture of Berardino's firm had as much to do with the pickle he found himself in as did the admittedly shocking fraud that seemed to have been perpetrated by his client. What I and millions of others saw was a firm and its leader casting about for someone else to blame. "The op-ed was a disaster," said Lynn Turner, former chief accountant of the SEC. "It conveyed a message of 'we've done nothing wrong,' and it detracted from needed industry reforms."

Berardino would soon come to regret those words and those appearances. In early January, his general counsel came to him and told him that internal lawyers' attempts to search computers of the auditors on the Enron account had discovered internal disk drives that had been completely erased of much relevant material. On January 10, Andersen announced that significant document shredding had taken place. Duncan never met with Bernadino, but instead had only a brief telephone conversation with Andersen lawyers, said Robert Giuffra, Duncan's attorney. Five days later, Duncan was fired, three Houston-based partners were placed on leave, and four other executives, including Gary Goolsby, head of the Risk Management Committee after Kutsenda retired, were relieved of management responsibilities. Berardino could no longer hide behind the business problem excuse: Suddenly, Andersen's involvement had gone from possible negligence or poor judgment to what looked like a criminal offense.

So the Firm worked to pin the blame firmly on Duncan as the rogue destroyer. On January 24, the House of Representatives's Energy and Commerce Committee's Subcommittee on Oversight and Investigations called Duncan, Temple, Odom, and several others to testify on the document destruction. Duncan invoked his Fifth Amendment rights, and Temple denied that her objective in sending e-mails to Duncan was to get him to shred information that might be damning to the Firm. C. E. Andrews, Andersen's global managing partner for business and advisory services, attacked Duncan under oath. "That was an extreme error in judgment that we as an organization don't support, don't condone, and don't encourage, and will not stand for," he said.

Few believed him. In just a few short weeks, Andersen had surpassed Enron as the symbol of corporate greed and lack of accountability run amok. Snide jokes, shredding references, and cartoons circulated around the Internet and on the Letterman-Leno talk-show circuit, and even President Bush jumped into the fray, although it was a long time before he appeared to realize the gravity of what was happening. Instead, he used the debacle as casual fodder for jokes. At the Alfalfa Club's annual dinner in Washington at the end of January, the President announced that he had good news and bad news from Saddam Hussein. "The good news is he is willing to let us inspect his biological and chemical warfare installations," President Bush said. "The bad news is that he insists Arthur Andersen do the inspection!"

The Duncan-as-scoundrel defense didn't go over too well. On February 1, 2002, a team of Enron directors went public with the results of an investigation into the collapse. Colloquially called "The Powers Report," named after an Enron director and the head investigator, it excoriated executives at both Enron and Andersen. Although Andersen's executives weren't interviewed by the investigators, the report had a few choice words for the Firm. "Andersen did not fulfill its professional responsibilities in connection with its audits of Enron's financial statements, or its obligation to bring to the attention of Enron's Board (or the Audit and Compliance Committee) concerns about Enron's internal controls over the related-party transactions." In other words, even without the document destruction, the Firm bore major responsibility for Enron's collapse.

Scrambling, Andersen announced that it had appointed Paul Volcker, the former chairman of the Federal Reserve Board, to lead an outside group charged with making fundamental changes to Andersen's business model. Already, many clients were dropping the Firm, and members of the worldwide alliance of affiliated groups began to wonder nervously if they, too, would be drawn into the mess.

Bringing in Volcker was a positive step, I felt, because it implied that the Firm understood—finally—that major changes were desperately needed. It was also the only time that the leadership seemed to admit to the possibility that there were serious problems inside the Firm. Volcker insisted that his committee would have the right to make any changes it deemed necessary, and within a few weeks named former U.S. General Accounting Office chief and Andersen partner Charles Bowsher and ex–Merck CEO P. Roy Vagelos to his panel. At the same time, Andersen began talks on settling the Enron case in the $700 to $800 million range, a sum that dwarfed what it had paid out in past audit failures.

It seemed as if Andersen might, with Volcker's help, turn itself into a new kind of audit firm, one not rife with conflicts of interest and one that could recapture the special responsibility it had to investors, a "model for the profession," in Arthur Levitt's words. But while Volcker tried his best, the Firm was deeply divided over whether to follow his recommendations and start over—knowing that many clients would not stick around for the reforms to take hold or simply to sell its various units to interested buyers on the cheap, thus saving at least some of the capital, including partners' retirement funds, invested in the Firm. In the meantime, Andersen's lifeblood—its large-company public audit clients that had stuck with them for half a century or longer, quality names like Colgate-Palmolive and Merck—were leaving in droves. In a business based on reputation, no company would want to be audited by a firm whose name had become synonymous with scandal.

As Volcker tried to unite the partners behind his plan, one that included the separation of auditing and consulting, better internal oversight at Andersen, and a "cooling-off" period before outside auditors could accept a job working directly for a client, the Justice Department began hinting that an indictment was inevitable. "At the age of seventy-five, I had the romantic notion that I could change things," Volcker said in a New York speech a few months later. "I thought they would accept change because they needed change. Many of [the partners] felt internally conflicted. They were making decisions that would hurt the partners that wanted to get out. Then the indictment took away their freedom of action."

Now the Firm was fighting a two-front battle, trying to keep its worldwide association of member firms together while scrambling to make a deal that would avert a criminal indictment. But it was too little, too late. Although Volcker was trying his best to hold everyone together, the internal leadership seemed divided and lost. According to several former partners, one internal faction, led by C. E. Andrews, wanted to go forward with the Volcker plan while another group, led by Lou Salvatore and other senior executives, felt the only hope was to try to pull off some kind of massive asset sale to a rival. "The Volcker Plan could have been great," said Baptist Foundation of Arizona and WorldCom litigator John "Sean" Coffey. "Andersen could have been 'scared straight.' But they didn't want to change how they did business. They figured, 'Screw this, I'm jumping ship.'"

The Firm would never manage to vote on the matter, as option after option melted away. "It seemed to many of us that you'd have to change the world for [the Volcker Plan] to work," said Bob Lorenz, who, as a 20-year partner just reaching retirement age, was in the group of partners most financially harmed by the Firm's collapse. His lost retirement savings and paid-in-capital added up to about $3 million. Talks with Deloitte Touche Tohmatsu got very serious at the end of March, then suddenly collapsed when they could find no structure that would protect Deloitte from Andersen's huge potential liabilities.

In the meantime, Andersen hired law firm Mayer, Brown, Rowe & Maw, a firm believed to have better government connections than Davis Polk & Wardwell, its existing counsel. Settlement talks continued, but again, Andersen refused to admit guilt—a key condition of the deal—arguing that doing so would kill the Firm anyway. The two sides came close, but Assistant Attorney General Michael Chertoff ultimately changed his mind, according to one person who spoke with him, because he was infuriated by what he saw as arrogance and a lack of desire to change. On March 14, Chertoff went ahead with the indictment, knowing full well that it could mean the end of an almost 89-year-old firm.

Berardino's worst fears became a reality when Andersen was indicted on one felony count of obstruction of justice. The Firm called the charge "a gross abuse of governmental power" and claimed it was being scapegoated for everything that had gone wrong in the business world. Berardino warned that the indictment was equivalent to the death penalty. And he was right. By this point, the Firm was caught up in a horrendous Catch-22. If it settled the charges—which the Justice Department said would require an admission of guilt—its reputation was already so besmirched that it could be impossible to recover. If the Firm went to trial and lost, it clearly was over. The trickle of client defections turned into a flood, and entire country groups of partners such as those from Spain and Chile began to sever their ties, leaving Arthur Andersen LLP, the U.S. unit, increasingly isolated.

For all intents and purposes, Andersen was dead. So why not go for broke? Andersen pushed for an early trial date and won a small victory: It would begin on May 6. In the meantime, the Firm launched a last-ditch battle for public support, organizing those orange-T-shirted pep rallies around the country and starting a campaign to lobby congressmen. One sample letter, which I received as a former partner, read:

> Dear [Senator/Representative NAME]:
>
> As one of your constituents, I am writing to express my utter shock and outrage at the indictment of Andersen for obstruction of justice. This is a politically motivated action, and is a disgrace to our justice system.
>
> I am an employee of Andersen in the _____ office.
>
> [*Insert personal story here.* For example, you might note how long you've worked for Andersen, how ethical you've found the people to be, how shocked you were when you first heard the allegations against us. . . .]

In Chicago, Androids organized a rally for March 25. Eugene Delves, the former Arthur Andersen partner, decided to call Berardino, angered that the senior leadership of the Firm wasn't there to support the protesters. "I said he should get his ass down here and be the leader," Delves said. What he didn't know was that Berardino had made up his mind to resign, unable to continue playing what he called "ten-dimensional chess." The calls for Berardino to leave had mounted, including an e-mail from former

Arthur Andersen managing partner Dick Measelle sent to all partners on March 26, supporting the Volcker Plan and harkening back to the courageous decision of Brian Peoples to publicly challenge Harvey Kapnick back in 1979. "In your heart of hearts . . . ," it read, "do YOU think Joe Berardino has more influence over the Federal government than Paul VOLCKER?" Berardino announced his resignation the same day, as that rain-soaked rally of his desperate New York employees carried on twelve floors below his office. Yet the resignation failed to have the desired effect of uniting the Firm or getting some leniency from the government. Andersen sailed on, rudderless.

Then, on April 9, Duncan pleaded guilty to one felony count of obstruction of justice. Justice now had a key actor willing to testify that his decision to shred documents and to order others to do so was indeed a crime. The Houston-based trial began with a flourish on May 6. Celebrity lawyer and Andersen defense attorney Rusty Hardin amused the court with his cowboy boots and inflammatory language and managed to anger the judge, Melinda Harmon, more than a few times. But Hardin also took advantage of a harried group of prosecutors and nearly pulled out a victory. Nancy Temple, the Chicago-based lawyer who had testified in January before Congress, this time chose to take the Fifth. Duncan, however, testified in great detail about how that e-mail from Temple influenced his decision to shred. "Obviously, the thought of litigation, whether that be the SEC or some other kind, was on our minds," he said.

Duncan also testified that he and his team originally had decided not to require Enron to attribute its $1.2 billion write-down in shareholder equity to an accounting error, because, at 8 percent of shareholder equity, the amount was "not material." Materiality, according to these Andersen accountants, was still a fluid concept. It reminded me of a story a former Andersen client at a Fortune 500 company told me about Paul Volcker, who served on that company's board's audit committee. At a board meeting, Volcker asked the Andersen engagement partner what constituted a material amount for that company. "Thirty million dollars," the partner responded. "You mean if we have a problem," Volcker said, stunned, "I'm not going to hear about it until it's $30 million?" "That's right," said the Andersen partner. Although Andersen's Enron team ultimately changed their minds and didn't allow the omission, it looks as if Duncan still had been willing to play the same game his colleagues had at Waste Management and elsewhere: Let it go and hope it fixes itself later.

For Andersen to be convicted of obstructing justice, only one person in the Firm had to be found "the corrupt persuader," the person who acted with intent to deceive. It was not, apparently, an easy call. After the jury announced that it was deadlocked despite deliberating for more than 60 hours, the judge instructed them to continue to try to reach a decision. The next day, the jury wrote a note that startled everyone involved with the case. "If each of us believes that one Andersen agent acted knowingly and with corrupt intent, is it for all of us to believe that it was the same agent," it read. It was a question that required legal research by the judge, who ultimately answered that the jury did not have to agree that it was the same person.

Hardin and Andersen's other defense attorneys began to salivate, sensing a hung jury, but they misread the tea leaves. On June 15, the jury suddenly came forward with a guilty verdict. To the surprise of everyone, the jury had essentially ignored the reams of shredded material in its decision and focused instead on an e-mail Temple sent to Duncan in October, asking him to doctor a draft memo sent to Enron that had originally shown Andersen disagreeing with Enron's characterization of its huge write-down as "nonrecurring." Temple was the corrupt persuader. "It's against the law to alter that document with the intent to impair the fact-finding ability of an official proceeding," said jury foreman Oscar Criner.

It was a bizarre end to a bizarre trial, and the jury's logic confused many. But everyone knew that even should Andersen appeal, it was over. Soon after the conviction, Andersen announced that it would stop auditing publicly traded clients as of August 2002. Even before the verdict, most of its most valuable partners and staff had been sliced off, piecemeal, and sold to the other four major auditing and consulting firms. I would never have imagined that all that would be left of Andersen by the fall of 2002 was a shattered brand and a few office buildings. Yet even without the guilty verdict, what came next would have obliterated any remaining shreds of its reputation.

Like dominoes falling, one Andersen client after another announced restatements and/or bankruptcy, from Global Crossing—like Enron, touted internally as an ideal client—to Qwest Communications, to, in June 2002, a scandal that dwarfed even Enron: the restatement of an incredible $9 billion in revenues by telecommunications giant WorldCom and the subsequent arrest of its CFO and controller. "They can never clear their name," said Lynn Turner. "In the court of public opinion, they have been tried, convicted, and hanged. And after WorldCom, there was just nothing you could say."

For a few months after the verdict, Enron continued to operate in Chapter 11, while Andersen got down to the business of dismantling itself, wrapping up audit engagements, selling off groups at firesale prices, and preparing for sentencing on October 16. It seemed unfair to some—why weren't the actual fraudsters getting in trouble too? But the Justice Department was working carefully behind the scenes. On August 21, Enron executive Michael Kopper pled guilty to two charges of money laundering and conspiracy to commit wire fraud and surrendered $12 million in ill-gotten gains. Less than two months later, on October 2, Andrew Fastow surrendered to the FBI and was charged with fraud, money laundering, and conspiracy.

In the end, the collapse of Andersen had uneven effects on its partners and staff. Many Andersen partners who had a good reputation and a strong client list were eagerly snapped up by other firms, and in many cases, the acquiring firms made up for the capital those partners had lost (getting a new audit client made it a relative bargain). Much worse off were the retirees, many of whom saw their pensions evaporate, and new partners that didn't find a new home. Many of them were deeply in debt because they had taken out loans upon becoming partner, at which point you had to put as much as $250,000 into the Firm as your own equity.

But for all the pain and suffering, Andersen never seemed to accept responsibility. Proud or simply deluded, the Firm clung to the witch hunt mind-set. In June 2002, Turner was at an accounting symposium at Northwestern's Kellogg School of Management and noticed three retired and current Andersen partners sitting alone. "Not a single person went up to talk to them," he said. "They were like pariahs." Finally, Turner decided to say hello. "We got to talking about what had transpired. They showed not one iota of remorse. One person said, 'Through all of this, we have not done anything wrong.' I said, 'Waste Management? Sunbeam?' The guy looks at me and says, 'You know, Lynn, on not one of those cases have we been found guilty in court.' That tells it all. The arrogance never changed."

A visit to the old headquarters of Arthur Andersen during the 1940s yields an interesting perspective. Today, the twenty-second floor at 120 South LaSalle holds the remains of an abandoned dot-com. Aeron chairs, exposed pipes, and brushed-metal cubicles litter the space that once was home to Arthur Andersen. Walking through this empty floor, it seems that here are two ironies wrapped in one—that the site of Arthur Andersen's greatest expansion is now just another New Economy disaster, and that in the end it was that manic energy that proved to be the Firm's ultimate downfall. It is the disintegration of Arthur Andersen, a real-life company with real revenues and real employees—not some dog-welcoming, pool-playing dot-com—that puts the ultimate exclamation point on the collapse of the New Economy. Enron was, indeed, a tragedy on many levels. But one enormous level belongs solely to Arthur Andersen.

# Other People's Money

10

*I love money. I love money more than the things it can buy. . . . There's only one thing I like better . . . other people's money.*

—LARRY "THE LIQUIDATOR" GARFIELD, the character
played by Danny DeVito, in the film *Other People's Money*

OTHER PEOPLE'S MONEY. That's really the only thing that corporate executives, accountants, boards of directors, bankers, analysts, and government leaders actually have in common. Whether we use the word "fiduciary," as banks do, or "stewardship," a favorite phrase at Andersen, the meaning is crystal clear: In the United States of America, when people part with their money—be it voluntarily, as with investments, or forcibly, as with taxes—they do so with the expectation that the receiving hands will use the money responsibly and honor their trust. Before we were engulfed in the flood of business scandals in late 2001 and 2002, most of us took this trust for granted.

Not anymore. In the summer of 2002, the American public, furious and betrayed, abandoned the stock market in droves and put an end to the free money that had lubricated the economy for most of the 1990s. Why, after all, should *anyone* have faith in a system that allowed so many business leaders to loot their companies for so long? One of the most glaring breaches of trust was the failure of the accounting system. Whatever the behavior of businesses and their top executives, investors should have had at least some protection from the early warning system of the public accounting industry. But we didn't. While there is sufficient blame to tarnish investment banks and analysts, corporate executives, and ourselves as starry-eyed investors, and, of course, the Big 5 firms, of all of those groups it is Arthur Andersen that lies in ruins today. Was it a coincidence that so many of the biggest and baddest wrongdoers of the era were Andersen clients—Waste Management, Sunbeam, Enron, the Baptist Foundation of Arizona, WorldCom? I experienced enough at Andersen to believe that the answer is no, but that doesn't mean reform isn't desperately needed throughout the industry.

I feel sad as I watch the vultures pick over the carcass of this once-great firm, and our president and others suddenly rush to implement reforms they resisted for years, proclaiming solemnly—and in tidy sound bites—that this will never happen again. As I watch stage-managed "raids" on white-collar criminals that end with them led off in handcuffs on national television, I also feel cynical. These earnest-sounding events and proclamations have an all-too-familiar ring. In them I hear echoes of the speeches and see the television images I remember from the last wave of scandals in the 1980s.

The late 1980s also featured a spectacular market crash and a series of scandals—this time with Wall Street as the epicenter—that ultimately led to the fall of investment bank Drexel Burnham Lambert and the imprisonment of Michael Milken, Ivan Boesky, and a handful of others. U.S. Attorney Rudolph Giuliani made a political career for himself by nailing Milken and Boesky (represented by Harvey Pitt, who headed the SEC during the fall of Andersen and then resigned in a political scandal over whom to appoint to the new Public Accounting Oversight Board), as well as some others who had gained personally through insider trading and manipulating markets. The rotten-apple theory won the day; some bad guys were caught and punished, and the world was supposedly made safe once again for the investors of America. But the underlying culture was left in place, where it could spread like mold on a piece of bread. Certainly, some of the "creative" financing treatments used to help Enron and the telecom companies seem a partial tribute to Milken's brilliant but sometimes illegal use of other aggressive techniques.

But the tough talk went only so far. Because he could not be sure of a conviction, Giuliani chose not to prosecute the investment bankers Richard Wigton, vice president of Kidder Peabody, and Robert M. Freeman, a partner in Goldman Sachs, after leading them prominently from their offices in handcuffs and charging them with insider trading on behalf of Kidder. Four months later, Kidder Peabody paid a fine of $25.3 million—a pittance for an investment bank—to settle charges of insider trading. The fire-and-brimstone threat of public arrest and the promises of radical change in the investment banking business dissipated into a few prominent jailings, a fine, and the liquidation of one firm—Drexel. And here we are again! Parading handcuffed executives like John Rigas of Adelphia Communications, Samuel Waksal of ImClone Systems, and L. Dennis Kozlowski of Tyco International in front of a phalanx of cameras with tough-talking prosecutors leading the way is a bizarre déjà vu. Government and corporate leaders suddenly discover widespread wrongdoing, send a few bad guys to jail, and huff and puff self-righteously about cleaning up the past and moving nobly to the future.

•   •   •

In 1987, while teaching at the Harvard Business School, I was asked to sit on a panel on business ethics at MIT with Harvey Pitt—then Ivan Boesky's Washington lawyer as well as a lawyer for Arthur Andersen, and Fred Joseph, the head of Drexel Burnham Lambert. Boesky had already been fined $100 million by the SEC for insider trading (he would later serve two years in jail), but Drexel hadn't yet gone under, and both men were very much celebrities.

We sat in the pit of an incredibly hot, overcrowded amphitheater sardine-packed with Sloan Business School students, most of whom were salivating at the chance to be in the same room as these "Masters of the Universe." The students were standing in every aisle and sitting cross-legged on the floor. The other two panelists—I and one of the first corporate ethics officers—were little more than filler. Each speaker was given fifteen minutes to present his view on ethics to the future business leaders of America, but Pitt's comments are the ones that have stayed with me all these years.

Pitt said that some people get away with some bad stuff for a while, and that some very smart people get away with some of it for a long while. Then he emphasized to the students that, in the long run, they were not going to get away with unethical behavior. If they did something wrong, if they broke the law, they were going to get caught and they would go to jail. In terms of ethics, he said, that was probably the only thing that was important for them to know.

I was astounded that such a well-respected lawyer would take such a cynical approach to ethics, particularly in front of impressionable young M.B.A. students. As the future business leaders of America looked on admiringly, neither Pitt nor Joseph had a word to say about the values of the firms, the culture of Wall Street, the responsibilities of investment bankers, and how the ethical lapses would only happen again if root causes weren't addressed. Certainly, we all agreed that "bad" individuals would and should be punished—but they must have known as well as I did that the insider-trading scandals of the late 1980s came more from a corrupt culture than a few bad guys. I look back at it now, and the similarities of the Wall Street era to the problems that ultimately destroyed Enron, WorldCom, and, of course, Arthur Andersen are amazing. In all of these cases, a culture developed in which making money was glorified at the expense of anything else.

Are we doomed to live the same scene again and again, like in the film *Groundhog Day*? Certainly, politicians who once defended big business at all costs have appeared to be changing their stripes— and fast—yet it seems as if many of the wrong lessons are being learned by Corporate America all over again. I don't claim to be an accounting or regulatory expert. But I do know something about what motivates people to act responsibly—or not. Some of the moves that the government is making today, such as requiring chief executives and chief financial officers of all SEC-registered companies to attest to the truthfulness of their financial filings or risk huge fines and long jail terms, and, finally, mandating a truly independent oversight board for the accounting industry—make sense, although there are already some major snags.

But it's not just about finding the bad guys: It's also about helping strong leaders create cultures in which good guys can do the right thing. There are things that we *can* do to try to restore that public trust—and, perhaps, to avoid more such lapses in the future.

## It's Not the Bad Apples, It's the Rotten Culture

"We want the bad guys exposed and the bad guys punished." With these words, WorldCom CEO John Sidgmore echoed much of Corporate America and the government's solution to the crisis that threatened the economic stability of our country and turned the American dream into a nightmare for thousands, if not millions, of people. Everyone seemed to be fixated on the same concept, which not coincidentally allowed them to declare victory. Just find the bad apples, punish them, and everything will be fine. This, I believe, is wishful and dangerous, if simple and efficient, thinking. It precludes examining destructive corporate cultures and instituting real change.

When Andersen CEO Berardino decided to fire David Duncan, it may well have been a response to the Firm's previous lack of action against other partners who had crossed the line. But it also was a panicked reaction to a public outcry for someone's—anyone's—scalp. When it came to the tougher stuff—trying to implement Paul Volcker's vision of a new, trustworthy accounting firm, for example—the Firm was paralyzed. Its leadership stonewalled for too long, reverting to the defensive strategy that had seemed to serve it well in the past.

Tossing out the bad seeds misses the real point—that a great deal of wrongdoing in American business is the result of systemic problems. I am not saying that people don't do wrong: They most certainly do, and individuals who have done wrong should be punished. But more and more often, ingrained cultural practices—pressure to meet targets, implicit ways of dealing with clients, information and how it is used—shape the behavior of more and more employees. Stories that are passed around the organization, career "moves" of the people who are promoted, and successes highlighted at meetings help to establish the culture.

When a group of young audit managers learn from their partner that they should charge entertainment expenses back to the client, and then teach that to their staff who continue the practice, we see the way a belief takes shape. A few more years of this practice, and it becomes "The Way We Do Things Around Here." Then, years later, when one unfortunate young auditor gets caught by a careful client, should the response be to fire the young auditor, or look to the practice that has caused the problem? The answer is both. Individual wrongdoing must be punished, although if pressure from a boss or culture played a part, it can be less severe than for the corrupt actor. When that happens, it's best to treat it as you do when you spot a mouse: Assume there are more, and try to find and plug the hole in your wall rather than setting mousetraps for years to come.

Changing the culture is hard, but it's not impossible. It simply takes long-range thinking and a commitment to something other than quarterly earnings and today's stock price. In the aftermath of billions in shareholder losses and the rubble of several once-proud firms, we have an opportunity.

## Think Straight, Talk Straight—Do Straight

"So, Barbara, how long are you going to go on being the entertainment at the Fall Festival?"

Wick Simmons, the then-CEO of Prudential Securities, stopped me cold. It was September 1994, a year before I joined Arthur Andersen and the year Prudential's parent, Prudential Insurance Co., was being skewered daily in *The New York Times* for unethical and illegal acts that ranged, over several years, from tax violations to ongoing deceptive sales practices. I had been invited, for the third time since 1988, to conduct a half-day ethics session at Prudential's annual Officers Council, a meeting of the top 110 officers of the company, and I was meeting with Wick at his office near the South Street Seaport to brainstorm for the session.

LIBRARY
*check it out!*

Check your due dates by:
Clicking "Your Library Account" on **www.icc.edu/library**. Log in to use to track due dates, request items from other libraries, see any fines that have posted to your account and more!
Calling any ICC Library:
East Peoria Campus 694-8463
Peoria Downtown Campus 999-4611
North Campus 690-6837

Need help? Ask us! Our friendly staff will be more than happy to help you get there.

Due Date: 11/22

"Through learning, minds change.
We believe by changing minds,
we can change the world."

# Create your library account online!

www.icc.edu/library
Click on the yellow "Your Library Account"
Click on "Create New Account"
Fill out your account information.

Your "Borrower ID" is on the back of your
ICC ID *(Include "ICC" in borrower ID)*

**Property of Illinois Central College**
**Library ID Number**
IIIIIIIIIIIIIIIIIIIIIIIIII
**ICC 1016589**

Select ICC as your library
Submit

Choose *"Checked out items"* from the menu on
the right side to see when your materials are
due!

In the past, I had used cases about various Prudential "problems" written in consultation with the company's employees. One concerned the Abbreviated Pay Plan, a life insurance policy with what appeared to be a fixed number of payments. It turned out that the number of payments was actually tied to the prime interest rate—although that had not been explained to the purchasers—so that eight payments suddenly became 12. I wasn't sure that more of the same types of case studies made sense. But before I said anything, Wick followed up that first line with another biting comment: "How many of the things written about in the *Times* have we talked about in your sessions?" "Every one of them," I said. "And," he continued, "how many of them have we done anything about?" "As far as I know," I said, "none."

His comments shook me to the core. I had been feeling proud of the work I'd done helping to bring to the surface some significant problems and getting the top executives to discuss them. But Wick was right. Awareness and discussions were meaningless if the company took no remedial action. (I had twice received notes from the CEO of Prudential Insurance thanking me for giving the group "something to chew on.") I resolved that this year would be different. I would spend the last 40 minutes of the session confronting the group and trying to force them into action.

"We've got to stop meeting like this," I said. "For the last six years we've met at many Prudential programs, and for the last six years we've discussed many troubling issues within this company." I then read a list of the topics we'd discussed since 1988. "This year, 1994, every single one of these issues was detailed in *The New York Times*. Not one of them has been addressed by you. You knew about all of this. Had you dealt with these concerns in a timely fashion, there would have been no newspaper stories, and Prudential's reputation would still be worthy of its history." There was dead silence. Then one fellow raised his hand. "If what you say is true," he said, "it's a terrible indictment of us." There was another pause, and then, from the back of the room, a sepulchral voice said, "It's true." "Tomorrow," I continued, "you will be introduced to a new million-dollar, state-of-the-art control system. But you know what? That system will do nothing if you all continue to put your heads in the sand. It's not just technology; it's people taking action that will make the system work." After the session, the internal auditors thanked me profusely for addressing their biggest problem with the new control system. They said that the deliberate withholding of information by employees had become part of the company's dysfunctional culture, which meant that the system wouldn't work.

I'll never know whether my comments made a difference. But I would like to believe that they contributed to the radical changes that began to take place. Coincidentally that same day, the board asked the CEO to retire ahead of schedule and selected Art Ryan, then the president and COO of Chase Manhattan Bank, to take charge of Prudential and the cleanup of the company. The process took several years, but Prudential ultimately paid out more than $400 million in fines and reparations, as well as $2 billion to policyholders who had purchased their policies under the Abbreviated Pay Plan.

After years of ignoring the problem, Prudential got serious, thanks in large part to Ryan, a smart, shoot-from-the-hip street fighter. Right off the bat, he acknowledged that Pru was in the wrong. No bull. No full-page ads claiming that "our values include a total commitment to continue talking straight," like the ones Andersen took out. Ryan made the rounds of Prudential offices. He talked openly to sales reps, to agents, to VPs, to auditors, trying to absorb as much information as he could. He worked with the regulators at the State Insurance Department to develop plans for making reparations and to change some regulatory requirements that had unintentionally resulted in unethical behavior. Then he tackled an array of deceptive practices, some of which were endemic to the industry. Ryan made a commitment to action and to changing the culture.

Fortunately for Pru, its pockets were deep enough and it had a lot more time than Andersen did. It not only survived, but rebuilt its reputation and, in 2001, became a publicly held corporation. Is it now the perfect company? Probably not. The insurance industry is full of unnecessary products and high-pressure tactics. But Prudential's story is in so many ways like Andersen's, except, of course, for the ending. The company addressed its failings, stopped dealing in platitudes, and committed to change. Would Andersen have done the same if it had as much time as Prudential did and had truly strong leadership? Unfortunately, we will never know.

Arthur Andersen's own mother taught him to "Think Straight, Talk Straight," and he used his Puritan approach and strength of character to transform that simple message into the cultural imperative of his firm. The implication of the phrase, however, was also to Do Straight. That's the difference between Mr. Andersen challenging his clients and telling several of them that he simply would not go along with their faulty accounting, and the partners on a February 2001 conference call deciding not to push Enron on its "aggressive" accounting because the star client could soon be worth $100 million annually. Somewhere along the way, Arthur Andersen's message—that you could make good money using good principles—got lost. People still constantly quoted his famous phrase, but their actions implied very different beliefs.

Look at the sentence displayed prominently in Andersen's 1999 Annual Report, published just as I left the Firm:

> After all, to be successful in the future, we must hold fast to our core values: Integrity, Respect, Passion for Excellence, One Firm, Stewardship, Personal Growth.

No one could ever disagree with such a statement. Every company has core values, and every company knows it must hold fast to them. But in terms of *action*, every one of these principles was in question. Integrity seemed to be suspect, as Waste Management, Sunbeam, the Baptist Foundation of Arizona, and so many other accounting problems bubbling just under the surface showed. Respect was shown for the biggest clients, but not for the ultimate client—the investor. The Passion for Excellence had been severely challenged by internal fighting and a pressure not to lose the client. One Firm? I almost never experienced it. Stewardship? The billions lost in the collapse of so many clients made a mockery of the concept. And Personal Growth, in a period of excessive turnover and an unending pressure to meet unrealistic goals, did not seem to be very high on the Firm's to-do list.

## Fess Up, Deal with It, and Learn

Every strategy consultant, PR guru, and ethicist gives the same advice: If you do wrong, own up, clean up, and do all you can to see that the same thing never happens again. So what happened to Andersen? Before there was Enron and Global Crossing and WorldCom, there was Waste Management and Sunbeam. Before there was a criminal conviction, there was an SEC sanction, a huge fine, and the public humiliation of the Firm and many of its partners. There was an internal awareness that the Firm was at risk. Yet at no time that I am aware of did any Andersen leader stand up and say to employees and the public: "We have done wrong and this is what we are doing to make sure it never happens again."

Instead, after the SEC announced its settlement with Andersen on Waste Management, managing partner for North America Terry Hatchett said publicly, "This allows the Firm and its partners to close a very difficult chapter and move on. The SEC has not questioned the underlying quality or effectiveness of our overall audit methodology, nor has the SEC limited our ability to conduct audits for other public companies." The same day, Hatchett wrote a confidential internal memo that talked about litigation as inevitable but urged partners to reduce risk by working harder on client selection. In other words, if we pick our clients right, we'll be fine. There was no acknowledgment that it was the partners themselves who had made the critical decisions.

There were many junior employees who were aware of practices that created trouble for the Firm at Enron and elsewhere. But combined with a culture that often saw the healthy questioning of partners as insubordination, this information didn't always make it to people who might have made a difference. In part, it's an American issue: We are a country that dislikes "tattletales." Even the moral arbiter of the masses, the late Ann Landers, had no sympathy for them. Responding to a "Grandma in Arizona" whose grandson had reported two classmates for cheating on a test, and who thought the child was wrong although the child's mother praised his action, Ann wrote, "I'm with you, Gram. When we were in school, they called kids who snitched 'stool pigeons.'"

Yet Andersen's path wasn't predetermined. There have been companies that, faced with serious evidence of wrongdoing, eventually did take a hard look at their own actions, such as Exxon. On March 24, 1989, the Exxon tanker *Valdez* ran aground on Bligh Reef, spilling 11.2 million gallons of oil into Alaska's Prince William Sound. The fury unleashed by environmental groups quickly turned into a national condemnation, spurred partly by the hostile, defensive response of then-CEO Lawrence Rawl. Rawl, like Berardino and the Andersen leaders before him, refused to acknowledge the company's responsibility, foisting it off on one individual actor (in this case, a drunk ship captain). After months of finger-pointing at various individuals within Exxon, from Exxon USA's president to the captain of the ship, the leadership came to the conclusion that while there was individual blame to be laid in a variety of places, the *Valdez* spill was, in fact, caused by conditions systemic to the organization. They were all, ultimately, responsible. So the executives decided to try to identify the problems and address them.

Since well before the accident, in the early 1970s, the Exxon Corporation had required that every division conduct what the company called Business Practices Reviews at least once every four years, or more often if necessary. These reviews were intensive discussion sessions, organized by the company's controllers and delivered by teams of Exxon managers to groups of fifty or fewer employees. In 1991, the Exxon USA leadership decided that a Business Practices Review was the way to identify and address the problems that led to the *Valdez* mishap. Our firm was hired to work with the company. We conducted interviews across several functions and levels with a number of key employees and executives, and we developed a vignette-based video using real Exxon situations and teaching and discussion guides. The vignettes pulled no punches, nor did they point fingers.

The message was simple: We were in this together, and together we were going to understand what had happened and work our way out of it. The top six executives of Exxon USA also participated in a 90-minute roundtable discussion that was edited and included in the final videotape. Granted, that discussion was probably more about public relations than in-depth analysis, but the fact that these six people took the time to participate supported the message. Although the Business Practices Reviews material was not available to the public, Exxon permitted me to show the videotape to executives of another client in a related business. After watching it, one of their executives said, "I'm really impressed. I've been thinking Exxon is a pretty sleazy company—haven't bought their gas in some time. But if this is how they're dealing with what went wrong, well, maybe I've misjudged them."

Arthur Andersen's approach, by contrast, was misguided from the get-go. When the Enron story broke, identifying Andersen as the company's auditor and raising the ire of the media and the public, CEO Joe Berardino wrote an op-ed piece for *The Wall Street Journal* on December 4, 2001, stating, "We take seriously our responsibilities as participants in this capital markets system," then laying the blame for Enron on a variety of causes and players by citing needed changes like "improving accountability across our capital system." This was a bad mistake. What Berardino and Andersen needed to do at that point was to make a clear acknowledgment of their *own* accountability. What's more, the piece cried out for a strong recognition of the role of the public accounting firm, and the Firm's responsibilities to the public and to the investor. Acceptance of that responsibility could have gone at least part of the way toward having the public, and possibly even the Justice Department, see Andersen as a potential part of the solution rather than a key part of the problem.

To take the difficult steps discussed here, a company in trouble needs good leadership more than anything else, someone who can take responsibility in front of the public for what has happened, but who, just as important, can gain the faith of the employees that he intends to do the right thing for everyone. Again and again at Arthur Andersen, we saw the absence of a coherent leadership strategy, and in its place a type of paralysis. Arthur Andersen was arrogant, not ignorant—a proud old company that knew what it should be doing but didn't make the effort to change until it was too late. No one stepped forward to own up to problems, to find solutions, and to address the sickness within the culture. Like Prudential, Andersen had a window of opportunity in which to act. But the Firm was distracted by internal problems, tensions, and the mad scramble for fees. It hunkered down instead, creating a fortress mentality that required fighting regulation attempts and denying accusations. At the end, Andersen's punishment was meted out quickly and severely—too quickly, say some defenders, for the Firm to be able to make any true changes. But strong leadership could have made a difference.

## Know What to Know

The unwillingness on the part of the leadership to hear bad news was also related to the desire "not to know." Again, this condition is not unique to Andersen, but its culture exaggerated both the condition and its effect. Far too often, common practice has supported the notion that ignorance is innocence. When former Attorney General Griffin B. Bell, in his report on the overdrafting practices of E. F. Hutton, exonerated CEO and chairman Robert Fomon in the 1980s, his words raised the ignorance defense to the heights of respectability:

> A corporate officer is, in the performance of his duties and functions, entitled to rely on the decisions, judgments, and performance of other officers and employees of the company if the officer believes that such decisions, judgments, or performance are with[in] the professional or other competence of such officer or employee.

The report says that the people employed were competent, and therefore the chairman bore no accountability or responsibility for what occurred.

In Bell's world, if a leader has reason to believe that the people hired by his company are competent, he's off the hook. In a culture like Andersen's, where the recruitment and hiring process that focused on bringing in people who were *inherently* ethical was a cultural touchstone of the Firm, the Bell defense rings loud and clear. But it is, at its core, absolutely wrong. Of course, no one person can know absolutely everything going on in a large organization. But the Bell response actively encourages leaders to *not know*. I have heard a division president explain why he didn't want his purchasing director to talk to him about the obligations to his supplier after a product was suddenly discontinued: "If he tells me, then it's my problem. So I don't want to know about it." When I asked the CEO of a global company how he would respond to a sales rep in a developing country who was hampered in meeting sales targets by the fact that the U.S. Foreign Corrupt Practices Act doesn't let him pay bribes, as some of the company's competitors from other countries do, his response was, "That's not my problem. I can't know what's going on six thousand miles away. We have people who deal with that." This practice has allowed leaders like Enron's Kenneth Lay and WorldCom's Bernard Ebbers, it seems, to assume that by professing ignorance, they bear no responsibility for their companies' collapse.

Finally, both Congress and the SEC are dealing directly with these issues. New SEC regulations require the CEOs and CFOs of all public companies to certify the accuracy of their financial statements. The rules say that your signing off on your company's financial statements attests to your *knowledge* that the statements are accurate. Still unclear at this writing is the meaning of the word *knowledge*. Does that mean what you do know, what you know as far as can be determined, or what you should have known? If the standard becomes the "as far as I know" interpretation, then the Bell defense will simply be reinforced. Much as it terrifies executives (and their lawyers), the standard should be what a CEO *should* have known, in order to give the law some teeth. Still, the fact that there is bipartisan agreement on the accountability of the leadership of a corporation is a good sign for Corporate America. Maybe there is hope, after all.

## Watch Out for Unintended Consequences

A truism of almost every institutional culture is that from inside, it's very hard to know when practices that once were effective no longer work, or when issues that were once innocuous have become problems because of changes in the outside world. Many in the oil patch remember that the trading of seismic data, once an industry practice of bartering, evolved between the 1970s and the 1990s into a brokered exchange with monetary values. Because of the slow pace of that change from a barter to a broker system, some companies ended up owing taxes simply because they hadn't realized that what was once barter had become taxable income.

The same was true, to some extent, in the accounting industry. As transactions became ever more complex and more and more clever people devised new treatments, the standards folks didn't always move quickly enough to rule on whether a new approach was legal or not. At Andersen, the fresh voices, wherever they were, didn't always get a hearing. And in the environment we all lived in, what was not officially verboten was fair game. While no company can be completely prescient, every business should have individuals charged with scanning the environment; assessing the consequences (intended and unintended) of new laws, regulations, and standards; and informing the leadership in a timely fashion so that the company doesn't cross the line. Those individuals or groups must have the respect of the leadership and be seen as important to the success of the firm.

Arthur Andersen's Professional Standards Group, its Risk Management Executive Committee, and its Global Risk Management Committee should have played that role. And at the level of identifying future risks and potential liabilities, they did. But the leaders who emerged from the chaos did not seem to respect these groups, did not listen to their warnings, and appeared to openly disparage their guidance. Andersen's removal of the Professional Standards Group's Carl Bass from the Enron account after he criticized Enron's accounting was just one more such move. The Firm's resolve crumbled in front of the client, leaving everyone horribly exposed.

Whereas my experiences at Arthur Andersen have left me more than a little cynical, I do believe that a carefully selected, knowledgeable, and experienced consultant can sometimes be invaluable in helping senior management assess and anticipate future concerns by understanding the experiences and perceptions of employees. The consultant must be expert at conducting in-depth interviews of individuals and groups and at effectively analyzing and feeding back the data in a way that leads to real action. He or she must also be capable of gaining leadership's trust, so that the always-painful process of change can begin.

There is one problem with the plan I've just outlined. In the *Stender v. Lucky Stores* court decision in 1992, an employee's comments in a supposedly confidential group session for company training and development purposes were found to be discoverable, meaning that people participating in such meetings could be subpoenaed and required to say what they heard in those meetings. That wrongheaded decision has meant that many kinds of self-exploratory processes within an organization have become fraught with legal risk. This is a sad and unfortunate outcome, making it in many cases too risky for individuals at a company to take effective action to prevent an Arthur Andersen–like meltdown from occurring.

During the writing of this book, the U.S. Sentencing Commission was revising the now 10-year-old sentencing guidelines for organizations. As part of that process, the Commission requested input from interested parties, and several—including PricewaterhouseCoopers—have suggested that the Commission provide some kind of "privilege" or exception that would allow an organization to do the kind of self-examination necessary to support a truly effective ethics program. If that self-examination is allowed, there should be greater penalties for leaders who claimed not to know about problems within an organization. And it would be a signal that the government was serious about changing the present environment.

## Ethics Is Not Just for Show

Enron, Andersen, and WorldCom all had principles and ethics codes that ostensibly guided their behavior. Each had a Web site prominently displaying their carefully crafted visions. Yet they all ultimately failed. They all knew what it meant to talk straight, at least. But ethics codes on their own have little meaning. Most companies have them, and many of them have been swiped from some other company. A quick survey of corporate values will tell you which ones guide most companies in the United States: honesty, integrity, trust, respect, and then maybe commitment, or teamwork. No problem there. But do a little detective work with employee groups and they'll laugh you out of the room. "Honesty? Ever see our budgeting process?" "Commitment? To the almighty dollar!" "Teamwork? Yeah, right. The guys in the trenches do the work, and the execs get the bonuses."

Every company needs values and principles to guide the actions of the people who work there. But every idea must connect to a way things are actually done in the organization. Leaders *and* employees must participate in the development of their companies' values statements. Leaders need to understand how the world looks from the employees' perspective. In one pre-Andersen consulting project, we conducted a daylong exercise that brought together groups of employees from every level with top executives to discuss the gaps between what the company said and what it did. At the end of the day, a 35-year veteran executive said to me, quite emotionally, "My God, I had forgotten what it was like [to be an employee]."

Sometimes the right idea can be executed in the wrong way. I remember well the defense industry government contracting scandals of the mid-1980s, complete with their notorious $800 toilet seats and $500 screwdrivers. General Dynamics was, briefly, that era's poster child for bad ethics: Its sin was the abuse of time-card reporting by unionized shop-floor workers. David Packard, chairman of an advisory group to the Department of Defense, recommended the establishment of the Defense Industry Initiative (DII) in 1986 to do away with fraud, abuse, and waste in government contracting. The DII mandated ethics officers; mechanisms for detecting, preventing, and reporting criminal activity such as hotlines; and ethics training for all employees in the defense industry. General Dynamics established one of the first ethics training programs and invited *The MacNeil-Lehrer NewsHour* to film a session in the late 1980s.

But behind the scenes, things quickly returned to business as usual. There were some benefits—the entertainment policies, for example, weren't abused as much—but ingrained habits proved tough to break, particularly when there was no strong motivation to support a change. For example, General Dynamics had been barred by the government from contracting with the Defense Department for a few months because of the time card and various other problems. Before we knew it, they were back in business and Uncle Sam was waggling his finger and saying, plaintively, "Just don't do it again." While some companies, such as Texas Instruments, took the Initiative to another level by giving their ethics offices real power in making critical decisions, for the most part, ethics experts are still battling an entrenched culture and focus more on enforcement than on change.

The hypocrisy of much of the Initiative really hit me around 1990, when I got a frantic call from the Ethics Officer of a small defense contractor that made gas turbine engines. The union was threatening a wildcat strike, and one of the biggest issues was that ethics program. As required by law, the company had established an ethics office and officer, who was training shop-floor workers in honest time-card reporting. Yet it soon became clear that much of the misreporting had come not from dishonest union workers but rather their bosses, who had told them to charge hours to contracts that were under budget to avoid overruns on contracts that had been won by lowball bids. After training, workers reported their hours honestly, and subsequently many were punished or harassed by their bosses for changing the "system" that had worked so well.

I'll never forget walking through the plant and seeing big orange stickers plastered on almost every machine that read: "Be Ethical, Get Screwed." I actually did a session with senior management in which the CEO announced that if I planned to talk about lying, he would cancel the session "right this minute." Needless to say, there was a strike. And the Defense Industry Initiative went on to become the model for the Federal Sentencing Guidelines for Organizations' "mitigating factors," the types of programs that would lessen the fine should a company get in trouble. This resulted in almost ubiquitous ethics officers, hot lines, and ethics training across Corporate America, with the results, or lack thereof, that we are presently witnessing. What is needed rather than a boilerplate program is a serious exploration of the vulnerabilities of a company and a program to remove them.

What had been ignored, in the design of the Defense Industry Initiative and all that followed it, was the overall culture of defense contracting, embodied perfectly by that angry union shop. At that time, almost all government defense contracts were awarded strictly on a lowest-bidder basis (Now the government usually looks at quality and delivery too.) So defense companies won business by submitting low bids that they knew would never cover the cost of production. But then they had to find creative ways to cover actual costs—hence the $800 toilet seats and misreported time cards. Sadly, while industry leaders were hailing the Initiative as the renewal of corporate ethical behavior, the culture that had produced the problem stayed firmly in place.

## The Big Picture: Some Suggestions from 15,000 Feet

Arthur Levitt Jr., the former chairman of the Securities and Exchange Commission, had it right in 1998 when he said:

> Increasingly, I have become concerned that the motivation to meet Wall Street earnings expectations may be overriding commonsense business practices. Too many corporate managers, auditors, and analysts are participants in a game of nods and winks. In the zeal to satisfy consensus earnings estimates and project a smooth earnings path, wishful thinking may be winning the day over faithful representation.

It was all too true. And everyone bears some responsibility for letting it happen, from the investment banks to the compensation experts to the day traders. Levitt was only partially successful in his drive to bring more accountability to these groups, but ironically, his push combined with the financial devastation around us today has created a consensus that big changes are needed in every part of the corporate governance system. Here are some broad-brush suggestions that I feel would have a salutary effect.

## The SEC and Other Regulatory Agencies

One of the most critical issues is the oversight of public accounting firms, which fought hard for self-regulation and are now paying the price for their own judgment calls. Is increased regulation the answer? At the present time, the answer for all but a few of the most ardent free-marketers is a resounding "YES!" I may sound like the parent of an out-of-control adolescent, but until the public accounting industry can show itself capable of exercising sound judgment and managing its own behavior, better rules and more oversight is necessary to restore the public's confidence. Yet the critical issue is not regulation as a form of punishment, but instead to develop clear definitions of responsible standards.

There is a fundamental question of fairness that must be addressed. Working with companies in regulated industries, I repeatedly heard the complaint that those who self-reported wrongdoing often suffered more than those who didn't own up. It's like the elementary school teacher who tells the students who cheated on a test to come forward and admit it. Those who do are kept after school. Those who keep their mouths closed get off scot-free.

This is one issue where I find myself, surprisingly, in agreement with Andersen's Joe Berardino. He protested that the Firm had in fact reported the document shredding in the Enron case to the Justice Department, only to have that evidence used against it in an indictment. Andersen did the right thing, he said, by reporting the shredding—and then suffered devastating consequences. Of course, in many cases the Firm did not do the "right thing," and that came into play as well, but Berardino's specific point is well taken. As strongly as I feel that management was ultimately responsible for the Firm's demise, that doesn't justify the pain felt by so many thousands of Andersen employees that did do the right thing, and I wish that the Firm could have carried on—albeit in a totally new form. In the future, regulation can manage this by making punishments for self-reporters less onerous than for those caught. Yet for federal criminal violations, that would require giving judges greater latitude than the federal sentencing guidelines presently allow them. It's a tough problem, but one that demands a more equitable solution.

Finally, whatever the structure of regulation or oversight, the key factor is independence in both perception and fact. While it is essential that members of regulatory and oversight groups be highly knowledgeable about the industry, it is even more critical that they not have played a partisan or adversarial role in relation to it. Harvey Pitt's role as lawyer to many of the major audit firms should have immediately disqualified him from serving on, never mind heading, the SEC.

## Executive Compensation

One of the starring roles in the Corporate Follies of 2002 goes to our distorted system of executive compensation. It is not a recent discovery that money can be an aphrodisiac, a destroyer of common sense, and as dismissive of intelligence and compassion as any form of power. But the sheer number of corporate leaders taking home literally hundreds of millions of dollars in pay and bonuses, including benefits and stock options, is hard to comprehend as we look back. Compounding the excessive pay was unbridled greed, which led some of these filthy rich individuals to borrow even more from their companies, and allegedly in some cases, like that of Tyco's L. Dennis Kozlowski, to loot what was left to feed their insatiable addiction. The supporting cast in this production was made up of enablers such as less-senior executives, lawyers, and, of course, auditors. Like kids with their faces pressed against the candy store window, the auditors saw the goodies their clients were enjoying and wanted to share the bounty, to get close to what counted for greatness. Giving the green light to risky transactions was the accounting equivalent of providing Viagra to a sex addict; it fueled the desire to push harder.

We live in a capitalist system, and high executive compensation as a reward to those who create positive *and sustainable* results is a great thing. But tying the majority of executive pay to the stock market has worked too well. Executives saw what they were to be measured on, and sacrificed long-term goals for short-term decisions that moved the stock. It was an entirely logical response, since that's how most of their compensation was determined. The same was true of Andersen's employees, who were measured in terms of fees and punished if they were involved in any restatement. What incentive was there to blow the whistle if that meant fewer fees and docked pay?

What can be done? Start by linking CEO compensation to the actions that characterize good leadership. Does the CEO make elegant pronouncements and then follow up to make sure that his employees have changed their behavior? Is he willing to seek out, and then truly hear, unsavory news? Ironically, we can learn something from Arthur Andersen's hiring process. Critical behaviors—those things that are essential to success in a particular organizational role—should be more than just hiring criteria. They must be measures of effective job performance. So the development of critical behavior measures for CEOs, CFOs, COOs, and all top executives, and the tying of compensation to an index that includes both such behaviors and company financial performance, would take Andersen's principle one step further. Also, if stock options are used, why not tie compensation to a company's stock outperforming a group of its competitors, rather than simply going up $1 or $2? Using this technique of indexing options was long ignored by Corporate America because an accounting rule meant that these types of options had to be counted as an expense on the income statement, while normal options did not. But now that such major companies as Coca-Cola and General Electric have decided to expense all options, creating a system that rewards you only when you outperform others makes perfect sense.

It is also essential that the board's compensation committee monitor and review the performance measurement system on a regular basis. I have often said that I never met an incentive system I liked, since all of them eventually will be gamed. People will figure out how to manipulate the factors that affect their pay. So board members, HR specialists, and maybe even the accountants should be systematically assessing the impact of incentive systems on the behavior of senior executives to make sure that the means doesn't become an end in itself.

## An Accounting Firm for the New Millennium

I don't think it's controversial to say that despite the bubble economy of the 1990s, the greed of corporate executives, and the game-playing of analysts, the collapse of the market and the loss of public trust would not have been nearly as terrible had the accountants done the job we expected them to do. Big changes need to be made at *all* of the firms—and the demise of Arthur Andersen, unfortunately, does nothing to help the problem.

### Rethink the Partnership

The partnership structure does not serve the public accounting firm—nor the public—particularly well. It makes decision making, rapid response to change, and crisis management extremely difficult. While comparing an accounting firm partnership to a socialist society may seem odd, particularly in an era where corporate greed ruled the roost, it's instructive to look at philosopher Michael Walzer's *A Day in the Life of a Socialist Citizen.* Walzer's key point is that the socialist citizen spends so much time participating in meetings about the activities of his community that he has no time to actually do anything. Of course, the partners of Arthur Andersen did not spend all their time in meetings, although there were scads of committees and task forces. But when a Firm's oversight system is diffused, concerns become everybody's business but nobody's responsibility. The partnership structure also undercuts the effectiveness and control of the leader, because the power and authority resides in the group.

The partnership structure in professional services is supposed to put accountability and liability individually and collectively on every equity partner of the firm. Originally, the American Institute of CPAs and state regulators did not let audit firms incorporate because they wanted accountants to have individual responsibility and not be protected by a corporate shell. When my husband, Chuck Powers, as executive director of an organization audited by Arthur Andersen, saw that the audit report was signed "Arthur Andersen" rather than by the engagement partner, he expressed concern that no individual was ultimately responsible for the audit. "Oh no," said the partner, "you misunderstand. Because we are a partnership, every partner stands behind every single audit. Everyone takes responsibility."

In 1991, largely as a result of huge damages imposed on partners in partnerships during the savings-and-loan debacle, the Limited Liability Partnership (LLP, a state-by-state statute) was established to protect partners from personal liability in the event of another partner's negligence or other type of wrongdoing. Audit firms were included under these statutes. In 1991, Texas was among the first states to install the LLP designation. Ironically, Andersen's present situation is the first big test of the strength of the LLP structure, which may not hold up in court. I think that for accounting firms, it's worth revisiting the partnership structure altogether.

## Know the True Client

During my time at Arthur Andersen, I frequently heard that the goal of the Firm was to become the client's "Trusted Business Advisor." As recently as May 1, 2002, Joe Berardino appeared on the PBS show *Frontline*, where he stated, with a gentle smile, that the auditor's job was "to help the client achieve its business goals." These two statements represent the gross distortion of the role of certified public accountant, and the complete abandonment of the commitment to their primary stakeholder, the public investor, that Andersen's earlier leaders clearly understood.

It is no wonder that Andersen managers forgot their obligation to the investor. Their leaders and mentors focused on the sources of income and on wooing the client as much as they did on providing accurate information to the public. "At the end of the day," said Lynn Turner, former chief accountant at the SEC, "you have got to understand that your customer is the investing public and deliver a very high-quality product to them. If you do that, you will also take care of your business issues." Audit firms must reaffirm their mission and role in the business community. They must change their exclusive focus on client happiness and begin to concentrate on client accountability. Their goal cannot be to be loved by the client, but to be respected—and, perhaps, even a little feared.

## Drop Consulting

Arthur Levitt's challenge to the accounting industry to separate most audit and consulting services is now largely a fait accompli, thanks to the Sarbanes-Oxley Act. Yet it hasn't gone far enough. Still not included in the new rules is a restriction on much of the kind of consulting that at Arthur Andersen fell under the heading of risk management and litigation support services. Having experienced it firsthand, I believe that the pressure to sell consulting services may have been the single most powerful factor in creating this culture of greed. Make the audit work for the client so it will stick with you and then buy more consulting services; pit your consultants against one another so they will do anything to get the engagement; create needs in the client that don't exist, then provide services to meet those needs; turn your partners into salespeople instead of careful analysts, and pray to the God of revenue. The new regulations are a good start, but we have a long way to go.

## Accountant, Heal Thyself

Accountants are good at playing tricks with numbers. So it's no wonder that the way they account for their own business is one of the most twisted, impenetrable systems out there. While at one time there may have been a solid rationale for recording gross revenues even though virtually no one pays the full price, the practice has evolved into a game of self-deception, one that distorts the measurement of partner and manager performance. I remember when a senior audit manager proudly announced a new $4 million audit client, then softly added that it came with a 75 percent Planned Fee Adjustment. In other words, the client agreed to pay $1 million, but the office, the partner, and the senior manager recorded a new $4 million client.

The most dangerous thing about this kind of numbers game is that over time it encourages a culture of both aggressive and deceptive accounting. Few Androids questioned the method, but almost every experienced hire was startled and perplexed by what seemed a misleading system. An accounting firm's fee and revenue structure should be both clearly understood internally and transparent to the outside world. It should be a model to its clients and the public.

## Limit the Goodies

After Watergate and the Lockheed bribery scandals of the 1970s, the government put in place significant reforms, from the Foreign Corrupt Practices Act to the almost ubiquitous corporate gifts and entertainment policies to manage the relationship between buyers and sellers and the regulators and the regulated. Until that time, buying influence through dinners, parties, lavish gifts, and even prostitutes was simply part of doing business. Some fifteen years ago, I was seated on a plane next to a retired purchasing director of a Fortune 500 company. When I said I worked in business ethics, he cheerfully told me that it was people like me who had destroyed the wonderful way business used to be done. "Back in my day," he said, "the guideline for purchasing people in regard to gifts and entertainment was simple. If you can eat it, drink it, or take it to bed—though that's not the way we said it—within twenty-four hours, take it!"

Unfortunately for my seatmate, those scandals forced the government and the corporate world to look at the impact—real and potential—of such relationships. A buyer is an agent of her company. If a supplier entertains or woos the buyer, what prevents the buyer from acting, or being perceived to act, in her own best interest as opposed to what is best for the company? Likewise, a regulator is an agent of the government. If an employee of a regulated company entertains a regulator, isn't the regulator more inclined to help his benefactor? Slowly, over the last 20 years, companies have developed policies to limit the giving and receiving of gifts, entertainment, and favors. The government has put in place extremely sensitive rules that restrict even modest perks to any employee. Yet somehow all of this missed the big public accounting firms. As I see it, they are both suppliers (selling services to companies) and regulators (overseeing the accuracy of financial statements reported to the public). At Andersen, virtually none of the gift-giving guidelines we prepared for clients ever appeared in our own materials.

It's quite the paradox: A contract officer from the U.S. Department of Defense can't take a free ham sandwich and a Coke from an engineer at a defense contractor. A regulator from the Environmental Protection Agency has to leave fifty cents on the table if he pours a cup of coffee while visiting a power plant. And even a corporate purchasing agent is rarely allowed to accept skybox seats from a supplier. Yet a partner of an accounting firm can fly a client CFO to the Olympics or to a center-court box at the U.S. Open tennis championships, put him up in a five-star hotel, and wine and dine him. These acts imply a friendship, a personal relationship, a collaboration. But the relationship between a company and its external auditor is none of those things. Every action that has the potential to affect the auditor's obligation to the public must be avoided. It's not very much fun, but after having been so tainted by scandal, the auditor, like Caesar's wife, must be above suspicion.

## Stay Out of the Campaign Finance Game

During the last presidential campaign, Arthur Andersen, through its PAC, contributed enough to George W. Bush's campaign to become one of his top five corporate contributors. Rival Ernst & Young was also in the top five. Between 1989 and 2002, Andersen contributed to the campaigns of 94 of 100 U.S. Senators and more than half of the members of the House of Representatives, according to the Center for Responsive Politics. The Firm gave far more than Enron did, and the numbers for the rest of the Big 5 are equally outrageous. Such contributions imply the desire for access to government influence and, of course, the hope that politicians will adopt policies that work in their interest. If certified public accountants are to be independent and responsible to the public, they must remain absolutely clear of the political process in every way.

It is more than ironic that the biggest recipient of Andersen's generosity was Representative Billy Tauzin (R. Louisiana), one of the most vocal opponents of Levitt's attempts to limit the consulting offerings of auditing firms and other much-needed reforms. As head of the House Energy and Commerce Committee, he helped lead the congressional investigation into Enron and Andersen, doing his best to convince the public that he was out to save the day from those dastardly devils that funded his campaign. In the end, Andersen got itself in such hot water that even all that political largesse didn't help it. But had there been more pressure on the Big 5 beforehand, it's possible that our financial system wouldn't have taken the body blow it did this year.

 • •  •

When I left Harvard to start Resources for Responsible Management, the hardest thing to accept was being called a consultant instead of a professor: A consultant, I had always joked, was someone who borrows your watch to tell you what time it is. Now I was one of *them.* Some time after I had joined Arthur Andersen, my husband and I were strolling through an antiques show on one of the Hudson River piers when we ran into the general counsel of a client I had worked with on a three-year project. After our hellos, he introduced me to his wife. "This is Barbara Toffler." He paused, clearly thinking of a concise identifying label. Then he smiled and continued. "She made us a better company."

It was a lovely compliment at any time, but a sorely needed one at a moment when I was caught up in an organizational culture that did not bring out the best in me as a person or as a professional. I was fighting with my colleagues, as willing to steal a client as anyone else in the Firm, overseeing work that often was shaped more by time and fee constraints than by thoughtful expertise. But I liked the money I was making, the St. John suits I was wearing, and the riverview Manhattan apartment we lived in. I remembered that at the end of my first meeting on that consulting project in 1993, my client walked me to the door. He didn't smile as we shook hands. "I hope you know what you're doing," he said. I answered the only thing I could. "I hope so, too."

One of the powerful personal lessons of my Arthur Andersen experience is that, despite my self-image as a debunker, my frequent battles with my bosses, and an occasional outbreak of "my way," I basically went along with the culture. I didn't break any laws or violate regulations, but I certainly compromised many of my values. Some of that was the money talking, but some of it was the fact that if you hang around a place long enough, you inevitably start to act like most of the people around you. I was older, had a lot of experience, and had a natural inclination to challenge the status quo. But if I got caught up in much of the culture, what can we expect from young people entering an organization with no idea whether what is happening is normal or not? As I was writing this book, I conducted an M.B.A. orientation session on ethics, and one student made a very powerful statement. He said, "I believe anyone has the potential to be a bad apple." One lesson: Organizational cultures are powerful and few organizational members are completely immune. I believe that that was the situation at Arthur Andersen.

Similarly, while I have emphasized the importance of individuals speaking out when they see problems, it is clear that those of us who did try to get a "senior person in authority's" attention were not terribly successful. Changing a dysfunctional or destructive culture is very difficult. That is not to say that individuals should not be conscious of their own values and control their own actions. Nor is it to say they shouldn't attempt to speak out when they see wrongdoing. But it does acknowledge the limits on any one individual to change an institutional culture. More likely, he or she finally will walk away rather than succumb. So given those realities, it falls upon the leaders and senior executives, who do have the power to effect change, to be keenly aware of the culture they create—and to take action when that culture is causing harm.

•   •   •

In his eulogy for Arthur Andersen, delivered on January 13, 1947, the Rev. Dr. Duncan E. Littlefair closed with the following words:

> Mr. Andersen had great courage. Few are the men who have as much faith in the right as he, and fewer still are those with the courage to live up to their faith as he did. . . . For those of you who worked with him and carry on his company, the meaning is clear. Those principles upon which his business was built and with which it is synonymous must be preserved. His name must

never be associated with any program or action that is not the highest and the best. I am sure he would rather the doors be closed than that it should continue to exist on principles other than those he established. To you he has left a great name. Your opportunity is tremendous; your responsibility is great.

It is not too much to expect that principles have a place in business today. They do. It's too late for this once-great Firm, but there's still time for the rest of us.

# NOTES

## Chapter 2: The Making of an Android

**9** *My own mother:* Arthur Andersen & Co., ed., *The First Sixty Years: 1913–1973* (Chicago: Self-Published, 1974), p. 141.

**12** *He had been right:* Many of the details of this period come from two sources: Arthur Andersen & Co., S.C., *A Vision of Grandeur* (Chicago: Self-Published, 1988), and *The First Sixty Years, 1913–1973* (Chicago: Self-Published, 1974).

**14** *There was the introduction:* Kenneth Morris, Marc Robinson, Richard Kroll, *American Dreams: One Hundred Years of Business, Ideas and Innovation from* The Wall Street Journal (New York: Lightbulb Press, 1990) pp. 50–52, and www.pbs.org/wgbh/aso/databank/entries/dt13as.html.

**14** *This was a city:* F. Richard Ciccone, *Chicago and the American Century: The 100 Most Significant Chicagoans of the 20th Century* (Chicago: Contemporary Books, 1999), p. 97.

**16** *The same year, Congress: A Vision of Grandeur,* p. 54.

**16** *If the confidence of the public:* Arthur Andersen, speech, "The Accountant and His Clientele," in *The Ethical Problems of Modern Accountancy,* a published lecture series delivered in 1932 by the William A. Vawter Foundation on Business Ethics, Northwestern University School of Commerce (New York: Ronald Press Co., 1933), p. 96.

**17** *I used to tell him:* Leonard Spacek, *The Growth of Arthur Andersen & Co., 1928–1973: An Oral History* (New York: Garland Publishing, 1989), p. 9.

**19** *I firmly felt:* Ibid, pp. 40–41.

**19** *He got lots of publicity:* Leonard Spacek, speech, "Professional Accountants and Their Public Responsibility," before the Milwaukee Controllers Institute of America, Feb. 12, 1957, in *A Search for Fairness in Financial Reporting to the Public* (Chicago: Arthur Andersen & Co), pp. 22–23.

**22** *But there was a catch:* www.nysscpa.org/cpajournal/1999/0299/0299toc.htm.

24 *Teach your children well:* "Teach Your Children," *Déjà Vu*, Crosby, Stills, Nash & Young, 1970.

25 *We would tell them:* Spacek Oral History, p. 124.

## Chapter 3: The Cult in Culture

37 *These are not billboards:* Spacek Oral History, p. 73.

38 *If [Arthur Andersen] had known:* Spacek Oral History, p. 279.

38 *And it struck me that:* Spacek Oral History, pp. 279–80, and *A Vision of Grandeur*, pp. 106–7.

45 *Thus in effect, I said:* Spacek Oral History, p. 122.

45 *Starting in the 1970s: A Vision of Grandeur*, p. 110.

46 *It is exceedingly embarrassing:* Leonard Spacek, internal memo re: "Appearance in the Office," Arthur Andersen & Co., June 28, 1954.

52 *Fees continued to grow:* Ashish Nanda, Harvard Business Review Case 9-800-064, "Family Feud (A): Andersen v. Andersen," pp. 7, 9.

## Chapter 4: Cain and Abel Andersen

71 *We found that everywhere:* "History of the Management Information Consulting Practice," Arthur Andersen & Co., self-published, 1988, p. 49.

71 *With a new name:* Ibid, p. 67.

71 *It was a lot of money:* Leonard Spacek, *The Growth of Arthur Andersen & Co., 1928–1973: An Oral History* (New York: Garland Publishing, 1989), p. 202.

71 *A son of a California:* Eileen Prescott, "Organization Man: Victor E. Millar: Why Saatchi Chose a Stodgy Ad Chief," *The New York Times*, March 27, 1988, p. C8.

73 *In 1970, there were: A Vision of Grandeur.* Arthur Andersen & Co., 1988, p. 136.

73 *By 1978, consulting contributed:* Arthur W. Bowman, *Bowman's Accounting Report.*

73 *An impeccably dressed:* Mark Stevens, *The Big Six: The Selling Out of America's Top Accounting Firms* (New York: Simon & Schuster, 1991), p. 115.

74 *A public accounting firm: A Vision of Grandeur,* p. 137.

74 *The compensation would be shared:* International Court of Arbitration Case No. 9797, Final Award in the Arbitration of Andersen Consulting Business Unit Member Firms. Vs. Arthur Andersen Business Unit Member Firms and Andersen Worldwide Société Cooperative, July 28, 2000, p. 11.

75 *The growing array:* Securities and Exchange Commission Accounting Series Release No. 264, June 14, 1979.

79 *In 1986, Kullberg, who liked:* Mark Stevens, *The Big Six*, p.121.

80 *By 1988, consulting's growth rate:* Duane Kullberg, "1988 Message for Our People," Arthur Andersen & Co.

81 *We knew we couldn't stop people:* Mark Stevens, *The Big Six*, p. 132.

82 *I hereby relieve you:* From interviews with Gresham Brebach and Duane Kullberg.

83 *Arthur Andersen promptly sued:* Mark Stevens, *The Big Six*, p. 149.

83 *Only after his son:* Interview with Eugene Delves.

84 *By the end of 1988:* Eric N. Berg, "C.P.A. Turned CEO: Lawrence A. Weinbach: Maintaining a Delicate Balance at Arthur Andersen," *The New York Times*, April 9, 1989, Section 3, p. 6.

85 *We are Arthur Andersen:* David Snyder, "New Andersen CEO May Face Old Woes," *Crain's Chicago Business,* January 16, 1989, p. 1.

87 *Fortune described him as:* David Whitford, "Arthur, Arthur . . . ," *Fortune,* November 10, 1997, p. 169.

87 *A growing pie:* Doug Bartholomew, "Reshaping Corporate America—Andersen Consulting Wins the Hearts of Many U.S Firms; It Has Given Others Heartburn," *InformationWeek,* July 22 1991, p. 30.

88 *At the same time:* Andersen Worldwide Executive Summary, Fiscal 1998 Operating Plan and Capital Budget, "Worldwide Highlights," p. 2.

91 *But Shaheen, who was never much:* From interviews with partners at the meeting.

92 *Just over a month later:* Ashish Nanda, "Family Feud (A): Andersen v. Andersen," Harvard Business Review Case 9-800-064, p. 11.

92 *Nobody ever conceived:* Ashish Nanda, "Family Feud (B): Andersen v. Andersen," Harvard Business Review Case 9-800-210, p.1.

93 *A few months later, Andersen Worldwide:* Michael Rapoport, "Andersen Worldwide Unit Files Suit Alleging Parent Is Scuttling Arbitration," February 17, 1998, *The Wall Street Journal,* p. 18.

97 *So he turned the deal down flat:* Interview with Jim Quinn.

98 *But they had lost more than that:* "Devastating Decision Leaves AA Billions Short, Growing Slower," August 9, 2000, *Public Accounting Report Extra.*

## Chapter 5: Billing Our Brains Out

101 *Italians hate Yugoslavs:* Sheldon Harnick, lyricist, "Merry Minuet," recorded by The Kingston Trio on *From the "Hungry i"* album, 1959.

116 *The company ultimately pled:* Federal Reserve Bank press release, July 19, 1999.

118 *We didn't make those investments:* Arthur Andersen & Co., S. C., *A Vision of Grandeur* (Chicago: Self-Published, 1988), p. 91.

123 *It was about how to maximize:* Interview with Mary Gottschalk.

## Chapter 6: Lord of the Flies

130 *A public accounting firm has:* A Vision of Grandeur, p. 137.

132 *Imagine an audit that focused on:* Andersen promotional material, from online Web page http://www.magnoliatree.net/clients/ArthurAndersenRetailing/retail_practice/services/business_audit.html.

136 *That is because the Firm:* Superior Court of the State of Arizona, County of Maricopa, *BFA Liquidation Trust v. Arthur Andersen LLP,* "Plaintiff's Separate Statement of Facts in Opposition to Defendant Arthur Andersen LLP's Motion for Partial Summary Judgment (Punitive Damages) and Motion for Summary Judgment (Statute of Limitations," Case No. CV 2000-015849, p. 2.

142 *Yet at the same time:* Arthur Andersen press release, January 23, 2000, "Arthur Andersen Positions Itself to Guide Clients in the New Economy."

142 *Given that Business Risk:* Arthur Andersen U.S. 1999 Annual Report, p. 6.

145 *Over time, most:* From 1988–1991, my company, RRM, consulted to Waste Management and a subsidiary of the company, focusing on sales and competitive practices.

146 *Buntrock was feted:* John A. Byrne, "The Flap Over Executive Pay: Investors, Em-

ployees and Academics Are Asking, How Much is Enough?" *Business Week*, May 6, 1991, p. 91.

146 *No company in this business:* Timothy Jacobson, *Waste Management: An American Corporate Success Story* (Washington: Gateway Business Books, 1993) p. 5.

147 *Chairman Dean Buntrock had a concept:* Ibid., p. 11.

147 *His job included consulting:* Securities Exchange Act of 1934, Release No. 44448, June 19, 2001, Accounting and Auditing Enforcement Release No. 1409, Administrative Proceeding File No. 3-10517, June 19, 2001, in the matter of Robert G. Kutsenda.

147 *Just a few years later:* Securities and Exchange Commission Release 2002–44, "Waste Management Founder, Five Other Former Top Officers Sued for Massive Fraud," March 26, 2002.

148 *Robert Allyger, the engagement partner:* Securities and Exchange Commission Release 2001-62, "Arthur Andersen LLP Agrees to Settlement Resulting in First Antifraud Injunction in More Than 20 Years and Largest-Ever Civil Penalty ($7 Million) in SEC Enforcement Action Against a Big Five Accounting Firm," June 19, 2001.

148 *The CEO of Arthur Andersen:* Interview with senior ex-SEC Official. Also David Ward and Loren Steffy, "How Andersen Went Wrong," *Bloomberg Markets*, May, 2002.

149 *He also kept his job: The Starfish Report*, "Alumnus profile—Walter Cercavschi talks about why CBA students are special." January 2002, Volume 4, Number 1.

149 *Maier, who headed up:* Bill Richards and Scott Thurm, "Boston Chicken's Andersen Suit Has Similarities to Enron Case," *The Wall Street Journal*, March 13, 2002, p. C1.

151 *According to John A. Byrne's:* John A. Byrne, *Chainsaw: The Notorious Career of Al Dunlap in the Era of Profit at Any Price* (New York: HarperBusiness,1999), p. 271.

151 *Arthur Andersen was forced to admit: Chainsaw*, p. 346.

151 *According to Chainsaw: Chainsaw*, p. 169.

151 *He would stick to that belief: Chainsaw*, p. 292.

152 *In a statement:* CNNfn, "SEC Charges Al Dunlap," May 15, 2001 (http://money.cnn.com/2001/05/15/companies/sunbeam/).

153 *According to the evidence provided:* Terry Greene Sterling, "Legerdemain Man?" *Phoenix New Times*, March 2, 2000.

153 *I regret to inform you that the Lord:* Report exhibit 111 98 230, from *BFA Liquidation Trust v. Arthur Andersen*, letter dated August 5, 1996.

154 *In public accounting, we were taught:* Testimony of Deeann Jo Griebel, May 1, 2002, in *BFA Liquidation Trust v. Arthur Andersen LLP*, Phoenix, Arizona, p. 36.

155 *This is Dee Griebel, my CPA number:* Ibid, p. 37.

155 *When asked during the trial:* Dr. Dan Guy in *BFA Liquidation Trust v. Arthur Andersen LLP*, May 2, 2002, pp. 67–68.

156 *There was McKesson-HBOC:* Securities and Exchange Commission Release 2000-145.txt, "Civil and Criminal Charges Filed Against Former Executives for Massive Financial Reporting Violations at McKesson-HBOC," September 28, 2000.

156 *Two years later:* Bill Richards and Scott Thurm, "Boston Chicken's Andersen Suit Has Similarities to Enron Case," *The Wall Street Journal*, March 13, 2002, p. C1.

156 *And in July 2002:* Simon Romero, "Echoes of Other Scandals Haunt a Chastened Qwest," *The New York Times*, July 30, 2002, p. C4.

156 *Qwest paid Andersen $8.3 million:* Qwest Communications International DEF 14A Filing, April 8, 2002, p. 35; Global Crossing DEF 14A Filing, April 27, 2001, p. 8.

157  *Not even counting Enron: Public Accounting Report,* March 15, 2002, page 3.
157  *It appears very clearly that Andersen failed:* United States House of Representatives Financial Services Committee Hearing on WorldCom, July 8, 2002.

## Chapter 7: Arthur the Terrible

159  *You find out these things:* Richard Melcher, "Where Are the Accountants? Why Auditors End Up Missing So Many Danger Signs," *Business Week,* October 5, 1998, p. 146.
163  *With these the SEC had much:* A *Wall Street Journal* reporter: "New Rules from SEC Define Misconduct for Accountants," *The Wall Street Journal,* September 24, 1998, p. A2.
170  *In a 1996 speech, Levitt said:* Arthur Levitt, Jr., "The Guardians of Financial Truth," June 6, 1996, speech at the University of Southern California, Pasadena, CA.
171  *If a company fails to provide meaningful disclosure:* Arthur Levitt, Jr., "The Numbers Game," September 28, 1998, speech at the NYU Center for Law and Business, New York, NY.
172  *I need not remind auditors:* Ibid.
173  *In December 1999, the requirements:* Report and Recommendations of the Blue Ribbon Committee on Improving the Effectiveness of Corporate Audit Committees, 1999.
173  *Audit committees alone have the combination:* Joseph F. Berardino and Gregory J. Jonas, "Power to the Audit Committee People," in *Financial Executive,* November 1, 1999.
174  *We just wait for the catastrophe: A Vision of Grandeur,* p. 108.
174  *PricewaterhouseCoopers settled and accepted:* Securities and Exchange Commission Release 2000-4, "Independent Consultant Finds Widespread Violations at PricewaterhouseCooper," January 6, 2000.
176  *Ultimately, the suspension:* www.andersen.com/website.nsf/content/MediaCenterNewsReleaseArchivePeerReview113001!opendocument.
178  *What empirical evidence:* Letter from U.S. House of Representatives Commerce Committee, April 17, 2000, to Arthur Levitt, Jr.
178  *The Commission is rushing to judgment:* Statement by Arthur Andersen, LLP, Deloitte & Touche, LLP, and KPMG, LLP, regarding proposed SEC rule on auditor services, July 26, 2000.
179  *The future of the profession is bright and will remain bright:* Joseph F. Berardino, in SEC Comment File No. S7-13-00: September 20 Hearing Summary of Intended Testimony of Joseph F. Berardino and Gail Steinel, Arthur Andersen, LLP.
180  *A month earlier:* Melanie Austria Farmer, "HP Mulls $18 Billion Bid for PricewaterhouseCoopers Arm," *CNET.com,* September 11, 2000.
182  *We would have sued:* Robert Manor, "Arthur Andersen Marches Ahead in the Consulting Arena: Accounting Firm's New CEO Defends Strategy," *The Chicago Tribune,* January 21, 2001, p. C1.

## Chapter 8: The Cobbler's Children

198  *Twenty years ago, employees:* Andrew W. Singer, "For Coopers & Lybrand, a $1.5 Million Ethics Program Totals Up," *Ethikos,* November/December 1997.

## Chapter 9: The Fall of the House of Andersen

210 *Berardino was a bit concerned:* Adrian Michaels, Michael Peel, Peter Spiegel, and Peter Thal Larsen, "Seven Months in the Death of a Global Giant," *The Financial Times*, April 11, 2002, p. 26.

211 *Ultimately, the conclusion was reached:* Michael Jones, Internal Andersen memo to David Duncan and Thomas Bauer, "Enron retention meeting," February 5, 2001.

212 *Andersen would be issuing:* Report of Investigation by the Special Investigative Committee of the Board of Directors of Enron Corp. (Powers Report), February 1, 2002, p. 203.

212 *After noting problems as early as 1999:* Mike McNamee, with Amy Borrus, and Christopher Palmieri, "Out of Control at Andersen," *Business Week*, April 8, 2002.

212 *The alarm bells came:* Jeff Leeds, "Andersen Trial Yields Evidence in Enron Case," *The Los Angeles Times*, June 30, 2002.

213 *The first page of his e-mail read:* Tom Fowler, "Witness Says Duncan Tried to Toss Key Page," *The Houston Chronicle*, May 23, 2002.

213 *The stock plummeted:* From Motleyfool.com, closing prices 10/15 and 10/22, 2001, for ENRN.

214 *Let me know if you have:* Internal Andersen memo, October 12, 2001, from Nancy A. Temple to Michael C. Odom.

214 *Three days later:* Kurt Eichenwald, "Andersen Misread Depths of the Government's Anger," *The New York Times*, March 18, 2002, p. A1.

215 *Enron's collapse, like the dot-com meltdown:* Joe Berardino, "Enron: A Wake-up Call," *The Wall Street Journal*, December 4, 2001, p. A18.

217 *The good news is he is willing:* Liz Smith, January 13, 2001, column in *Newsday*, p. A13.

217 *Andersen did not fulfill its professional responsibilities:* Powers Report, p. 24.

218 *It seemed as if Andersen might:* Floyd Norris, "Arthur Andersen Needs Help to Survive," *The New York Times*, March 8, 2002, p. C1.

218 *At the age of 75, I had:* Paul Volcker, speech at Baruch College Financial Reporting Conference, May 2, 2002, "Reforming the Accounting Profession in the Post-Enron Era."

219 *In the meantime, Andersen hired:* Kurt Eichenwald, "Miscues, Missteps and the Fall of Andersen," *The New York Times*, May 8, 2002, p. C1.

220 *One sample letter, which I received:* "Employeeletter2.doc," in series of letters circulated by Andersen employees.

220 *What he didn't know was that Berardino:* Ken Brown and John R. Wilke, "Andersen Partners Grasp at the Volcker Plan," *The Wall Street Journal*, March 28, 2002, p. C8.

221 *Obviously, the thought of litigation:* David Greising, "Duncan Tries to Shed Idea He Acted Alone," *The Chicago Tribune*, May 15, 2002 p. 3A.

221 *Duncan also testified that:* Jonathan Weil and Alexei Barrioneuvo, "Duncan Says Fear of Lawsuits Drove Shredding," *The Wall Street Journal*, May 15, 2002, p. C11.

222 *If each of us believes:* Kurt Eichenwald, "Andersen Jury Startles Court with Question," *The New York Times*, June 14, 2002, p. C10.

## Chapter 10: Other People's Money

229 *We want the bad guys exposed:* Jonathan Krim and Christopher Stern, "WorldCom CEO Apologizes for Scandal," *The Washington Post,* July 3, 2002, p. E1.

232 *The process took:* Penny Cagan, "Standard Operating Procedures," ERisk.com, March 2001, p. 8.

232 *No full-page ads claiming:* "An Open Letter from Joe Berardino, Managing Partner and CEO, Andersen," full-page ad in *The Wall Street Journal,* January 29, 2002, p. B5.

234 *Instead, after the SEC announced:* "Held to Account," June 21, 2001, on www.stockpatrol.com.

234 *The same day, Hatchett wrote:* Terry Hatchett, internal Andersen memo to all ABA partners, June 21, 2001, "Client Acceptance and Retention."

237 *A corporate officer is:* Quoted in Barbara Ley Toffler, *Managers Talk Ethics: Making Tough Choices in a Competitive Business World* (New York: John Wiley & Sons, 1991), p. 331, from *The New York Times,* September 6, 1985.

240 *In the* **Stender v. Lucky:** www.orrick.com/news/emplaw/diverse/4.htm.

243 *Increasingly, I have become concerned:* Arthur Levitt Jr., "The Numbers Game," September 28, 1998, speech delivered at the New York University Center for Law and Business.

248 *In 1991, Texas was among the first:* West's Legal Dictionary, www.wld.com/conbus/weal/wlimlcom.htm.

248 *Ironically, Andersen's present situation:* Philip Mattera, "The Buck Doesn't Stop Here: The Spread of Limited Liability Companies," Corporate Research E-Letter No. 27, September 2002 (www.goodjobsfirst.org/crp/sep02.htm).

251 *Rival Ernst & Young was also:* Top Contributors to President George W. Bush, Opensecrets.org.

251 *Between 1989 and 2002, Andersen contributed:* www.opensecrets.org/news/enron/index.asp.

253 *Mr. Andersen had great courage:* "Behold the Man," *Harper's,* June 2002, p. 16.

# ACKNOWLEDGMENTS

We are truly indebted to the many people who shared their experiences and thoughts to help us tell this story. Though many prefer anonymity, we thank them collectively for trusting that we would fairly describe their points of view, even as they suffered through the collapse of their firm. Our deep appreciation to Gail Rentsch, who instinctively felt we would make a good team, and introduced us to each other. Susan Ginsburg, our smart, supportive, and savvy agent, saw the need for this story immediately. She sharpened the proposal and got it into the hands of Charlie Conrad, our editor at Broadway Books, who kept us focused on the forest when we were caught up in the trees. We also wish to thank the legal team at Broadway. Linda Steinman and Kathy Trager were sharp and wise and easy to work with. Lauren Field was a steady hand who helped us significantly before her untimely death in late 2002. Attorney David Korzenik provided the legal guidance that made our successful collaboration possible.

Among our most helpful sources were Dr. Lynn Turner, Jim Hatch, and Natalie Green Giles, all of whom assisted us in clarifying key events in the recent history of Arthur Andersen. Eugene Delves provided us with a treasure trove of old documents, clips, and Firm histories.

A few other people contributed enormously to the writing and production of this book, starting with Jay Akasie, our tireless and razor-sharp fact checker. He made endless phone calls and went over every word of the manuscript, making it better and stronger. Monica and Pat at QED Transcripts and Alan Kelly at Verbatim Transcriptions helped make sense of hundreds of hours of interviews.

Although this book is truly a team effort, each of us has some special personal acknowledgments, as well.

## Special Acknowledgments from Barbara Ley Toffler

The decision to write a book of this sort is not easy. So I am grateful for the unbounded enthusiasm of my long-time friend and colleague, Jeff Sonnenfeld, whose suggestion launched me on this adventure. I must specially acknowledge the Arthur Andersen Ethics & Responsible Business Practices team—my group—who lived many of the experiences described in the book. Every one of them joined the group with a genuine desire to make the corporate community more responsible and responsive to the public it served. That many of their goals were not achieved is unfortunate, but they planted many seeds that I hope bear fruit in their future work.

I am so lucky to have had the opportunity to work with Jennifer Reingold. Who would have believed that a collaborative writing project could be as full of energy, satisfaction, and fun as this one has been? It's been a great time!

My thanks, and love, to my family. My parents, Ted and Clarice Ley, always encouraged me to stand up for what I believed in. They also taught me to take on the tough stuff, no matter how difficult—something my Dad has done so well these past few years. My very special appreciation to Garnell Miller, and to Runetta Gamble and Rose Cartwright, who give such caring support to my Florida family.

My children, Judith, Aaron, Sam and his new wife, Dorian, and my stepchildren, Catherine and Laura and her husband, Josh, add more to my life than I can ever thank them for.

Finally, my thanks beyond all measure to my husband, Chuck Powers, who not only lived through the Arthur Andersen years with me, but also relived them again and again as he read the manuscript and offered wisdom, practical advice, and loving support. This book is dedicated to him.

## Special Acknowledgments from Jennifer Reingold

Barbara Ley Toffler deserves a very special thank you, most of all for having the guts to tell her very important story. It was a wild ride and a great experience, and I thank her, too, for choosing me to lend a hand. I can only hope that any future collaborations go as smoothly as this one did.

I'd also like to thank several friends and colleagues who offered a comforting suggestion or some much-needed support when it seemed we'd never finish. John Byrne was always generous, both with time and the wisdom that comes from writing eight terrific books. Tony Bianco read the manuscript with an author's attention to detail and made it better. Peter Spiegel was of great help with Enron-related sections. In five seconds, Nina Munk solved a structural problem we'd wrestled with for months. Paula Dwyer helped us with SEC-related information.

Thanks, too, and love to my brother, Guy Reingold, to my mother and stepfather, Jacqueline and Rodney Shapiro, and to my stepmother, Susan Reingold. My father, Mark Reingold, served not only as my attorney but also as a first reader, noting inconsistencies and offering helpful solutions to frustrating problems while still being the great dad that he is. Finally, I'd like to thank my wonderful then-fiancé and now-husband, Randall Lane. Rand used his storytelling skills to improve the book while managing to be supportive and patient with a fiancée whose wedding day also happened to be the book deadline. It's good to be hitched.

# INDEX

# ABOUT THE AUTHORS

Formerly the partner-in-charge of Ethics and Responsible Business Practices consulting services for Arthur Andersen, **Barbara Ley Toffler** was on the faculty of the Harvard Business School and now teaches at Columbia University's Business School. She is considered one of the nation's leading experts on management ethics, and has written extensively on the subject. She lives in the New York area.

Winner of a Deadline Club Award for Best Business Reporting, **Jennifer Reingold** has served as management editor at *BusinessWeek* and senior writer at Fast Company. She writes for national publications such as *The New York Times, Inc,* and *Worth* and co-authored the *Business Week Guide to the Best Business Schools* (McGraw-Hill, 1999).